# Everything Happens in Cable Street

*by Roger Mills*

D1423802

Five Leaves Publications
www.fiveleaves.co.uk

**Everything Happens in Cable Street**
*by Roger Mills*

Published in 2011
by Five Leaves Publications,
PO Box 8786, Nottingham NG1 9AW
www.fiveleaves.co.uk

Five Leaves acknowledges support
from the Barry Amiel and Norman Melburn Trust
for all our titles related to Cable Street

Five Leaves acknowledges
financial support from
Arts Council England

Five Leaves is represented
to the trade by Turnaround
and distributed by Central Books

Typeset and designed by
Four Sheets Design and Print

Printed by Imprint Digital in Exeter

# Contents

# 4. The Basement

# 5. Cable Street on Film

# 6. The Art of the Battle

# Acknowledgements

For the interviews featured in this book, I thank the following: Roberto Bangura, Kate Beresford, Sam Berkovitz, Gerald Broer, Paul Butler, Sidney Cass, Gertrude Cass, Walter Coleman, Louis Collin, Jil Cove, Tony Crisp, Brook Cronin, Nita Freedman, Derek Gadd, Gladys Galdeano, Manuel Galdeano, Alfred Gardner, Julie Gershon, Alan Gilbey, Mr & Mrs Ginsberg, Millie Grotham, Richard Humm, Tunde Ikoli, Dan Jones, Denise Jones, Gertrude Jones, Helen Katin, Connie Lang, the Reverend Kenneth Leech, Alfred Levitt, Henry Lipman, Vivien Lovell, Frances Mayhew, Kim McGee, Hymie Mesnick, Ray Newton, Maggie Pinhorn, Phyllis Rose, Harold Rosen, David Savage, Chris Searle, Jane Sill, Jenny Smith, Celia Stubbs, Liz Thompson, Liane Venner.

Thanks to Alexander Gander, George Jones and Mrs Shaw whose letters I have quoted from, to Jim Wolveridge for his essay on the Cable Picture Palace, to Arnold Schwartzman for the photograph he sent from America, and to all those who gave interviews or wrote letters whose words I just didn't have room for. Sadly, some of those mentioned are no longer with us. They are fondly remembered.

Thanks also to the following who supplied information, gave comments or support: Alice Bigelow, Eamonn Burke-Duggan, Joe Collins, Sally Flood, Tony Harcup, Hazuan Hashim, Maggie Hewitt, Chris Lilly, Phil Maxwell, Leslie Mildiner, John Tunstill, Ken Worpole, Carole Zeidman. Also, Chris Lloyd and the rest of the staff at the Local History Library and Archives in Tower Hamlets.

I am indebted to the Society of Authors for an Authors' Foundation award which enabled me to continue my research. Thanks to Ross Bradshaw of Five Leaves Publications who trusted in this book when it was little more than a collection of random ideas. Also, to the Cable

Street Group for permission to use the tape-recorded interviews made by them. And thanks finally, to Sir Arnold Wesker. A line from his play, *Chicken Soup with Barley,* provided me with the title for this book. He was consulted about its use and kindly gave his blessing.

*Roger Mills*
August 2011

# Introduction

I've lived along Cable Street and its various tributaries ever since moving into East London in the late 1970s. My first residence there was a squatted flat, half way up a tower block on the western edge of Swedenborg Gardens, named after Emanuel Swedenborg. The Stockholm Christian mystic, who claimed to be on speaking terms with both angels and demons, lived in the area, on and off, from the early 1700s. The Swedish community raised a church here, in which Emanuel was buried in 1772. The building is long demolished and with only a small stone protrusion — easily mistaken for a vandalised drinking fountain — to mark it. This part of the street was also the birthplace of boxer Jack 'Kid' Berg, who in 1934 won the British Lightweight Championship, wearing the Star of David on his trunks.

Later, I moved to another tower, further east, beyond the crossroads where the suicide John Williams, supposed perpetrator of the Ratcliffe Highway Murders of 1811, was tossed into a hole. His bones were left to rot for a century until disturbed by workmen, the skull gifted to the landlord of the corner pub, now closed and shuttered like all the others along the entire stretch. The current location of Williams' head is unknown. My new abode was a rented GLC 'hard to let' flat which overlooked Watney Market, just off Cable Street. The tall metal skeleton of the structure was clad in a hard, white plastic material. With ill-fitting window frames rounded at the edges, unkind visitors were keen to remark on its resemblance to a pile of illegally dumped washing machines, abandoned at some forgotten roadside in a clapped-out and toxic condition. The only difference was that when it rained, the water leaked in. In the old, dying market below, 'Joe the Grocer' was still having anti-Semitic slo-

11

gans daubed on his shop-front as recently as the late 1970s, many years after Sir Oswald Mosley's fascist Blackshirts were frogmarched out of the area in the Battle of Cable Street of 1936.

Oscar Wilde came to Cable Street too. Or at least the main character in *The Picture of Dorian Gray* did. The novel was first published in book form in 1891. It's the one where the portrait in the attic withers while its subject's face remains unblemished despite a lifetime of sin. The 'sordid room of the little ill-formed tavern near the docks' that he frequented was located in that section of the street that was once known as Bluegate Fields. Wilde was said to have visited opium dens in the area and would have known of its reputation. Whether those who chose the name of Blue Gate Fields for the new primary school there were aware of its previous associations is unknown.

Another housing step found me, now with a family, in my current location at the far eastern end of Cable Street, tapping the computer keys in a ground floor maisonette. The estate, where satellite dishes seem to outnumber the residents and teenage boys nightly sow the flowerbeds with emptied cans of *Red Bull* and miniature vodka bottles, is on Stepney Causeway, running between Cable Street and Commercial Road. It was on this exact site in the winter of 1870 that the Dublin-born evangelical Christian, Dr Thomas John Barnardo, opened his Home for Destitute Boys — although for some reason, Tower Hamlets Council, when erecting a plaque to commemorate the event, attached it to a building on the wrong side of the road.

I have probably lived along Cable Street and its off-shoots for longer than most of the other people contained in these pages. I use that thought to justify myself in writing — from a personal perspective — about the street and the people who have lived here. But who are they? And for that matter, what is Cable Street?

Before Brick Lane, there was Cable Street.

That is, a thoroughfare which merely by the mention of its name will evoke an image. Brick Lane is trendy clothes shops, bars, clubs and curry houses, right? Think of other places. Think King's Road, Chelsea. Think Covent Garden. There is already a picture forming in your head, isn't there?

But wait a minute.

There are certain factors which will determine if we are all seeing the same image. Age is one of those factors. Is your King's Road teeming with colourfully dressed 1960s hippies or with safety-pin punctured, gobbing 1977 punks? Are you watching trucks hauling fruit and vegetables from Covent Garden Market or is your personal movie camera panning along stalls of fashionable bric-à-brac, buskers and bustling coffee shops? And, for that matter, for a dying generation it will be Mr Katz's string and paper bag wholesalers that comes to mind when Brick Lane is mentioned rather than a wild night at the Vibe Bar.

In the same way, for people of a certain age, Cable Street will serve as shorthand for a time-specific milieu. Jewish. Poor. Sometime in the 1930s. And in the main, that is still the approved view. For others who have made it their home since that time, it will summon up different associations.

Cable Street is where we beat the fascists!

Cable Street is a Red-Light district!

Cable Street is full of social workers!

For many more recent arrivals there may be no picture immediately to hand at all: nothing that differentiates Cable Street from any other rather dull-looking concrete highway in the nation's capital. Having said that, in years to come, there surely will be tales to tell about the drug-related turf wars in the area around Shadwell station, the first glimpse of the gleaming, driverless

Docklands Light Railway trains snaking along the periphery of the street. And some inevitably hazy recollections of the fetish nights at Stunners, based in the Cable Street Studios at the very tip of its eastern end.

\* \* \*

In his essay, *A Necessary Myth: Cable Street Revisted*, the late Harold Rosen was referring to the famous 'Battle' of October 4th 1936, when he calls into question the role of fallible memory in written and verbal reconstructions of that day. But he is not over-worried by it because 'mythical versions have their own kind of truth'. That the telling of a story depends who is telling it, when they are telling it and who they are telling it to is inevitable: the teller incorporates not just attitudes present at the time of the event but those derived from life experience both before and afterwards. We are a product of our own — and collective — memory. Harold Rosen states towards the end of his essay: 'I am sure that there have been and still are thousands of stories of Cable Street in circulation which each express a participant's necessary myth.' And that put together they express 'a larger necessary myth.'

To read Harold Rosen's essay is a liberating experience. It gave me permission to compile this collection: a book composed of interviews, extracts, clippings, asides and maybe a few dodgy recollections gathered over many years. It is not just about the Battle, but also other, less well-known, events. Those in which I played a part are inevitably written from a personal perspective. I don't have to question the views in the stories presented here — bias is taken for granted — but I trust in the teller's version of events and the truth of their perceptions.

\* \* \*

This book deals in the main not with the distant past but with a more recent *remembered* time. When I started

14

work on it, I had to think hard about how I might try to present all those different memories that people told me about. It was as if there were a hundred Cable Streets, so different were the stories. And, unbidden, an image came to mind of an old-fashioned slide projector on a dusty wooden table. And next to it, a clutch of slides from the early twentieth century up to the present day. I imagined myself as the projectionist, feeding the slides into the slot, one after another. But in my haste, I fail to take any of them out: the result being an increasingly crowded montage on the screen, of shifting architecture and of different generations of Cable Street inhabitants. Pictures of Yiddish-speaking tailors with tape measures dangling round their necks, post-war US servicemen with a blonde hanging off each brawny arm, shelves of kosher food shops restacked with Halal product, outdoor toilets, rundown picture houses, dubious Maltese cafés, tower blocks — all along the same track that is called Cable Street, each successive wave of new arrivals adding to the jumbled scene.

These overlays are what I present in the following pages.

# 1. Coming to Cable Street
## Stepney Books

## A House in Cable Street

I can't think of a better place to start this journey than at
the house of Dan and Denise Jones, on Cable Street itself.
Denise responds to my knock on the bright red door and
leads me at a dash through to the back garden where she is
busy rescuing some washing from the incoming rain. The
tall, slim building is one in a row of surviving terraced
Georgian houses. 'The house was built in 1760,' Denise tells
me when I ask her about it. 'The people who originally lived
along this stretch were seamen and sea captains. When we
moved in we'd dig in the garden here and find oyster shells
— people would eat them and just throw the shells in the
garden — and lots of clay pipes that people would have
used for smoking. We've still got some somewhere.'

Denise married Dan in her last year as a student at
Brighton Art College. They moved to London in 1967.
'When we approached a local estate agent, there was a
vacant house in Cable Street. But he was shocked,
saying, "You don't want to live there! Cable Street is a
horrible place!"' Both politically committed, the couple
arrived in the area as teachers, decades ahead of more
recent middle-class incomers. A couple of doors down at
number 198 there is a plaque on the wall dedicated to Dr
Hannah Billig: 'The Angel of Cable Street', who opened a
clinic there and was awarded the George Medal for her
work during the Blitz. She later joined the Indian Army
Medical Corps and in the 1945 New Years Honours List
was awarded the MBE for her services to the famine-
stricken people of Bengal and Assam. This international
figure remained in Cable Street until her retirement in

1964. But to their solidly working class neighbours, the Joneses must have seemed very different.

Dan took up a job as a 'detached' youth worker for the local authority, all the while pursuing his passion of painting and sketching. He isn't at home today, away on some important mission for Amnesty International, his current employer — but even so, his presence is illustrated in the dozens of artworks on the walls. There is an international feel to this solidly English house; canvas upon colourful canvas provide portals to the furthest reaches of the earth — or something happening just up the road. A village celebration in Nigeria or a market in Bangladesh will butt up against a scene of banner-bearing trade unionists at Tower Hill. Because of Dan and Denise's contacts abroad, the house has sometimes felt like a sort of unofficial embassy. Over the years, a trail of asylum seekers and outcasts have arrived here requesting the Jones's support. They include a Peruvian lawyer who had survived several assassination attempts, ex-Death Row prisoners from the USA and Buddhist monks from the Chittagong Hill Tracts. Denise came home one day to find a stranger, a young Asian woman, making herself at home in the living room. The woman was Taslima Nasrin, the exiled Bangladeshi poet and writer who had become the subject of a fatwa because of her writings on the persecution of Hindus in her homeland. She had been temporarily accommodated by an obliging Dan, who had forgotten to mention it to Denise. Denise's memory of that encounter is of being irked that the fighter for human rights was puffing on a fag in the non-smoking household.

When I first arrived in East London, there didn't seem to be a single meeting, be it for an arts initiative or a coalition of community groups that wasn't chaired by the same tall, wild-haired man with a black bushy beard. I soon enough found out who he was. I'll be back to speak to Dan later. But today, it's Denise that I'm here to talk to, about her long-term involvement with the community publisher, Stepney Books.

# The World in a Room

After I've helped Denise into the kitchen with the damp washing we sit down with a coffee at the table of the basement kitchen. A collection of striking masks, gathered from across the globe, stares down at us from the walls. In a fanciful mood, I choose to see them as symbols of all those people who have made Tower Hamlets their home since Dan and Denise arrived. A five-minute walk away from their house is the Bishop Challoner Catholic Collegiate School. On its website, they express pride in its cultural mix and the seventy-two languages spoken there. East London tongues include Silheti, Panjabi, Gujerati, Turkish, Vietnamese, Urdu, Somali, Kurdish and more latterly Serbian and Polish. Multi-language leaflets are on display in the new Ideas Stores and the council's newspaper *East End Life* carries stories in English and Bengali. In the 2001 Census, 48% of the Tower Hamlets population were defined as coming from a non-white ethnic group, the largest being Bangladeshi, comprising 34% of the borough population. As Denise lays out the dozen or so titles from the Stepney Books list onto the table, published between 1976 and 1994, I realise that they are almost without exception stories from a different age when the dominant group in the area was the white working class.

## The Lost Library

Something of the art student still clings to Denise in her dark clothing and dark hair. But also, a trace of the quiet Sussex girl, intoxicated at being let loose in the big city. I imagine her kicking along the cobblestones of 1960s' Stepney. Free and fashionable. A Mary Quant girl, now grown up. Except that she couldn't have been all that quiet. Denise has been a local Labour councillor for ages now, was once the mayor (she features in one of Dan's paintings, reprinted on the cover of this book, in her official regalia) and finished a stint as the leader of Tower Hamlets Council not so long ago. She is proud of her achievements in office, including her work on the Mile End Millennium Park. In 2008 she was awarded an honorary Doctorate of Letters from the University of East London for her services to arts, literature and the regeneration of East London.

Denise starts to tell me about the origins of Stepney Books, formed in 1973, which took inspiration from the Centerprise Bookshop and Publishing Project in Hackney. But it wasn't the original intention to be a publisher at all. At that time there was no bookshop in Tower Hamlets; the borough which had spawned such novelists as Bernard Kops and Willy Goldman, First World War poet Isaac Rosenberg and playwright Arnold Wesker. 'So we realised,' says Denise, 'that we would have to start one — but start small. Stepney Books began as a stall operating on a Saturday in Whitechapel Market. We were just selling children's books then, as cheaply as possible. I'd had a baby by that point and he slept under the stall.' Denise's friend Celia Stubbs was amongst the rota of volunteer staff and while wandering along the row of stalls discovered one selling second-hand books and comics, up at the other end of the market. Celia became entranced by stallholder Jim Wolveridge's recollections of his upbringing in the East End of the 1920s and 30s, told with wry humour, and realised that there was a book there.

It's pelting down outside now and there's a knock at the front door. Jenny Smith has arrived, dripping a wet umbrella down the stairs into the kitchen. Like Denise, Jenny had been a teacher and describes her work with Stepney Books as 'a hobby'. Jenny's face in repose is very serious, but even the smallest crack, when recalling the self-taught scissors and glue technology behind the publications, reveals a mischievous interior. Some of those books were pieced together at the very table we are now sitting at. It is Denise and Jenny who were working on the publications when I first became aware of the slow but steady stream of life histories seeping out into the community. But initially there was a broader steering group which set things into motion, and both Denise and Jenny make it clear that the wellspring of the publications operation was Celia Stubbs. I had hoped to meet Celia today, but she is otherwise occupied at her current home near Brighton.

'Celia tape-recorded Jim's stories for hours and hours,' says Denise. 'It would have been on cassettes at the time. She transcribed it all and we assumed it would be the book. But Jim had other ideas. He felt it needed to be expanded and improved. He took it away and pretty much rewrote the whole thing.' It is an example of the loose, undefined author-publisher relationship that was to typify the Stepney Books list.

'We were making it up as we went along,' says Denise. 'About a thousand pounds was raised from various funding bodies and Centerprise gave us advice. This was all before computers, of course. We had to learn lay-out, paste-up and design skills. How to liaise with printers and things like

*Jim Wolveridge*

that.' Jim's book, which was eventually released in 1976 under the title of *'Ain't It Grand' (or 'This Was Stepney')* was followed by others, each one unique in its path towards publication.

Denise and Jenny shove the books about on the table top. *Victoria Park* by Charles Poulson is a history of the famous 'lung for East London', while *Under Oars* by River Thames lighterman Harry Harris (published in conjunction with Centerprise) arrived via the author's son as a copper-plate handwritten manuscript, written some forty years earlier. It would probably have remained a family heirloom if not for Stepney Books.

Others followed, amongst them: *Children of the Green* by Doris M. Bailey, an autobiographical portrait of a Bethnal Green family between the wars; *Tough Annie*, which chronicled the life of Annie Barnes, a suffragette friend of Sylvia Pankhurst, transcribed from tapes of Annie in conversation, and two self-explanatory autobiographies: *Looking Back — A Docker's Life* by Joe Bloomberg and *Memories of Old Poplar* by John Blake.

'You'd be surprised how many people had got manuscripts tucked away in the drawer,' says Jenny. 'They came through the letterbox, I should think, at the rate of about one a month. When we took a book on we'd sometimes help them edit it. Not taking away their voice but suggesting that something might have gone better elsewhere in another chapter.'

Denise says, 'Reviews appeared in *The Evening News*, the *Morning Star* and *Contact*, which was sent out by the Inner London Education Authority to schools. There were radio interviews, and radical bookshops were sympathetic. But mainly the attitude was: *Why don't you sell it in a local bookshop?* But there wasn't one! We had a network of unconventional outlets, The Half Moon Theatre, The Labour History Museum, and so on.' Celia was involved in the production of the first four books, by which time Jenny had already come along at Denise's invitation. As well as working on the publications Jenny also became chief rep: 'I used to go to bookshops in school holidays and half term. I had all the stock in my back bedroom and ran a mail order service from there.' Jenny recalls that even after several successes, publicity and distribution was problematic. 'Foyles Bookshop in Charing Cross Road were horrible to us! I used to join a long queue of reps on a staircase. They were there to see a man they all called "The Hun" or "Goebbels" — something implying he was despotic. And they joked that he was Christina Foyle's lover. We each got about two seconds with him. He looked at the covers, turned them over, said something caustic, and shouted, "Next".'

The homemade publishing house of Stepney Books was an early exponent of what became known as community publishing. There were similar projects in London and across the country. Leaving the Jones's house on that rainy day, I worry that the efforts of such groups have been washed away by a media that undervalues the lives of people documented in those books. Due to the limited print runs, born of financial restrictions, many of the titles have been unavailable for years, no longer there to be read by the people they were aimed at. And although I have entitled this section: 'The Lost Library' it should have perhaps been followed by a question mark — because the world wide web may yet provide an outlet to put this work back into the public domain.

## A Name on the List

When I spoke to Denise Jones and Jenny Smith about the genesis of Stepney Books, they told me that there had been a steering group prior to the first publications which included themselves and Celia Stubbs. When I finally unearthed some minutes from an early meeting, which took place in the Basement of the Town Hall in Cable Street, I was surprised at how many people had attended. Eighteen names are listed. There is one in particular that caught my eye. That name, Blair Peach, might also ring a bell for you. Blair was born in New Zealand in 1946, arriving on our shores in 1969 when he began teaching at the Phoenix School in East London, staying there until April 1979. But the termination was not planned. On the 23rd of that month, while attempting to leave an anti-fascist demonstration in Southall, he died after a blow to his skull by an unidentified weapon. It was wielded, Blair's friends and supporters claimed at the time, by a police officer attached to the Special Patrol Group. The press coverage was enormous. Blair Peach was a committed member of the Anti-Nazi League, which, along with the pictures in the press of a raggedy-haired man with a beard, might have caused some to write him off as yet another troublesome lefty. But those who knew him describe a gentle man, popular with the kids he taught. The blatantly biased inquest that followed, many felt, was part of a cover-up. No charges were brought against the police. That ten thousand people attended his funeral on what I remember as an overcast, drizzly day was an indication of the strength of feeling about what had occurred. Blair Peach had been Celia Stubbs' partner of ten years. Being unavailable when I interviewed Denise and Jenny, I arranged to meet her at a later date. It wasn't my intention to rake over the ashes of the case but to verify that I had got the beginnings of Stepney Books correct and to talk about the ferment in which Blair's kind of politics was allowed to grow. I have called it 'Cable Street Politics,' a mixture of poetry and protest, shared and personal experience.

## 'Cable Street Politics'

It's not a secret that many of the people I have spoken to in the course of writing this book, the movers and shakers, artists and activists, are politically left of centre. But I've found that politics — party politics — doesn't count for much in Cable Street. Too many people around to deflate those who come with a set agenda. I've always been fond of the Bob Dylan song, *Tangled Up In Blue*, from his 1974 *Blood On The Tracks* album. His line about a 'basement down the stairs' and 'revolution in the air' brings to mind the hopes of those times when I was regularly attending Basement Writers meetings in Cable Street. Although very few of those attending the meetings would have seen themselves as revolutionaries, there were others who would have liked them to be. I remember one occasion when an earnest film crew from East Germany paid us a visit, trying to identify the source of all the mayhem being caused by striking schoolkids and afro-haired filmmakers. The interviewer set upon some of the writers. His questions were answered with blank expressions until, in desperation, he asked about their influences. At this, young writer Billy House, possibly as a wind-up but then possibly not, responded with a name with the interviewer took to be 'Lenin'. At this the German began to perk up, relief evident in his face. 'Yes,' Billy continued, 'John Lennon is definitely someone we can identify with.'

## A Meeting in the Park

I finally got to meet up with Celia Stubbs during one of her visits to East London. We sat outside the café at the edge of the lake in Victoria Park and watched the ducks splash in the water as we chatted. She confirmed what Denise Jones and Jenny Smith had told me; about how it was her interest in publishing Jim Wolveridge's memoirs that launched the Stepney Books list.

'Jim really jumped at the idea that it might be published. He was such an engrossing speaker and, yes, we initially taped the whole book. I remember typing it up and then him checking it in case I'd made mistakes. He had a natural talent and had a really good memory. He flourished during the process because basically he was a solitary person. He always said he had no relatives.'

Celia mentioned that Jim used to visit her and Blair Peach when they lived in Victoria Park Road, close to where we were currently sipping our teas. Inevitably, the subject drifted to Blair. As a teacher, he had produced small anthologies of his pupils' poetry in the school. Celia sees that sort of work as being a precursor of the whole community publishing movement. She told me that she was in the Socialist Workers Party although some wry asides on her part led me to understand that if she had her time over again... Anyhow, Blair became a member, but late, not really being a joiner. He was far more interested in trying to get things done on a local level.

Celia's determined features and questioning eyes have in the last few years been appearing in national newspaper articles and on television news reports. In the wake of the death of Ian Tomlinson, a passer-by struck down by a police officer during a G20 protest in London in 2009, the parallel Blair Peach case jumped back into media consciousness. And in 2010, the then Met. Commissioner agreed to release a long-suppressed internal police report which accepted that a policeman was likely to have been responsible for Blair's death. It was a victory of sorts but the report didn't contain the names of any of the officers involved. They had been 'redacted'.

'The new commissioner has said he'll meet me,' Celia told me. 'We're firming up a date. My solicitor is going to challenge the redactions. It's ridiculous, thirty-one years on there's no need for them. The police officers must all be retired by now. Some people say: *What's the point, why do you fight for all those years?* But the report proves our point, what we knew at the time, that a policeman had killed Blair and that the police covered up.' But still, at the time of writing, no one has been charged over the death of Blair Peach.

What I found interesting was that of the three Stepney Books women I spoke to, none of them had a ready answer to why they embarked on the whole business in the first place. You spent years, masses of time and energy publishing these books, I cajoled, *Why did you do it?* What I wanted them to say, for the sake of easy copy, was something like '... a fast disappearing culture which we felt needed to be preserved.' But it just couldn't be prised from their lips. I reckon they are just born story-gatherers, life-redistributors, anecdote-addicts — in a good, marvellous, brilliant way.

It was partly the inspiration of Stepney Books that led me to the writing of this book. But there were also other influences and different working methods, undertaken with different groups and individuals, as detailed in the following section.

# Recording Cable Street

## Gathering the Material

The transcriptions of interviews featured in this book have been selected from three different recording campaigns. The earliest date back to 1979, when I helped out with research towards the Cable Street Mural Project; talking to Battle veterans about their memories. I was also involved in the second surge, initiated by the Cable Street Group following the 1986 fiftieth anniversary of the Battle. Some extracts were featured in the publication, *The Battle Of Cable Street 1936*, published by the Cable Street Group in 1995 and reprinted by Five Leaves Publications in 2011. The third category of recordings were those that I undertook on my own during 2009 and 2010 for this book.

The Cable Street Group interviewees were mostly contacted through adverts in the *Jewish Chronicle*. The Group would take off *en masse,* usually on Sundays, in the couple of cars we had between us, and as individuals or in pairs, visit the homes of the people who had responded to our pleas for information and wanted to put their testimony on record. Quite a few had moved out to Edgware and other distant corners of London. The homes we were invited into were uniformly warm and comfortable, their owners proud of where they'd come from and where they'd got to, the neatness and tidiness of their surroundings perhaps a reaction to the less than perfect housing conditions they'd grown up in. All those we spoke to were welcoming and gracious, unfaltering in their attempts to help us understand their world as it had been.

The only technology available to us back then were cassette tapes, spooling away on a collection of begged and borrowed machines; the background hiss sometimes giving the impression that we were conducting our interviews in a fish and chip shop. We had the experience of microphones inexplicably conking out on us, tapes snapping mid-conversation and batteries — full of life only moments before — running flat the second we voiced our first questions. Environments were also unpredictable. Previous to my Cable Street experience I had worked voluntarily with Ken Worpole at Centerprise in Hackney, which published a series of oral histories in the 1970s and 80s. Ken recalls the preponderance of budgie owners amongst interviewees, their tweeting, ticking and bell-ringing forever preserved in the background of the tapes. And while the Cable Street Group undertook the interviews in as professional manner as we were able, our recordings are still punctuated with ticking clocks, rattling teacups and the rustling of our own notes. The preservation of our work was not something that occurred to us at the time. Maggie Hewitt, who had also worked at Centerprise told me about a visit from an oral historian who lectured them about the correct way to store tapes and even the temperature they should be kept at, all the while Maggie thinking guiltily about the tape she was transcribing — at home on a kitchen shelf amongst steaming kettles and bubbling foodstuffs.

## Chasing History

Any visions I initially had of sitting in a hermetically-sealed, temperature-controlled, budgie-excluding pod to grill my new interviewees were soon dashed. People were just too busy to sit still; many with little enough time in their day as it was, let alone carving out a chunk to speak to me. I took my opportunities where I could. As well as in people's houses, interviews took place on their way to work, in cafés and pubs. And I decided, after all, that this was how I had intended it. Best of all where those made in Cable Street itself. Me chasing people along the pavement with my little digital recorder. Out go busy budgies and tick-tocking clocks; in comes a cacophony of revving cars, beeping horns and passing acquaintances of the interviewee stopping for a chat. Some people weren't available for face-to-face encounters. So for these, I organised a series of e-mail exchanges and phone calls. Then it was all down to transcribing their words, the most laborious part of the process, involving huge amounts of coffee. I then typed up and sent a copy to the interviewees. Maybe they wanted to add something. Perhaps they might want to retract something they had said. When I mentioned this part of the process to a journalist acquaintance, she was visibly shocked. The idea of running anything by an interviewee was totally alien to her profession. Where's the fun if you can't catch someone out with an off-hand indiscretion? But for me, an interview is a shared experience, as is the result. And, apart from a few typos and confusions on my part, nobody asked for any significant changes at all.

# 2. The Battle of Cable Street Before the Battle

## 'English Voodoo'

When the Royal National Theatre staged its 1990 production of Shakespeare's *Richard the Third*, the setting was transposed to Britain in the 1930s. Richard, as played by a black-uniformed Ian McKellen, was an elegant (minimally-humped), moustachioed adventurer. This interpretation, directed by Richard Eyre, also provided the basis of the 1995 film adaptation. In both instances, reviewers identified Oswald Mosley, the founder of the British Union of Fascists, as an influence on McKellen's interpretation. The play's original audience, some four hundred years earlier, would already have been familiar with the archetype at the root of the Richard character. The 'Vice' was a well-known theatrical personality, a representative of evil who — like a pantomime devil — sets the stage alight by his very presence. And it might even be comforting to see Mosley himself as something of a stock character, a mad strutting figure to scare the kids, a shallow one-off upper-class loony with delusions of grandeur. And that might, in part, be true. But the jack-booted toff in a Nazi-inspired outfit was very much a feature of the established political scene prior to his eager embrace of fascism.

Sir Oswald Mosley, Sixth Baronet of Ancoats, a Winchester College student and Sandhurst soldier: a First World War veteran who in 1918, entered politics as a twenty-one year old Tory MP. After a falling-out — there would be many of these — he crossed the floor to sit as an independent. He retained his seat in Harrow, having already gained a reputation as a powerful orator. In 1924, however, when the Labour Party formed a minority government, he decided to throw his lot in with them. Then, when they fell that same year, he spent some time kicking economic policies around with the Independent Labour Party, only to return as a Labour MP for Smethwick in 1926. When Labour won the general election in 1929, Mosley must have thought that his time had finally come. But his progress within the party was not as speedy as he felt was his right and he founded the New Party in early 1931. Disillusioned by the failure of all its candidates in the General Election that year, he went to Rome in order to take a look at what the fascist party in power was doing there. He liked what he saw.

## 'Mister Oswald with the swastika tattoo'

In 1977, purchasers of the debut single by New Wave singer-songwriter, Elvis Costello, listening to its somewhat oblique lyrics, might have wondered about 'Mister Oswald with the swastika tattoo'. But for many East Enders, and politicos in general, the inference in *Less Than Zero* was clear: the spirit of Mosley was once again on the march. Costello's anti-fascist message spoke of its rise as a form of 'English Voodoo'. The songwriter was, if you like, taking the temperature of a recurring, self-induced, national fever. Were we witnessing a resurgence of the extreme right? In 1932, Mosley created his own British Union of Fascists (BUF), modelled on the Italian prototype and adopting the black shirt as its uniform. In 1934 Viscount Rothermere's *Daily Mail* ran the headline: 'Hurrah for the Blackshirts', although when a number of hecklers were beaten up at a BUF rally at Olympia that year, some of the movement's upper-crust supporters became concerned about being associated with what was coming to be seen as a bunch of brawling thugs. At first, the BUF denied being anti-Jewish, but in his 2005 history, *'Hurrah for the Blackshirts'*, Martin Pugh, notes: 'During 1936 the BUF had discovered the value of anti-Semitism as an expedient for rejuvenating their movement, at least in the East End of London.' Some within the party built up a large following with hoary old tales of rich and powerful Jews pulling financial strings on the international stage. And whether he believed it or not, Oswald Mosley in his ruthless pursuit of power allowed such propaganda to become prominent in his movement.

## 'The biggest load of nonsense ever'

Living in the Cable Street area at the time, Henry Lipman wouldn't have been able to recognise any of the BUF's powerful Jews amongst his family and friends. In an interview recorded with the Cable Street Group, he said:

> *I've heard people say that there's no thing as a poor Jew. That's the biggest load of nonsense ever, I can assure you. Those years had more dinner times than dinners. It was very difficult for my parents at that time. We didn't get a dinner every day and there was a lot of hand-me-downs. There were some very poor Jewish people there that lived from hand to mouth, brought up families. They were all clean, tidy, went to their schools and their religious schools and what-have-you and there was not an ounce of trouble. Everybody got on with everybody. Everybody knew everybody's business. Everybody stuck by everybody else. If I kick you, it hurt her up the road — that sort of thing. That's how it was.*

Harold Rosen spoke to the group about the separate communities and how politics sometimes provided a bridge between them:

> *Cable Street has certain powerful associations for me. It marked a kind of frontier territory. I always thought of it as being close to the ethnic boundary — where you moved into gentile land. Our house was frequented by gentiles in a way that none of the other houses were because my mother was active in the Communist Party. That meant*

*we had dockers and seamen in the house at number 14
Cable Street. There weren't any Jewish dockers — nice
Jewish boys didn't become dockers — they were almost
totally Irish. I always remember my mother when she was
canvassing in elections and often her beat would be in the
gentile area. It struck me as a child that it seemed the
gentile people were very much harder up than we were,
even though my mother was on public assistance because
I had no father. The poverty struck me as greater, these
great big Catholic families; dockers out of work.*

In another interview, Walter Coleman spoke of how the
influence of the BUF started to be felt in East London:

*When I was a child there was very little anti-Semitism. In
those days the home was quite open. Everybody came into
your house. We'd have the rabbi but at the same time the
priest would come in or we'd have the reverend from the
sailor's home in Dock Street. But as the fascists came
along, close friends who I went to school with became
well-known fascists. It was distasteful to my parents. To
my mother it was very hurtful because she'd seen them
grow as babies and now they had become anti-Semitic.*

# The English Test

Anti-Semitism wasn't restricted to the streets of East
London, as Gertrude Jones, whose parents had a bakery
shop in Cable Street, explained:

*I left school at fourteen and went to Pitman's in
Southampton Row to train to do secretarial work. I knew
that if I didn't get certificates I would never get a job so I
used to sit on the tram and learn shorthand going back and
forth and I went to night school as well. I did very well and
got a medal and a typing certificate. And then when I
started to look for jobs I had terrible trouble because
although my father traded in his bakery shop under the
name of Harris, my surname was Hertz. As soon as I
handed in the paper, they'd say, 'Are you German?' 'No.'
'Are you Jewish?' 'Yes.' 'Sorry, we don't employ Jews.' It
happened so much it used to get me down.*

*Well, one lady — her name was Tillie Flynn — I said to her, 'I don't know, I'm intelligent enough to do the job yet I can't get started'. There was this company in Chancery Lane. They'd interviewed fifty-two girls and didn't employ anybody, so she said to me, 'Don't worry. You know what, Gertie? I'll phone this man up'. He was an ex-Sergeant Major and she said, 'I've got a little Jewish girl here. I'm sure she'll do the work that you want. She's very intelligent, very clean looking.' This is how he answered her, 'We don't want Jews.' She said, 'But you haven't seen the girl. Interview her and then if you don't want her, fair enough.'*

*At that time they were offering seventeen shillings and sixpence a week. I said to her, 'If I've got to work with people that really resent me, I'm not starting for under a pound a week! And when I've been there three months he's got to give me a raise in the salary otherwise I don't want the job!' She told the man that so he said, 'Oh, she's got a business head on her.' So I went for the interview. I had to do a geography test, an arithmetic test, an English test with spelling. I got the job and they were thrilled but after a couple of years they wouldn't give me promotion. I went to see this Sergeant Major and said, 'Why don't you want to promote me?' He said, 'Well, we don't want Jewish people to advance.' I said, 'Well that's it. Now you can have your job. But you've put ideas in my head. If I'd have come to you with the name of Smith or Green or White, what would you have done?' he said, 'We'd have probably promoted you up the ladder.' It was something I had to learn the hard way.*

On the subject of acquiring the married name of Jones, she explained, 'My father-in-law had a tailoring shop in Notting Hill Gate and on the shop front was the name W. JONES. He was a Russian, a first-class tailor who couldn't speak a word of English. He took the name of Jones for a business name.'

Alfred Levitt, another interviewee, said, 'The Mosley organisation was a problem at that time. They used to have meetings every Saturday. I think one was in Ridley Road in Dalston on a Saturday night. He had a van with a loudspeaker on it. They used to draw people round. The nearest meeting to us was in Whitechapel. Before the

Battle of Cable Street we knew there was going to be trouble.' Could it be happening here as it was elsewhere? Louis Collin's father, born near Warsaw, thought so: 'He said, "You must learn a trade. If anything happens in this country and you need to get out quickly and you haven't got a trade in your hand, you're completely lost!" That was his argument. He wouldn't even let me join the Boy Scouts because he had a horror of uniforms. He used to tell me about how in the small villages the soldiers used to come in and drag the elderly men along by their beards.'

The tales of beard-pulling soldiers were no longer scare stories, the men in black were no longer mere bogeymen to a new generation of British Jews, but a real and tangible threat.

# The Day of the Battle

## Were It Not For the Battle

For some readers it may come as a surprise to find that the section here on the Battle of Cable Street is not particularly large and that it doesn't even appear to be the main focus of this book. The Battle is, after all, the single most famous event that occurred in the street, the immediate area, and perhaps the whole of East London. But its influence, directly and indirectly, seeps out into the subject matter of the larger part of all the other histories contained here. Many of them would not exist at all were it not for the Battle, and its story is also told through them.

It is not my aim to try and set down a definitive account of the Battle. It is my intention to let the people in the book speak for themselves (although some readers may think that I stick my oar in far too often). Also, I'm not sure that a definitive account is even possible. But because the Battle is so central to the Cable Street story, I feel that a brief description of the events of the day is necessary. And I can't think of a better one than that reproduced below, concluding on page 37, from the book *The Battle of Cable Street 1936*, compiled by the Cable Street Group; a concise thumbnail sketch of the day when the high-born Sir Oswald Mosley, creator of the British Union of Fascists, personally gathered his Blackshirt army at the borders of East London in an attempt to intimidate its people. A day when history was made.

# A Brief History

Throughout the summer of 1936 tension mounted in London's East End as marches and meetings were organised in response to the BUF's anti-Semitic propaganda and the often violent activities of its Blackshirts. The announcement, on 26th September, of a massive BUF march through predominantly Jewish Stepney was greeted with alarm and dismay. A petition signed by 100,000 was organised by the Jewish People's Council calling on the march to be banned. Local Labour MP George Lansbury and the mayors of the four East London Boroughs appealed directly to the Home Secretary, Sir John Simon, but his answer was that such a ban would be undemocratic.

Mosley's intention was that BUF contingents from all over the country would assemble in Royal Mint Street near Tower Bridge to be inspected by him before dividing into columns which would march to meetings in Shoreditch, Limehouse and Bow and finally to a rally in Bethnal Green. The Left was at first uncertain how to respond. Moderate elements rejected the inevitable violence of a confrontation and called upon the march to be ignored. Labour Leaders, the newspaper *The Daily Herald* and The Board of Deputies of British Jews all followed this line. The Communist Party was caught in a dilemma. On October 4th, the day of the planned march, a rally in Trafalgar Square had been organised by the Young Communist League in solidarity with the Republicans in Spain's Civil War and they were reluctant to cancel it. But the pressure from local activists was intense and the Communist Party's leadership gave way. The headlines in their newspaper *The Daily Worker* on October 2nd ran 'East End rallies against Fascism... prepares to answer Mosley's march... Youth Meet transferred'. The Spanish Republicans' slogan 'They Shall Not Pass' was adopted and anti-fascists urgently set about using the little time they had left to prepare to stop the march.

Mosley's exact route was not known and the anti-fascists designated four assembly points, Leman Street,

Gardiners Corner (Aldgate), Cable Street and St George's Street (now The Highway). Fights broke out as groups of fascists began to converge on the area. However the major confrontation was between anti-fascists and the six thousand police, including the entire mounted division whose task it was to clear the roads to allow Mosley's march to get through. Baton charges were made to clear Leman Street to Gardiners Corner from where Commercial Road led into the heart of Stepney. But at Gardiners Corner an unexpected obstacle was encountered — a tram, one of four immobilised by their anti-fascist drivers. This obstacle and the sheer number of people made this route impassable. An eye-witness compared the scene to Wembley Stadium on Cup Final Day with a huge crowd cheering and singing. The *News Chronicle* reported 310,000 but some eye witnesses put the figure at over half a million people.

To the south of St George's Street was unattractive to the fascists. Where it was not lined by warehouses it passed through Catholic Wapping rather than Jewish Stepney and attention was turned on the one remaining available route — Cable Street.

According to a pre-arranged plan a lorry was overturned to form a barricade with material from a builder's yard. In the ensuing battle police were pelted with fruit, bottles and the contents of chamber pots from the upper windows of houses as they launched repeated baton charges. The barricade was cleared only for the police to encounter further blockades and be forced back by anti-fascist attacks. Injuries and arrests mounted as the police made little headway and eventually the Metropolitan Police Commissioner, Sir Phillip Game, ordered Mosley to abandon the march. The three thousand Blackshirts turned about and marched through the deserted streets of the City of London to disperse on the Embankment. Mosley issued a statement seething at the 'surrender' of the British Government to 'red terror'. In London's East End the anti-fascists' celebrations went on long into the night.

# 'The difference between a riot and an achievement'

Three first-hand accounts by veterans of the Battle, not previously published in their entirety. The first two interviews were undertaken as part of the research for the painting of the Cable Street Mural. The following, with Sam Berkovitz, was carried out by artist Dave Binnington and Denise Jones, in 1979.

## Sam Berkovitz

*I was a member of the Communist Party at that time and make no mistake, the Communist Party were the force behind it. They were organising a big demonstration at Trafalgar Square in an effort to push the national government into doing something about the Spanish Civil War. The Stepney Communist Party at that time was big, three quarters of it or more was Jewish and we were more anti-fascist than communist. The only people who were actively opposing the fascists was the Communist Party. There were little groups like the Independent Labour Party, there was the AJEX [The Association of Jewish Ex-Servicemen and Women] and there was Father John Groser. Father Groser was a big man here, he was great. He was based at the non-denominational Christ Church in Watney Street. He was not a communist but he would support any progressive action.*

*The Communist Party organised this big meeting about Spain for Sunday but the Jewish communists were the tail that wagged the dog. I was in the St. George's cell where Joe Jacobs was the secretary — he was also the secretary of the Communist Party in Stepney — and I was the agit-prop man. We had about three hundred members. We called an emergency meeting in a little café in Manningtree Street and we decided it wouldn't do for us to leave Stepney if Mosley was coming. We had two weeks warning.*

There would have been a response without us but we gave it direction and we gave it impetus. Joe was a disciplined communist. He went up to the [Party] centre and he argued the case. He told them that everyone was stopping him in the street — people were worried. But they said, 'No, this is a Party decision, you must all come to the Trafalgar Square rally.' Joe came back and we had our Monday night meeting, the next Sunday was going to be October the 4th and he says, 'What shall we do?' Joe was a powerful chap, about twenty or twenty-one, ten years younger than me. His reading was deep but narrow, Marx, Engels, Plotkin, the lot. For me, one page of Marx is enough. There were about eight of us around the cell, about two or three women. He says, 'I want a unanimous vote — we stay in Stepney!' There was us, a load of Yiddisher upstarts telling the centre what to do! Joe went back one more time to give them the ultimatum — 'Do what you like with us, we're not coming to Trafalgar Square!' All the others, the official Labour Party, their line was 'Stay away from Stepney on October the 4th.' Some of the religious bodies also said stay away.

He went there Wednesday. He stated calmly that whatever happened we were not leaving the East End because people looked up to us. We'd have a go. And I've no doubt he pointed out to them that it wouldn't be the first time the minority had been proved right. Then, something happened that night. We were waiting for him in the café and he said, 'The Party's agreed to switch.' That gave us Wednesday to Sunday, only four days. But we had all the whitewash ready. Before that we were pasting up: 'Go to Trafalgar Square'. Now we put up: 'No Pasaran', the Spanish Civil War slogan. I think that not only was Joe very persuasive but they were conscious of the powerful Jewish support they had here. The dockers wouldn't have turned out in Stepney to save Spain but they turned out to have a go at Mosley. In those four days we whipped up the biggest agitation you ever saw. We painted the slogan: 'Meet here at 12 o'clock. All out Gardiners Corner, all out Cable Street, all out Leman Street'. Mosley was a bad tactician. He got himself into a corner where he couldn't get out. Only the Communist Party had the ability to do it. We had a centre in Manningtree Street which would act as the HQ and there was an office in Great Garden Street. A key member at that time in getting it going was Phil Piratin. There was Alan Cohen — part of an association *of Jewish ex-servicemen — and a hardcore of toughs who came out of the billiard halls. They were not particularly socially conscious but they knew what fascism meant. They came out with their cues, you know?*

*By and large it was nobody but the Communist Party. I won't say the dockers wouldn't have had a go on their own but when they brought in the whole of the London Communist Party with groups of Jewish ex-servicemen coming from Manchester, from Leeds — they came by train specially — you had the hardcore of what we might call experienced people. Veterans. Without the Commun- ist Party there might have been a mêlée and a riot but it wouldn't have been a disciplined riot, which is the differ- ence between a riot and an achievement. The Party organised the demonstration, they ran it, they controlled it. And if there was any weakness anywhere they could whistle up twenty of the heavy mob. And that's all you needed. Mosley was a very capable person as a narrator but he didn't have the brains. We knew he wouldn't get through. He was humiliated. It was the biggest setback he ever had.*

*There were no banners at the event. You know why? Although the Communist Party organised it and directed it, it was not a Communist Party political stunt. It was a social reaction to a political threat. There was not a single banner because there were a lot of people there who would not have anything to do with commu- nism. There was a community at the time and everybody knew everybody in Stepney. So through our personal connections we could bring enough people to block the three entries into Stepney. I could go around the street and pick up a dozen pals right away. We could block any one street at any one time. I think they had a couple of lorries in reserve where the wheels were going to come off. Now, Cable Street can be blocked by a single lorry because it's narrow. We had mobs waiting in Brick Lane and all round the area. Nothing could get by them in a million years. The police charged once or twice so we backed up a bit but they were having difficulty them- selves with the amount of things being thrown on the floor. Things like glass marbles and stone marbles. The horses would slip and fall on them. The police were highly regarded in Stepney. But nevertheless at that place and point in time they were the enemy. They didn't have an enviable task.*

40

*All the main fighting went on at the top of Royal Mint Square, a big vast open space leading to the Tower. The BUF were all lined up ready but they couldn't go until the police gave them permission. They said, 'We'll clear the streets but at this stage you can't get through Cable Street and you can't get through Aldgate and you can't get through Whitechapel Road, you won't get through Commercial Street.' We had reserves in Commercial Road too. If he had got into Cable Street, I tell you, he would never have got out again. This went on for about two and a half hours by which time it was too late for him to go. It was about half past four and it was beginning to get dark. The police came over to where I was in Commercial Road and said, 'The march has been cancelled. I give you my word it's not a trick. They are marching back through the City. They're going back to their headquarters and we are going to start gradually evacuating the town and go back to our duties.' So we hung around a bit longer to make sure and then we had time for a march all round here. We had a party and a dance at one of the local town halls and that night I went out collecting money round the workshops. Three days later I was in Salmon Lane and Mosley was speaking there in his uniform and when he spoke about all the alien riff-raff who dared to prevent a free-born Englishman the very rights on which the English constitution was founded, the crowd didn't cheer, they bayed. That's the thing I remember most.*

## Julie Gershon

The following interview with Julie Gershon was recorded by me, also in 1979. I went to her flat in Upper Clapton. Julie was a charming and friendly woman, who spoke at length about the Battle and her growing political awareness throughout the 1930s and 1940s.

*I was the youngest of twelve children. My father was born in Belgium of French parents and my mother was Dutch. She was in the circus and got married at about sixteen or seventeen. My father was a tailor, he was a cripple. He got wounded in the arm in the African Congo when he was in the Belgium army. He was a coppersmith originally when*

41

*he met my mother and when he came over here he became
a tailor. It was a poor living with twelve children.*

*At the time of the Battle, Cable Street was very old and
very narrow. There were little tiny shops and businesses,
tailors' shops with people living above them. Very, very
poor. I worked in the Cable Street area for years as a tai-
loress but I lived in Stoke Newington. It was hard work
but it was easier for women than men really because girls
could do a lot of jobs that men couldn't. I used to just sew
on buttons, for instance. I think it was on the corner of
Pell Street. It was a little shop that was erected at the
back of a house in the yard. My father-in-law rented that
little workshop with machines in it. There was myself, my
husband and father-in-law and a machiner.*

*Before the war everybody used to go and see Mosley's
rallies at Olympia to try and prevent him holding his
meetings. A lot of our boys got in and we didn't recognise
them when they came out, they were beaten up so bad.
Their faces were like balloons, you just didn't recognise
them.*

*The Battle was on a Sunday and I wasn't working that
day. A crowd of us met about eight, nine o'clock in the
morning at Whitechapel corner before we went into Cable
Street. The BUF wanted to go to Cable Street because
there were a lot of Jews living down there. They wanted to
provoke them, you see? We stood at the corner of Leman
Street and Whitechapel and I think Mosley was supposed
to come along at about eleven o'clock but thousands of
people were there early in the morning. 'They Shall Not
Pass' was the slogan that day. I resented them marching,
obviously. We didn't like the Blackshirts. They might
have reached the beginnings of Cable Street but they
didn't get down there. People were throwing things out of
their windows, anything to build up the barricades so
they couldn't pass. There were Jews and Irish, the lot.
Everybody was down there.*

*I can see Mosley now, marching at the head of his
troops. One little old woman was standing at the side as
everybody was booing and shouting as he was marching
along and suddenly she gave him the [Sieg Heil] salute
and my brother-in-law who was standing by the side of
me shouted out, 'Mosley' — Mosley turned round — he
said, 'There's one for you here, look.' And there was this
dear little old soul giving him the salute. She didn't know
what it was all about, I'm sure she didn't. My mind can*

42

go back and I can see it. The people were terrific. It was the feeling of togetherness and the fact that they didn't get through, that was what was most amazing when they had all that police support. The only side fight I saw was a bunch of fascists trying to get through at Whitechapel. The dressmakers used to have black vans which they used for carting the clothes from one shop to another. And we used to let them though because they were going to their shops to deliver their goods. When one got half way through the crowd it opened and out came a bunch of about eight or nine Blackshirts. They thought they were clever. They didn't last long in that crowd, they were out before you could say Jack Robinson. That's when the police came in: they dragged them out of the crowd.

The only thing I didn't approve of — I'm soft, you see — was when the police came down the street on their horses and they started throwing marbles underfoot. Perhaps I was stupid, perhaps I was wrong but I didn't approve of that. The horses fell but they weren't hurt. When the police came down on horses, you see, we thought that Mosley was going to march after them, but they didn't. I don't know why they call it the Battle of Cable Street really because he didn't reach Cable Street. People were throwing bedding, tables, chairs, everything out of the windows to build barricades. It was terrific to watch. Something you could never forget. I can remember the old girls with their aprons on and the men's caps that they used to wear in those days with shawls round their shoulders and glory in their faces. I'd like to be able to do a picture.

There seemed to be thousands of police there. Everything seemed gigantic to me then, everything. If you asked me how many people there were I'd say millions. There weren't, of course. But the crowd didn't start with the police, they weren't concerned with the police. It was the Blackshirts they wanted and they were so well protected that we couldn't get to them. There were still people milling about at eight o'clock in the evening, meetings on street corners popping up. But the Mosley march just drifted away, they couldn't get anywhere. There was a terrific feeling that evening, the workers felt as if they'd won something, they really did, they didn't pass.

My husband was in the Communist Party. I met him through the Rego strike in Edmonton, the first strike after the General Strike. I was made a union delegate to the London Trades Council. But of course, I'm not a speaker,

43

*you see, and wasn't very politically minded. But I knew which side I was on. I went to Russia and was out there for eight months. Delegates went from all over the country, shirt makers, miners, factory workers. We all went to stay with people from the trades we followed here in England. I lived there on the same wage that a clothing worker in Russia would live on. I was taken around the factories and that sort of thing. I was close to the Party but I never actually became a member. I used to sell the* Daily Worker *in those days in dockland at about five in the morning by the gates and then I used to have to go all the way back to Edmonton where I was working to start the day.*

*During the war I joined the fire service and I was stationed in Whitechapel. Mosley was in jail then and fascism wasn't allowed. They weren't even allowed to wear their black shirts. No street corner meetings. They kept low, they kept very low. We never heard anything about them. They just died away. I never think of myself as anything but a worker. I say whatever happens now I know what side of the barricades I've got to go on when the time comes.*

# Mr and Mrs Ginsberg

The final interview in this section was carried out by the Cable Street Group in the late 1980s. We talked to Mr and Mrs Ginsberg jointly; they both had vivid memories in particular of the behaviour of the police on the day. During the conversation we also learnt that Mr Ginsberg, the son of a Russian shoe repairer, was a violinist in a small group who provided the musical accompaniment for silent films. During the Second World War he formed a group which played music 'entertaining the people' in some of the larger bomb shelters.

Mr Ginsberg: *I lived in Cable Street all the time up until 1938 when I got married. People by then were scattering all over the place. I didn't know my wife then but she was at the Battle. I was there right at the front. I saw the crowds so I went right through them. Foolish! Mosley's crowds were in Royal Mint Street. The police were lined up in Leman Street and Dock Street and the beginning of Cable Street so I went — Nosey Parker — right to the*

44

*front to see what was happening. I was foolish being in front because when they started pushing forward — the police were on horseback — they didn't care who they pushed or threw down.*

Mrs Ginsberg: *Policemen's helmets were flying and boys' teeth were being knocked out. They were banged on the head with truncheons. It was terrifying.*

Mr Ginsberg: *I went to help this chap, the horse had jumped on his stomach. He was in terrific pain. I went to help him but the police were saying, 'Get back, get back.' They were going to hit me, I had to go back; I couldn't help the man. But Mosley never got past. We all expected it — that was why there were so many people there. It was a very heavy atmosphere. Many people were afraid, they stayed in their houses and wouldn't come out. But a lot of us did. When they did turn back there were people on the floor, injured.*

Mrs Ginsberg: *I belonged to the Labour League of Youth — the Labour Party. The Blackshirts were going through our streets and a friend of mine said, 'Come on, join us.' So I did and we all went to Cable Street and that's how I became involved. I was there in the thick of it and saw all the horses coming at us. I was terrified. I went to the corner and said to the police, 'I want to go home.' He said, 'No, you can't go that way,' and he sent me back into the mêlée. It was like a war. They built a barricade in the middle, the men did. Everything they could lay their hands on — tables and chairs and God knows what.*

Mr Ginsberg: *It came as a great shock because the police were our friends. They used to walk along the street and we used to say hello. Every time the police walked they used to try the door. Every door they tried. They used to give advice and have a drink in the pub. They were very friendly the local police. But here they were from the Midlands — somewhere up north — goodness knows where they came from. They had strange policemen. And here they were banging people on the head. A great shock.*

Mrs Ginsberg: *They suffered too. We saw policemen with blood streaming down their faces. They didn't have it all their own way. It was their job to allow Mosley to march through. They tried but there were masses and masses of people and it was impossible to get through even with horses. They had to give up in the end and turn him back.*

# 3. The Voices of Cable Street
# The Cable Street Group

## 'A shadowy group'

The Cable Street Group is a 'small, unelected, unac-
countable, shadowy group of white middle class people'.
Or rather, that's how it was described in a Respect Party
e-mail in 2006 when George Galloway was the MP for
Bethnal Green and Bow. The group was also damned as
a 'New Labour clique', some of whose members were 'very
closely connected' to the Blair-led Labour Government
and to the local Labour Party. This electronically-
communicated kicking occurred in the run-up to the 70th
anniversary of the Battle of Cable Street, for reasons that
will be explained. As for the actual accusations? Well, it
must be said that some of them are true. And I speak as
a member of the Cable Street Group.

## The 50th Anniversary

Twenty years earlier, a 50th anniversary celebration of the
Battle had been organised by a coalition of the Tower
Hamlets Trades Council, local community groups and various anti-fascist and anti-racist organisations. In that year
of 1986, there was an increased resonance in the story of
the Battle. One of the organisers, Liane Venner explains,
'What we set out to do was recognise a great event in history and to link it to current issues; the idea that there were
parallels with the struggles of the Jewish community and
those faced by the new Bangladeshi community in a time of
increasing right-wing activity in the area.'

The event, on the actual anniversary date, October the
4th, started in Altab Ali Park on Whitechapel High Street,

where a speech from Battle veteran Phil Piratin set in motion a well-attended procession. With banners and placards held high, it made its way up Brick Lane, along Bethnal Green Road and down Cambridge Heath Road — heckled by the patrons of a couple of well-known fascist pubs on the route — and finally arrived at the wide expanse of Bigland Green near Cable Street itself. Here, on a stage hastily erected the night before, there was a rally that featured music from local Bangladeshi groups, youth bands and those politically hard-edged representatives of the New Wave, The Men They Couldn't Hang. Such was the concern about the growth of right-wing activity in East London that volunteers slept on site overnight to defend it from possible sabotage.

The event had been a huge undertaking; from the mammoth task of fundraising (from unions and elsewhere), liaison with the police and local council, down to organising a beer tent and portable loos. Problems sprung up at every turn: a flyer for the event caused outrage amongst Bangladeshi groups. It included a montage of images from the Battle alongside contemporary black and white photos featuring the scarred bodies of Asian youths; and although intended as a warning on the evils of racism it seemed to cast them as victims. Other pictures of aggressive 'White Power' skinheads, could have come straight from a National Front recruitment poster. The flyer was hastily withdrawn. But despite all this, after the event, it was felt that the aims of the organisers had been achieved.

Then, after the celebration and self-congratulation had died down, what next? Simply wait around for the 60th Anniversary before reminding people of this proud chapter of East London history? Nobody is quite sure who first suggested it, but it was proposed — somewhat ambitiously — that what to do next was to compile a book dedicated to the oral history of Cable Street.

# The Idea of a Book

In its initial stages, the make-up of the Cable Street Group was liquid — without even a name — but it quickly solidified around the task of contacting past Cable Street dwellers and interviewing them on tape. In the original plan, the Battle would only occupy a section of the book. Rather, it would focus on the lives of the people who lived there at that period. However, during the planning of the anniversary event, group members had been surprised at just how few people had heard the story of the Battle, or had only a vague notion of what had actually happened. It was decided therefore that a small booklet, explaining it all, and using extracts from the tapes we had made, would be a useful stop-gap until the production of the much bigger compilation. The latter never actually happened, though the book you are holding is a distant relative of that original idea. Dan Jones was one of those who collaborated in the writing of *The Battle of Cable Street 1936*; the core group members steering it through to publication being Jil Cove, Richard Humm, Liane Venner, Derek Gadd and Denise Jones. I had worked with Denise previously and she suggested I be invited into the group because of my oral history and publication experience.

## *'Cable Street?'*

All of the group members have strong connections with Cable Street and retain vivid memories of their introduction to the area. Jil, the lynch-pin of the group, was based at Whitechapel's Royal London Hospital in the early 1960s. She recalls, 'Four of us trainee midwives decided to explore the area. I'd heard about Cable Street and we asked a woman the way. And because we were nurses she said that she wasn't going to give us directions — it wasn't for the likes of us to go down there! Which, of course, intrigued us even more. We eventually arrived in Cable Street. It was seedy but it was quite fun.' Jil later became a probation officer until taking early retirement. As previously mentioned, Denise and her husband Dan have lived in Cable Street since 1967. And even though many of the slums and dodgy cafés had already been bull-dozed, Denise remembers that the place still had a reputation. On entering a local pub after going to see what became their house for the first time: 'Dan went up to the bar to get a drink and this woman came up to me and asked if he was bothering me. It turned out that she thought I was a prostitute and Dan was my pimp.'

According to my theory that you can only be sure you are doing the right thing in Cable Street if you get sacked, vilified or arrested for it, group members have form: both Jil and Derek were arrested during what became known as the 'Wapping dispute'. The year-long action, starting in 1986, was one of many which drew on the power of the Battle. And this one had the cachet of happening just round the corner. Following Rupert Murdoch's News International move to East London and the effective lock-out of his skilled unionised print work-force — in order that he could take on less bothersome unskilled ones — a group of local people picketed with disgruntled ex-workers, attempting to halt the lorries bringing out the dailies. Derek, an archaeologist and one-time Museum of London worker, was part of this night-time haunting of 'Fortress Wapping'. Police cor-dons, horses and barriers once more made parts of Cable Street into no-go areas as the late-night lorries thundered past and the bussed-in coppers waved their overtime pay at the demonstrators. A year into the turmoil, banner-bearer Derek was hauled by the lapels through police lines, banged up (for a few hours, anyway) and fitted up as the victim of a less than competent 'canteen conspir-acy', accused of all manner of things, before eventually emerging triumphant, vindicated and in pocket via an out-of-court settlement. The boycott itself was not successful, finishing after a year with not a day's newspaper production halted.

Liane, by this time, had moved into the borough. Then a worker for the USDAW union, she also became a fixture in the world of Tower Hamlets politics and threw herself into a variety of local campaigns ('I'm a serial joiner'). Richard Humm is certain that he first entered Cable Street on the back of a lorry — singing. 'I was involved in running a folk club called The Knave of Clubs in Bethnal Green during the early 1970s with Michael Rosen, Sandra Kerr and other people. We were working with Ewan McColl and Peggy Seeger but split with them in 1971 to set up our own group called Combine.' They performed benefits for various actions, such as the building workers' strike of 1972, sometimes from the back of that lorry. Later on, Richard became a social worker, based in the Street itself. And as for myself, the announcement to my family that I was moving to Cable Street brought about a not dissimilar reaction to that received by Jil more than twenty years before. 'Cable Street?' — my dad said, screwing his face up in horror, recalling the days of long-gone ponces and knocking shops — 'Cable Street!'

The Cable Street Group, as well as promoting its book, has administered an ad-hoc programme of educational workshops, bookstall promotions and veteran get-togethers. It has also taken on itself the job of lobbying for the maintenance of the Cable Street Mural and provided speakers for a variety of events. The group also took ownership of the banner produced for the 50th Anniversary event — regarding it with the sort of reverence usually reserved for holy relics such as the Turin Shroud. It is unfurled every year next to the International Brigades Memorial to the casualties of the Spanish Civil War. An annual event takes place there, under the gaze of the slowly turning London Eye, in the South Bank's Jubilee Gardens. It is always well-attended, younger generations of supporters supplementing the handful of actual veterans, fading fast like their Battle of Cable Street contemporaries.

## The 70th Anniversary

During 2005, The Cable Street Group, in conjunction with Alternative Arts, began to make plans for the 70th anniversary the following year. 'I don't think we had ever stepped back and said — are we accountable to anybody?' says Liane. 'Should we think about the fact that we're an all-white group, some of us who don't live here anymore? But on the other hand, isn't it legitimate that people in a community, holding strong beliefs, should have the right to organise things?' But it was the seeming lack of accountability that Respect seized upon when they launched their attack on the group. Yes, some of the group were Labour Party members. Indeed, since the group began, Derek had met, married and begun to raise a family with Ruth Kelly, then a Cabinet Minister in the Blair government. But, contrary to criticisms, others in the group were not in the Labour Party at all, never had been, were not middle class and, given their very visible and vocal promotion of various events, could hardly be described as 'shadowy'.

Derek explains, 'We had decided that we didn't want the standard kind of political rally with dignitaries making speeches. Instead, we asked Harold Rosen, who had been at the Battle and his son, children's writer Mike Rosen, to give their perspectives. Then, once we started to get the publicity out we got contact from Respect, offering George Galloway to speak. We replied — thanks but no thanks. Then, an acrimonious exchange of e-mails started to take place which culminated in Respect adopting a position in which they supported the event but not the organisers. They saw the exclusion of Galloway as a deliberate snub. The irony being that one of the only

51

speakers on the day, Michael Rosen, had become a member of the Respect Party!'

The event, held on a sunny autumn Sunday, was focused around the Battle mural on the side of St. George's Town Hall in Cable Street. The open space behind the building provided space for a stage, stalls and marquees. Festivities began at noon with the inevitable march and a piece of street theatre by the Cardboard Citizens group (brilliantly realised from an idea on the back of an envelope by myself). There followed music from the Jewish, Bangladeshi and Irish communities. And to his credit, George Galloway came to show his support even without the opportunity to speak and was welcomed alongside the 10,000 crowd that attended during the day. When the event overran and the electricity was finally cut off, it was left to the Grand Union Orchestra, who had composed a specially written jazz piece, *No Pasaran!,* to perform an improvised jam amongst the crowd. The sun dipped behind the trees as the music continued, an appropriate display of people power on which to finish the day.

As for the future of the Cable Street Group, Derek observes, 'In terms of staying power, the group has been quite remarkable. It's still in existence after twenty-five years and is currently making plans for future commemorations. We've linked up with dozens of groups and individuals during that time, so it's not a closed shop.' But he adds, 'It's just that we haven't invited anyone else in.'

# I Was Born in Cable Street

## Shopkeepers, Bakers and Boot-menders

*I was born at number 28 Cable Street above a shoe shop which belonged to my uncle. His name was Rabinovitz. My dad was an immigrant — a Russian. My mother came from Lithuania. They were brought over, I think, by my uncle who came here in about 1880 something. My mother had several sisters and several brothers all in the vicinity of Cable Street. And at the age of three or four we immigrated to Christian Street. Christian Street! I do not know of any non-Jew who lived in Christian Street! This is the paradox. My father died when I was ten years old and the house was condemned. They came round and offered my mother alternative accommodation in Hackney and she said, 'No way am I leaving the country at this time in my life.' She didn't know anything else existed.*

*This picture was sent by Arnold Schwartzman from Hollywood USA. It features his grandparents Mr and Mrs Michael Finkleson with daughter Gertrude and son Ben on either side, outside their boot repairers at 292A Cable Street.*

Those were the words of Hymie Mesnick, one of the Cable Street Group's interviewees, captured in the extended period of recording activity following the 1986 'Battle' anniversary. All the following extracts in this chapter derive from that time, detailed in the 'Recording Cable Street' section. Hymie Mesnick's perception of the ethnic makeup of the area was backed up by others. Alfred Levitt (whose original name was Lefervitch) said, 'In the area where I was, if you took a hundred shops to the left or to the right there might have been four families that weren't Jewish. All the rest were Jewish. We had nothing and didn't want too much. I wouldn't want to go back there but I enjoyed it at the time because I didn't know any different. I liked the people — we were always in one another's houses. It was a very friendly place.'

These two interviewees were typical of those that the group spoke to: first generation British, born into families of incoming shopkeepers, bakers and boot-menders. Many had more than one occupation. Alfred Levitt's father was born in Poland, his mother in Stepney Green. They ran a tobacconists and sweet shop but were quick in spotting new opportunities: installing pinball machines to satisfy the sailors who dropped in, and flogging slot machines to the Maltese cafés. The illegal 'one-arm-bandits' they kept in the backroom of the shop.

I have reproduced several of the interviews at length, giving a sense of the spirit of those engrossing encounters. The following account is by Kate Beresford.

## 'That's not our fish and chips'

*Our shop was a fried fish and chip shop: H. Lascombe, Luncheon and Supper Bar, at 32 Cable Street. My parents came from Poland. My father, Harry, came here in about 1910. He was eighteen or nineteen and he met my mother here. She was brought over as a baby, so she knew more of England than Poland. My father managed to get this shop and he was there from 1911 until the time that he died in 1955. There were six children and I was the eldest. We were all born in Cable Street, upstairs to the shop where we lived.*

*I started working in the shop immediately I left Christian Street School at fourteen, selling fish and chips for tuppence. And it wasn't a half a piece of fish — it was a whole piece of fish! We used to sell skate, plaice, haddock, rock salmon — there are two kinds, catfish and dogfish — and cod. Also, small haddocks that they used to call chats and we used to sell them at a penny, penny ha'penny, tuppence. But the favourite was skate because we had a Catholic trade and middle skate is the favourite. We had a kosher home and my sisters wouldn't eat skate — I myself ate all the fish! My day started at eleven o'clock till two, had a break in the afternoon, and then from five o'clock till half past eleven. Until twelve o'clock at night I was working, every day — Saturday included — bar Sunday. It was such a wonderful atmosphere. It was a long day and life carried on later on. We had an eating area in the shop with twelve or fourteen little marble topped tables with four chairs each to sit on. Previous to that we had wooden tables with wooden seats. In the summer when we'd finished serving our customers we used to get our chairs and sit outside our shop and be there till two or three o'clock in the morning. Other neighbours like the bicycle shop further along the road were doing it. This one would go and make tea and then this one would go in and make tea. It was a real party. It was a real family. It was wonderful. It was my life. It was all I knew and I loved it.*

*Pre-war my father never used frozen fish but lots of other shops were using it. He got his fish from Billingsgate and brought it home every day on a barrow. There were other fish shops near Watney Street but 'Ginger's' was still the favourite — my father was called Ginger in his younger days — and people knew him as that. If they sent you out as a child to go and get the fish and chips and you were lazy, even before it was opened the parents knew that it never came from Ginger's. And they'd say, 'Take it back.' Or they'd come back with it, saying, 'Why did you give them this?' And I used to say, 'I never served her, that's not our fish and chips.'*

*During the war you were rationed. If you got fish one day, you couldn't get fish for another day. We were rationed with the oil, we were rationed with the flour and the coal. In the Second World War my life was in the shelter. If I was serving fish and chips when the siren went, up went the fish and chips and I was off. My dad used to say, 'Where's she gone again? She's off!' I lived in the shelter, I slept there. It was in Commercial Road at the top of Alie Street. We had a very lucky escape one night. The siren had gone about twenty to seven. Well, it took time for us to get out although I was all ready to run and I used to say, 'Come on Mummy, come on Daddy.' They used to say, 'Well, you go.' Because they weren't keen on going to the shelter. I said, 'No, I can't go without you.' Well, gradually the people got to know that we had the fish shop. It was difficult for them to have a meal when they came home from work before getting in the shelter. So they used to say to us, 'Will you fetch us in fish and chips — that'll be our supper which would be lovely — into the shelter?' Anyway, this night we must have had about four bags between us. There was about twenty or twenty-five packages of fish and chips. And we're chasing up Gower's Walk. We could see them all and hear them all above us. The flares are coming down. I'm saying, 'Come on Mummy, come on Daddy.' I'm running on ahead. 'Go, go,' they said. I said, 'No!' Well, thank God we just managed to get in the shelter because if we'd have got caught outside, nobody would have known who, what and where we were. We got down to our place and people were all coming round to us, they were wanting their food. All of a sudden, through the lift shaft came a bomb. Up went the fish and chips. Nobody had fish and chips that night.*

# The Eccentrics of Cable Street

Sometimes, our interviewees didn't seem clear about what we wanted of them. Some mentioned the various neighbourhood eccentrics they remembered from their childhood. I personally wondered if they presented us with these stories because they didn't believe that we could really be interested in the minutiae of their own everyday lives. But I realised that these figures represented shared memories; the same people kept cropping up. For instance, the Irish ambulance-chaser in a homburg hat and velvet collar — a pair of race-goers' binoculars permanently slung around his neck — who would seek out accident victims and split the damages by offering himself as a witness. A huge man, he also dealt in stolen property. On one occasion he was seen dangling two policemen — who had the temerity to raid his flat — by the scruff of their necks from his upstairs window. There was the jittery, shell-shocked Great War veteran who was able to magically talk up fallen horses. And another, 'Katy Warhorse', was a six foot tall Amazon, constantly downing huge jugs of water, egged on by the kids. Two of the women we spoke to recalled the regular visits of a group of street entertainers known as 'The Nancy Boys'. The troupe of female impersonators, in elaborate wigs and costumes, would cart a white barrel organ around with them and let the children turn the handle as they danced and sang, collecting coins outside the pubs. As children, one of our interviewees was thrilled by the outrageous glamour they brought to the street while the other fled in terror. And there were many, many funny stories: such as that concerning a family of feuding brothers, Ralph, Isaac and Sidney Sole. After their frequent rows they would remove the initial of the offending brother or brothers from above their clothes shop, on one occasion leaving the name R. Sole to greet the street in the morning.

## 'King of the Bakers'

The following is from an interview with Gerald Broer:

*My father came from Poland in 1926 and he worked his way up. He was a foreman baker at Lyons in Cadbury Hall. My mother came over in 1926 and they got married. She pawned her wedding ring to get the shop in 1930: one pound ten shillings a week it was — sixteen rooms. They didn't speak Polish at home. My father was very well-educated. My mother what she lacked in education she made up for in common sense. People used to come far and wide to see my mother, she was so clever. Marvellous woman. My*

*father was the best baker in London. When he was in the
Union of Bakers his nickname was the 'King of the Bakers'
and when he took over the shop he became a master baker.*

*I was born in Underwood Road in 1928 and we moved
to Cable Street on July the 4th, 1930. There was my mum
and dad and my sister. And we stayed there until
January, 1957. The bakery was a family business. I
worked there after school. It was my regular job to go
down to the cellar and bring out thirty buckets of coal.
Took about half an hour. It was continuous. When we got
on a bit we employed one or two bakers and a pastry cook.
But my parents worked night and day. The week used to
start on Saturday night and we worked continuously till
twelve o'clock on Friday, then we never baked anymore
till Saturday night again. On the Jewish Sabbath we
never worked. My father worked hard and earned a living
but it wasn't the kind of business where you could make a
lot of money. The government gave a subsidy on every loaf
so that you could keep the price down. Otherwise you
would have lost money because the bread was four and a
half pence a loaf and it cost six or seven pence to make
and sell it. The area was poor and bread was the main
thing the people bought — the backbone of their diet. It
was hard work. We never had money. My mother said if
people gave her all the money they owed her she could buy
a Rolls Royce. Everybody was like that. But we got on
because my father was this wonderful baker and my
mother was a wonderful cake baker.*

*Charrington's Coal Merchants had a long stretch of
Cable Street exactly opposite. They used to dump hundreds and hundreds of tons from the trucks on the
railway above. It used to be like you would picture in
Wales — mountains of coal! The dust used to blow all
over and my mother was forever washing the curtains:
they were always black from the coal dust. In the war we
got blasted out a few times. We had lots of incendiary
bombs fall on it. There used to be trucks carrying anti-
aircraft guns up and down the lines so the railway was
a target. The landmines used to come down on para-
chute. It never hit the ground, it used to explode, say, a
hundred feet above the ground and the blast used to be
devastating. One fell just outside one of the bridges. It
blew everything out of our place. Everything was blown
apart. A couple of times we went to the shelters but usually we used to go under the arches which had been*

*bricked in. But my father used to bake at night. He should have gone but he thought it was his duty to bake.*

Gerald Broer also told us about two very vivid childhood memories:

*There were one or two seaman's homes. And one of my earliest recollections — I must have been six or seven years old — was somebody running into the shop and saying, 'We've seen a black man.' I said, 'Where? I've never seen one in my life.' They said, 'He's a seaman.' So about fifty of us ran down to the seaman's home and we stood outside waiting and waiting. Then he walked out. It was a black man! We couldn't believe it. We'd never seen anybody with a black skin. We must have followed him for about half an hour, trailing behind him. It was the funniest thing, the most peculiar thing. But you can imagine, never to have seen anyone with a dark skin! It was amazing, the reaction.*

*A place that brings back bad memories: the corner of Cable Street and Back Church Lane. It was called the Prunella and you had to go there to see about your teeth. And most times they pulled them out! Downstairs there were lines and lines of benches and you'd sit on a bench and a bell would ring, and as you walked up the stairs four or five kids came down with towels soaked in blood. You had to go every six months and nobody got away without their teeth being pulled out. It was horrible. You went upstairs to the waiting room where there might have been another eight or ten kids. Then the bell went again and another four or five kids walked out with blood-soaked towels around their mouths. And you'd go into this surgery where they've got four or five chairs like barber's chairs and they'd strap you in and they would put the mask over your face — it was straight gas — and pull out all your milk teeth — except me. I bit his hand and they chucked me out. So I never had them pulled out. It was horrible!*

# Cholents, Card Schools and Evacuation

In his interview, Gerald Broer mentioned how on a Friday afternoon his father would take in up to two hundred dishes which would be baked in the shop's ovens and the 'fantastic smell' that would drift up to his bedroom. Nita Freedman also remembered this weekly ritual:

*Because they were orthodox, the bakers didn't bake on Friday night for Sabbath. The big thing, especially during winter, was the cholent. It's a wonderful dish. The women used to buy the fattiest cuts of meat and you would have great big deep pots that you'd throw your beans in with onion, carrots, potatoes and the meat. In the middle my mother used to have a little dish where she made a pudding with flour and carrots and sultanas and peas. And we kids used to take it along to the bakers on Friday before the Sabbath came in. They weren't cooking bread, you see, but they didn't let their ovens go out overnight so for a couple of coppers the cholents were cooked in the oven over Friday night and Saturday. All the kids would be seen trotting along the road with the dishes from their mothers. Saturday lunchtime we used to go and bring them back and that was our meal. The baker was really nice. When us kids used to go along he used to give us a piece of broken biscuit when we got there.*

Nita also had vivid memories of their old house, the activities in the cellar and illicit goings-on in the street outside:

*Both my parents were from Poland. My father was a tailor. He hated writing English. He always used to get us to write for him but he spoke English quite well, with an accent. My mother was quite well spoken. She went to evening classes when the kids were small because she wanted to be able to speak and write English properly. She also worked in tailoring. She worked very hard. We all had to help — when we were kids we used to do the bastings and turn the sleeves through. It was a very menial task. My brothers and sisters used to go and deliver the work because my father used to make suits for tailors' shops all round London. My poor eldest brother was always kept away from school to help in the workshop. But I suspect that was common for lots of people. I suppose it's a bit like the Asian families around London now.*

*I was born at home at number 80 Cable Street in 1931. There were five of us. It was an old Victorian pub, with a date on the glass windows and a crown and anchor in*

60

*frosted glass. We had a bendy staircase to go upstairs with a door at the bottom and a window in the stairs that you could look down onto the workshop. That was probably a big public bar originally because it had side doors and there was a small room at the front that was probably the saloon bar. And there was another little bar at the back. It had cellars underneath that the locals used as an air raid shelter. My father was a great gambler as they all were. All the men used to go down there to play cards when the air raids broke out. A lot of the police who were recruited for the war liked their game of cards. When the sergeant needed the copper who was missing he was generally there. At least that's the myth that's been told to me. The main games they played were Solo and Klabberjass. I don't ever remember my parents quarrelling all my life. Only once I remember my mother being really bad tempered. My dad and his cronies were playing cards after they'd finished work and she always had to make them sandwiches and once she was making kippers and she was muttering so much about the card players.*

*We didn't have betting shops; they only originated in the early 1950s. It was illegal until the Betting Act came in. Bookmakers were very undercover but they had their offices. As you came down from Leman Street into Cable Street on the right hand side there was a barber shop by the very first street there. There used to be a tall, well-built guy with a slightly balding head who was a bookie's runner standing on the corner. And he used to spend his time in and out of that barber's shop. The men knew where to find him if they wanted him.*

Nita told us about when she was evacuated, an experience shared with several of the others we spoke to:

*That week we had to go to school every day with our gas masks that we had been issued with in yellow tin cans. And we had to take a packet of sandwiches and sultanas and little packets of Sun Pat raisins. We sat in the hall every day and didn't do any lessons. The kids just sat there every day because presumably they didn't know what day they were going. It seemed to me like we sat there forever more. And then when we did leave school we all went out by a gate round the side. I suppose the head thought that the parents wouldn't wait there but all the mothers were*

*standing there crying. We went from the British Rail sta-*
*tion in Watney Street to a family in Brighton. My parents*
*used to come and visit us but we weren't there very long. We*
*actually went to a couple who'd never had any children.*
*Very tough on them I should think.*

## 'No such thing as payment'

Walter Coleman was born in Dalston in 1911 and his
family moved to the Cable Street area when he was two
or three years old. After a fire gutted their home the
neighbours rallied round to house them until they found
a combined accommodation and shop in Well Street, now
Ensign Street:

*My father was a bootmaker, which was very good because*
*we were near the docks and the labourers wore very, very*
*hefty boots with great hobnails in and they used to come*
*to have them mended. One pair would take him more or*
*less all night long. Around five or six in the morning he*
*would wake one of us three boys up. The boots were very*
*heavy — we could hardly hold them! We would put the*
*laces round our neck with a boot hanging either side.*
*That was the easy way of carrying them. We delivered*
*them because that would be the chap's only pair of boots*
*and without them he couldn't get to work. That was the*
*reason why my father stayed up all night — because when*
*the dockers finished work they would bring the boots in to*
*him and they'd want them back in the morning. We, the*
*children, would ask for payment and of course there was*
*no such thing as payment. After my father had worked all*
*night all we would return home with was a thick ear! It*
*wasn't often they had work in the dock area so if a boat*
*came in they were lucky — and if they were paid then my*
*father would get paid. They took it for granted that Jack*
*— which was my father's name — would pay for the*
*leather and mend the boots and that was it.*
*My father started work when he was twelve years old.*
*Because his mother and father had both died the chil-*
*dren were given into care of an aunt. One of his first jobs*
*was to push a barrow from Leman Street over to*
*Bermondsey, pick up the hides for a bootmaker, and*

*push them all the way back. A little boy of twelve years old! All the tanneries were over there. When my brothers and I got older we used to go over there and get the leather for my father when we came home from school. He established himself but we hadn't been there more than four or five years when somebody came along and thought the property was very good and were able to buy it. We were tossed out. So that was the end of his business. From there we found a little home further down Well Street in a courtway called Harad's Place, leading into Wellclose Square. There were four courtways leading into Wellclose Square. There was Ship Alley, Grace's Alley, North East Passage and Harad's Place. They were very narrow. In Grace's Alley every other house was a shop whereas Ship Alley and Harad's Place were just houses. North East Passage had no houses at all: there was a large factory there.*

*Houses in Harad's Place were made up of rooms on ground level off a passage, and rooms above, just one floor. But there were also stairs going down, and downstairs were your living quarters, your kitchen and the back room, which was more or less a cellar. You used it for living in as well as keeping the coal. So you lived above and below ground level. You also had a backyard where your toilet was and where the water was for washing. There were no indoor facilities, everything was uncovered even in the freezing winter. You'd go out there without a shirt on to wash — it would have no effect! When we were very young we'd have a bath out in the open in the copper. As we got older, of course, we had a bath indoors where the water was heated up. We had gas lighting but no gas or electric for cooking — we used to cook on this great big stove run by coal with an oven. At the back of it would be a little outlet where the flames could come up again to another outlet where you could put the kettle on. Everything was either done in the oven or on the hob. The water was boiled in great big iron kettles which were held over the top of the fire. So you had plenty of hot water because that was going as long as the fire was alight. Everything was done on the range, even roasting meat: they were experts at doing it. It would be done on a hook on a spit, turning it with the big tray underneath to catch all the fat running down. It was great because all that fat became your bread and dripping to take to school. Nothing was wasted.*

## Street Games

Walter Coleman also told us about how children used to regularly play in the street — but that the local police didn't look upon it kindly:

*Wellclose Square was our playground and when you played football it would not be eleven each side, you'd have fifty or sixty playing, but none of the neighbours complained that you were a nuisance for the simple reason their children were playing as well. They were all about fourteen years old and we were nine or ten, so we were used as lookouts at the beginning of each alley because the police would come along and raid you. Not only in uniform, but in plain clothes. They would come creeping along by the side of the walls but we had a signal — from one end of the alley to the other we would whistle. I'll never forget one day when they had come down Well Street and were going to rush through Harad's Place. I gave the signal and as I did this plainclothes man clouted me — and I didn't know anything more for a couple of days! I was completely out. It was taken for granted — one of those things. I think I can still feel the pain from that clout. The way to get away was down Neptune Street, which led into the Highway. One mad rush. The police just got bowled over, nobody was usually caught but my brother was snookered with this other chap who was charged for committing a nuisance. He was taken to court and fined two shillings and sixpence, and his father was terribly upset because he was a very straight-laced type person. And when he left school and he went for his first job in an office in the City this cropped up. He had forms to fill in and he could not get the job and he finished up working as a furrier, which he hated from the moment he went into it to the day he finished. That was the sort of thing that playing in the streets caused!*

## 'We were the Spanish family'

Manuel Galdeano's family ran a café in the Cable Street area. After the Second World War, he and his wife, Gladys, moved into 35-37 Cable Street, above a dry cleaners run by

a man named Mosley ('not to be mixed up with the fascist'),
who was a retired policeman, and his family:

Manuel: *The majority of people in the area were Jewish.
But we were the Spanish family. During the 1914-18 war
my grandfather, on my mother's side, was a steelworker
in the Basque part of Spain near Bilbao. The family name
was Pardelous. I believe it was the norm at the time for
steelworkers to bring all their families to this country,
and they came to a place in Wales. My mother, who was
the oldest daughter, went to work in a seaman's boarding
home in Swansea and my father, who was a seaman,
stayed in this boarding house. They got married there
and then once the war was over, the whole retinue came
to London to seek their fortune. They opened this little
café which was in the first turning in Cable Street. It was
called Well Street in those days. It was basically for
Spanish seamen. They made just one meal a day, usually
a Spanish meal, and everybody including the family
dived in, whatever it was. Then some time later my
grandfather decided he wanted to go back to Spain to live
and he took his two youngest children with him. My
mother and father took the café over.*

*My parents and grandfather were very sympathetic to the
Spanish government. In other words, they were anti-fascist.
My grandfather was a very jovial man and he played a very
good guitar. He formed a group called the Pardelous
Quartet and played at various fundraisers for the Basque
people and had quite a following. My father, apart from
having the café, also supplied goods to Spanish ships —
Republican ships — because he was a ship chandler. He
had various contacts with the Spanish people but the
British Government placed an embargo on the ships. They
were in the various docks and weren't allowed to leave until
the Spanish war ended and then they were all turned over
to Franco. That's when my father's business went kaput.
The ships didn't move so neither did his business. The captains who we knew in the London Docks came to live with
us. They daren't go back to Spain because they were
Republicans, known to be anti-Franco. It wasn't until many
years later that they could go back safely.*

On leaving the Merchant Navy and before joining the
RAF, Manuel met his wife to be while she was working in
a pub opposite the Ivory House in St Katharine's:

65

Gladys: *He wanted me to go to Weston-Super-Mare for Christmas where he was. He said, 'Why don't you come down and we'll get married.' You had to get a signature from your mother in those days if you were under twenty-one, I think. My mother drank a lot and at first she said I could go and then she said I couldn't. While she was drinking I guided her hand to sign the permission. I went down and we got married on the Christmas Eve. I came back a week later and got to the door, knocked to go in and when it opened she gave me such a fourpenny one. 'Where have you been?' she said. 'Where the bloody hell do you think I've been?' I said. 'Don't you remember? I got married!' She went mad: 'Got married?' I said, 'Well, you knew we were getting married.' I sort of talked her into it, and she was going, 'Well, I remember something about it.' So then I said, 'Can we rent a room off of you?' So she said, 'Well, I'll charge you half price.'*

*There were three flats over this cleaners — the Mosleys had the third flat — and as one of the others was vacant, we took it. We used one for sleeping in and the other for living in. I had visions of being a hairdresser or a sales lady but my mum said to me, 'You've got to get out to work, you've got to find a job. I need the money.' So I went to Louis London's in Alie Street for 11 / 8d a week and served my apprenticeship as a machinist there, but I think before I learnt to machine I learned to swear. We had this forelady and every word out of her mouth was a swearword. I was great at swearing in those days. Then I got called up. You either got called up for the Land Army or the ATS but being married you got a certain exemption. So I became a clippie on the 253 out of Fairfield Road, Bow. One day I started morning sickness and I found out that I was pregnant. So that was the end of the buses. I had two children in Cable Street. Being a machinist, the chap who had this cleaners used to let me do some alterations at home upstairs at night. I had a boy of five at school and then when my little girl was two I took her with me to work. She used to draw, sitting in the back kitchen and I used to work in the shop.*

Manuel: *We had a window cleaner named Connie and he used to do our windows on the second and third floor. He used to come in the shop and say, 'All right if I go up?' So he went up to do our windows at the top and a short while later, Gladys saw him coming out of the yard. He'd fallen out of the window right down into the yard and landed on*

66

*Mr Mosley's rabbit hutch, which had broken his fall — for-tunately for him. But he'd broken the rabbit hutch as well. Poor old Connie ended up with a broken leg and a broken arm.*

Gladys: *I put a tourniquet round the leg because his knee was really bleeding and, I mean, what did I know about tourniquets? I knew they used to put a handkerchief round and put a pencil in and that's what I did to stop the bleed-ing and ease it off till the ambulance came. I said, 'I'm sorry, Connie, I can't come with you. I can't leave the shop.'*

Manuel: *It was the quickest way he ever came down the stairs anyway!*

Gladys: *Mrs Mosley said, 'Damn cheek! He's broken our rabbit hutch!' I said, 'But Mrs Mosley, Connie's fallen out of the window!' All she said was, 'What about my rabbit hutch?' I don't know what happened to the rabbit but Mr Mosley wanted to sue him. He said he wanted some com-pensation.*

Manuel related his childhood memories of St. George's Baths in Betts Street:

*It had a swimming pool and warm baths. I went there as a boy and I was so little that they allowed two in a bath. I'd never seen an expanse of water so great as a bath of water and this boy I went with loved to show me how he could swim. He could actually swim from one end to the other. Of course, as I grew older I had my own bath and the funniest thing was the shouting out. If you were in number three you had to shout out, 'Hot water in number three,' and you very often did it to other people. They didn't want hot water but you'd shout out, 'Hot water in number six!' That was one of our favourite tricks. You can imagine the hot water coming in while he was laying in the bath. He'd be shouting, 'No, no. Not me! I didn't call for it!' So naturally they'd always open the door to confirm that it was you that wanted hot water. You got all your good bathroom barracking. You could hear everybody singing because there were only six-foot partitions from one bath to another.*

# Faith in Cable Street

The subject of faith arose naturally, threaded as it was in the day-to-day life of the Jewish families. Observation of the Sabbath was universal but attitudes to belief and practice differed. For Phyllis Rose, her father's role as a synagogue treasurer was a source of family pride:

*We lived at number 113 Cable Street. It was a leather shop and grindery. Grindery is all the things that shoe repairers would need — the polish, the laces, the nails, rubber soles and heels, a last, hammers that you bang the nails in with. My father was kind, generous, charitable. He had a home in Grove Road and was the treasurer at Grove Street Synagogue. He'd paid for all the repairs and decorations and they gave him the honour of reopening the synagogue. I'll never forget it. They said, 'We have a treasurer and we have a treasury. There's no money in the treasury but everything has been paid for!' The roof had been done, everything imaginable. He was very religious and used to shut at twelve when the Sabbath came early on Fridays. He was a very modest man and wouldn't want anyone to know what he was doing. He helped many a person.*

Less charitable was the father who beat another of our interviewees with a leather dog lead when, as a child, she wanted to skip a Hebrew class. Another, Nita Freedman, spoke about the confusions of assimilation: 'The Jewish kids used to go for Hebrew classes across the road — the Talmud Torah. The Torah is Hebrew for the Bible and Talmud is the learning of the Bible. My parents spoke Yiddish but I didn't very much. They were very anxious that their children shouldn't be foreign: they wanted them to be English.' And Sidney Cass discovered, at an early age, that religious barriers can be as strong as racial ones: 'There was a little Roman Catholic school in Wellclose Square. My best friend was a coloured boy — a black boy — and his name was Ernest. He had a white mother and a black father who was a sailor. I'd been at school a week or two when he said, "Come to my school." So I went to the school that he belonged to. I'd been there for a couple of weeks when suddenly the teacher said to me, "What's your name? You're not supposed to go to this school! We're Catholics." I was very upset.'

One of my favourite extracts from all the recordings we made is from an interview with Louis Collin. A life changing experience brought about through a chance encounter in the street:

*I must tell you this, the thing that changed my life. It took five minutes to change my life. My whole outlook was changed in the moment this happened. We were a family of seven and I used to go out and get all the breakfast things. I got up about seven every morning to go to a shop in Hessel Street where they sold milk, butter, cheese, bread and things like that. Behind the counter sat a fellow who must have had polio. He couldn't use his legs and used to sit in the corner of this shop. He had these two crutches and every time you came in he put them on and swung his feet forward and rested on his toes for a minute, bring his crutches forward again and swing his feet forward. Every time you went in he was reading a book. He never asked you what you wanted, never said please, thank you or anything, just took your money, gave you what you wanted, went back to the corner and read. I always remember this, it was the first day of Passover. My life was reading. I wanted to read out of this world. I was going to St. George's Library along Cable Street. And here for the first time in all those years I saw him walking along the street. He was flinging his crutches forward and coming towards me. I remember I had a feeling — what shall I do? Shall I walk past him or what? This was the most momentous moment of my life. It changed me entirely. He stopped me for the first time and spoke to me. He took the book from under my arm.*

*'What book are you reading here? A detective book,' he says. 'It teaches you in this book how to murder people, doesn't it? How they get away with it. It teaches you to murder. But a book about love, about sex, which is your future life, what do you know about it? There's no books to tell you. It's barred for you. There's no way you will know how to behave, how to live, love, aim for something. There's no books for you, yet murder you can read.' He said, 'I'm only telling you for this, whatever you read now I want you to enjoy but think about what you're reading.'*

*That night we had the Passover. We were all round the table and I'm reading the Passover story about the plagues coming, about how they attacked all the*

*Egyptians and left the Jews alone. It began to worry me. I started to think, you see? It didn't seem possible. It goes on to say that all Jews should mark their doors in case their first borns were killed. God told the angel of death to look for the marks on their doors. I couldn't puzzle how a plague can be informed not to attack the Jews, only the Egyptians. So I come to the conclusion I'm reading a fairy story. I began to get very frightened because as a young- ster to think there's no God and there must be a fairy story in the Bible, about Noah's Ark being a fairy story, about Joshua going into a town and wiping out women and children. I got to know and attended what was called a secular society in the City. They used to run a meeting every Sunday morning. I was sixteen years of age and I came back and told my father it was impossible for me to go to the synagogue anymore as I didn't believe. My father was absolutely shocked and shaken. He said, 'There's nothing I can do about it if that's the way you feel, carry on.'*

# Millie, Nancy and Lady Henriques

Millie Grotham was able to give us first hand information about the local boys' and girls' clubs set up by Basil Henriques. Henriques was a member of a Reform Jewish family, educated at Oxford University and although coming to London in 1913 to set up a club in Cannon Street Road, found himself whisked away almost imme- diately to serve in the First World War. He was in command of the first tank to be engaged in battle. Known affectionately as the 'Gaffer' or the 'Long-un' (due to his height of six foot five inches), he ran the boys' club while Rose Loewe ran an associated one for girls. They married, with Rose giving up her training as a pianist to assist him in the setting up of a club and settlement in Betts Street after the war. She maintained a strong interest in the arts, encouraging the young people she worked with to participate. Basil Henriques was later knighted, and Berner Street, the location of one of the settlements, has since been renamed Henriques Street in his honour.

Millie told us:

*Our family name was Schneider. My father was in the tai-*
*loring trade and we lived at Prince's Square, a turning off*
*Cable Street, at number 15. A Mrs Samuels lived at number*
*16. Her daughter Nancy was my bosom friend. We did every-*
*thing together. The first holiday that I remember was with*
*the Oxford and St. George's Club in Cannon Street Road. It*
*was run by Lord and Lady Henriques. They were very phil-*
*anthropic. They had a wonderful name. Afterwards they*
*moved to the Bernhard Baron Settlement in Berner Street.*
*Basil Henriques had a boys' section and Lady Henriques*
*had the girls. They used to organise holidays in places like*
*Goring-by-Sea in Sussex. Through the club I went to camp*
*for a week and Nancy was longing to go. I went there at four-*
*teen and we slept under canvas. Nancy's mother wouldn't let*
*her go and it broke her heart, but afterwards we went to the*
*Isle of Wight and Bournemouth. I called her mother toffee-*
*nosed. She thought that her children shouldn't mix. She*
*didn't mind me although I think she disapproved of lots of*
*things I got Nancy into, although Nancy was very, very will-*
*ing. She was just as bad as I was. The club subsidised*
*people. If anyone couldn't afford it they could go for less. I*
*think I paid less at the time because my father hadn't been*
*working. Some paid two or three pounds. I think I paid*
*about twenty-five shillings. And you were allowed six*
*shillings pocket money per week. If you had any more they*
*used to take it to make up what you hadn't paid to the full*
*amount. Lady Henriques was a wonderful person. She was*
*very, very clever. She used to make up all the camp songs.*
*She did such a lot of good work, really and truly. If anyone*
*was really in need they knew they could get help. They were*
*nice holidays. Of course, after we were married, it wasn't the*
*same. Nancy married a very wealthy man. But she still*
*came to see me.*

After her father died, Millie went to work in Houndsditch
as a saleswoman. 'My husband always used to say I could
sell snow to the Eskimos'. But it came as a shock to her
mother. 'She was waiting at the door for me. "Where have
you been?" — in Yiddish. My mother only spoke Yiddish.
I said, "I've got a job in Houndsditch." She said, "What,
you've got to go all the way to Aldgate on the tram?

Dangerous.'" Before that, however, Millie's first job hadn't worked out so well:

*I was fourteen and a half. My sister was a machine embroiderer and my mother said, 'Go and work with your sister Katy.' I got sent on all the errands. They used to do machinery and embroidery down the foreparts of the clothes that were sent from Farringdon Street where there used to be a lot of tailors who put them together. I was there about three or four months, getting the princely sum of 7 / 6d a week, which I suppose was good in those days. The guv'nor wanted me to take this great pile of clothes back to Farringdon Street but I had this new coat on with buttons all down the back that my father had made for me and I didn't want to go out in the rain. So he says, 'You've got to take this.' I said, 'No, I'm not going out in the rain, I've got a new coat on!' He was a little Yiddisher man. He said, 'What do you mean, you're not going out in the rain? You should go!' I said, 'Well, I'm not going!' So he sent another girl who was an apprentice there. And in the afternoon I heard him say to his daughter, 'Fanny, you should give that little girl notice because she would not do what I tell her.' He wanted to give me notice Friday of that week. This would be 1924 when my father was still alive. I went home that evening and said, 'Look Daddy, he's going to give me notice.' I said that I hated it there anyway and didn't want to work there. I said, 'Let me give* him *notice.' He said, 'What do you mean, give* him *notice? He's your guv'nor!' I said, 'Look, this is my first job. If anyone finds that my first job I couldn't keep after a few months, I'll never get a job anywhere.' Come Friday he handed me my 7 / 6d. So he says, 'And I want to say...' I said, 'Well, just a minute. Now that you're giving me my notice I'm telling you I'm giving* you *a week's notice.' 'What do you mean, you're giving* me *notice? I'm giving* you *notice.' I got there first. He was furious that I had the audacity to say that to him.*

Mille's account ended on a sad note however:

*When I married, my husband's name was Berenson. I didn't even get eight years with him, more like three or four because we got married in 1936 — war broke out in 1939 — and he got killed in 1944. I had one daughter who was only five years old. My husband was a cab driver and when war broke out they commandeered all the cabs. So he said that he was going to join the fire service. I said, 'Don't, it's so dangerous!' He said, 'I'll take my chances.' And, you know, he narrowly avoided getting killed three times. And then when the blitz was on and they returned all the cabs, he said, 'I'm going back on the cabs.' I said, 'Don't leave the fire service. They'll call you up.' He said again, 'I'll take my chances.' He was in Monte Casino. I had a letter from him the same day I got a letter from the War Office. I opened his letter first* — Don't worry about me, I'm not in the front line. I'll come back to you and the baby. We'll have a good life. *He was asleep in a tent. He was hit by mortar fire. He wasn't even in the front line. So I only had a few years. But some people had less. I remarried a few years later. Married his cousin. I wanted security for my daughter. I wanted her to have everything I didn't have. And thank God it worked out.*

# The Parrot That Spoke Only Japanese

Connie Lang told us:

*I was born in number 6 Well Street in 1920 where the old sailors' home used to be. My grandfather had a shop down there selling clothes for the sailors. He came from Russia and my grandmother came from Poland, although my mother and father were born over here. I had a brother and two sisters. When my grandfather died, my grandmother still kept up the seaman's clothes. In Back Church Lane there used to be a very big factory and they had to use hooks to lift the bales inside. She used to sell these bale hooks, dungarees and seaman's boots as well. There was a Japanese sailor and he didn't have any money. He came into the shop. And he said to my grandmother he'd leave his parrot with her and he'd come back for it. He wanted some dungarees and he left his parrot, which could only speak Japanese. It never spoke English at all. And he said he would come back for it. I always remember it sitting up in the kitchen in its cage. A beautiful parrot. Unfortunately, it got out and the cat must have got it in the yard outside. The sailor did come back — it must have been about a year after. He came back for his parrot and the parrot was gone. But he paid his money, after a year. He remembered it. My grandmother used to trust them, you see?*

73

# 'A good job in a way that they all got bombed'

All the stories were different, all were similar. They were unique within fixed points of reference. Family relationships and housing conditions were central to them all. Much of it was related with self-effacing humour. Sidney Cass told us, 'Very rarely was there an internal toilet in the house in those days, so you had to go down in the yard where there was a little outside toilet. It backed on to the house's next door's toilet. You could carry on a conversation in there. Very sociable! But when you think about it, having to go to the toilet in the middle of the night, it wasn't very nice.' There were a lot of mixed feelings about what had been lost and what had been gained. I was particularly taken by Helen Katin's recollection of her childhood wonder of the world:

> *What I remember is lying in bed when it was dark and hearing the sound of the boats on the river. You could hear the whoop-whoop and you could hear the horses and carts going along Cable Street. It sort of lulled you to sleep. It was interesting. I remember standing in the yard and looking at all the houses of all the people as you go along, who lived in which place. I used to know everybody's name who lived along there.*

But this was tempered with other memories:

> *Because of the bed bugs you couldn't sleep at night. In the summer it was absolutely awful. You'd have all lumps and bumps on you. They all used to come out from behind the wallpaper. Horrible! You daren't tell anybody, you were ashamed of it. And everybody had them! But you daren't say —* Ooh, we've got bugs at home. *It was a secret. And the mice! My sister and brother lived opposite and they used to have cockroaches. They were all infested. It was a good job in a way that they all got bombed, don't you think so?*

I suspect I find the following passage so affecting because it represents a physical and spiritual passing. Millie

Grotham was talking about an experience during the Second World War, when the world, and Cable Street, was changed forever.

*I remember during the blitz when I came up from Marlow where we lived during the war. I brought my daughter. She was a baby, just over a year old. I had her in my arms. I wanted to come and visit my brother and sister-in-law. They lived in Prince's Square opposite to where we lived and I remember getting off the bus and walking down Christian Street and the whole of Cable Street was alight and my brother came towards me up from Prince's Square. 'Millie,' he says, 'go back. It's an inferno here! Go back!' He wouldn't even let me get near his house. He took me right back to the station to go back to Marlow. Cable Street seemed to be a blaze of light.*

# 4. The Basement
## The Basement Project

## Dan Jones Comes to Cable Street

One of the people I spoke to for this book was only a teenager when he first met Dan Jones. He'd seen Dan trundling along the road on his pushbike a few days before our interview and it prompted him to tell me, 'It's strange, I'm in my fifties now but whenever I meet Dan I still feel like a little kid.' I knew exactly what he meant, given that many of us were just kids when we first met him. But it's

*Dan Jones, photo courtesy of The Gentle Author/ www.spitalfieldslife.com*

strange as well, because in his large frame, Dan retains something of the child himself in the form of his inexhaustible enthusiasms. This combination of innocence and experience hits you the minute you step through the front door of his Cable Street home (I've brought you here previously, when I interviewed Dan's wife, Denise). Stepping into the long hallway, on the right-hand side, one entire wall is taken up with an equally long mural, painted on heavy wooden panels and bolted into the brickwork, depicting children in the playground of nearby St. Paul's School. The rhymes they are chanting float into the air around them as in a comic book. The picture is reproduced in one of the books that Dan illustrated, *Mother Goose Comes to Cable Street*, which juxtaposed traditional nursery rhymes with contemporary illustrations: there are multi-cultural families pushing baby-buggies around in supermarkets, helmeted motorcycle cops at Tower Hill, turbaned pub-goers, mums on telly talent shows and old men gathering outside the betting office — all accompanying rhymes sometimes going back a hundred years or more.

Further into the house, Dan's other interests become apparent. His fascination with different cultures is reflected in the huge canvases that cover almost every surface. During the interview I was able to pump Dan for information about his inspirations: a trip to West Africa as a teenager is recalled in the colourful cloths and headties of women on market day and vivid sketches of village life chart his trips to Bangladesh: an equal number of the pictures represent Dan's lifelong association with the labour movement. He told me:

*A lot of my larger work is screwed onto the wall in various trade union places. I painted a huge picture of the Pentonville Five demonstration against the jailing of Bernie Steer and four other dockers. It hangs in the TUC. And when Blair Peach got murdered I did a painting of the protest demonstration which got made into prints. People would say, 'Could you do us a banner for our union branch?' I made a large purple and red one for the*

*National Union of Seamen depicting the 1966 seaman's strike. On one side was a four-masted galleon on a roaring ocean and on the other, dockside cranes and lots of activity, and instead of the circle that you would have drawn around the main picture on a traditional Victorian banner, I painted a lifebelt with writing on it:* Pull Together. *Although I had imagined the faces of the seamen I'd painted on to it, when we first took it out on a march people kept coming up claiming they'd worked with the crew members on it. Invented people became real in people's minds.*

Dan took me down into the kitchen area where I had interviewed Denise and where the dozens of masks on the walls had so beguiled me: from Nigeria, Mexico, Guatemala, Japan, Thailand, Cambodia, Sri Lanka, Korea and a Poro mask from the Dan tribe of Liberia. Many were collected on his trips on behalf of Amnesty. There is even a mask that looks like Dan: a character with wavy black unruly hair and big beard. Dan as he looked when I first met him. It occurs to me that this collision of politics and art, and perhaps even his location, is inevitable given Dan's background.

'My dad was Frederick Elwyn Jones who was the Labour MP for West Ham for twenty-nine years. From 1974 he served as Lord Chancellor in Harold Wilson's government. My mother had come to live in Whitechapel in the late 1920s. Her name was Pearl Binder, an artist and illustrator who did beautiful lithographs. She drew Pearly Kings and Queens, designed theatre costumes, travelled a great deal.' Dan also ponders (I assume tongue-in-cheek) if in her drawings, she had somehow imagined him and mapped out his life to come. 'She did extraordinarily accurate drawings of *me*, my mum; before she met my Dad, twenty years before I was even born! I appear among her skittish sketches of Bohemian London in the 1920s. And here I am amongst these slightly hippyish looking, effete people lolling about in Bloomsbury. And there's some hairy agitator, waving his fist on a soapbox. Extraordinary likenesses!'

# Burrowing Through the Basement

In the late 1960s Dan was teaching in Islington in a school for what, in those less-enlightened times, was called the educationally sub-normal:

*It was a very interesting school but a very depressing place. Lots of kids diagnosed as 'ESN' were sent there who shouldn't have been — not for a learning difficulty but for something like throwing a desk at a teacher. I always used to draw and was interested in pictures. The kids at the school would do a picture but they would get very destructive and tear it up. So I started painting to encourage them. I was also teaching at Holloway Prison in the evenings and volunteering to teach English at Toynbee Hall in Aldgate to old Pakistani machinists and newly arrived Sikh children. I wanted to get out of the school. Then, a job came up in Tower Hamlets as a detached youth worker.*

The Basement Project officially began in May 1970, when the Tower Hamlets Children's Department joined a nationwide project devised by the Home Office to further neighbourhood youth work. As part of the Family Advice Centre, two new workers, Dan Jones and Dave Findlay were appointed and accommodated in the basement of the neo-classical pile of St. George's Town Hall in Cable Street. A major element of the project involved working with young offenders, keeping them out of detention, and offering alternatives to hanging around on street corners. The brief was: keep the kids out of trouble.

*The basement wasn't the 'Basement' then, it was just piles of stuff. We initially got one room cleared out and gradually burrowed our way through more and more of them. Some were full of amazing and decaying records: petitions asking for the creation of Victoria Park and other lists. There were Deeds of Bastardy and endless Town Hall minutes. We went from room to room, clearing more space until we took the whole place over. I was to make contact with kids at risk and set up activities and programmes. Things emerged out of the kids' interest really.*

They had barely any resources to start with, which meant that from the beginning it relied on joint activities with sympathetic groups operating in the area. The number of rooms in use expanded to a total of eleven, including washrooms, toilets, meeting rooms and a space for school refusers. The problems of truancy — for the truants themselves and everybody else — were so great that after discussions with the Inner London Education Authority it was decided to set up what became one of the first off-site education projects in the country: the Basement Intermediate Education Centre, with two full-time teachers and up to fifteen young people at any one time. Things were organised in the freewheeling spirit of the time with a strong arts bias to the project. Drama and photography was on offer (they had a darkroom for developing their own pictures) and there was an emphasis on film-making, painting and pottery. There was a silkscreen printer — great for posters and T-shirts — and a Gestetner machine on which they produced a huge range of leaflets, reports, cards and booklets. Later on they had access to an offset litho printer. Young people developed musical skills, as singers and songwriters, and a steel band was launched. As well as being a lot of fun in itself, it helped to provide the users with skills and experience.

# The Great Escape

Dan told me:

> *We decided to do camping. We had no equipment at all! Nothing! But it developed into a huge exercise, finding camping sites and worming our way into places where you could go. We found that the East End Methodist Mission that ran the soup kitchen up the road had access to a place at Lambourne End out by Hainault Forest, a very nice little camping area on a hillside. We had no transport at the beginning but you could get there by tube, and whatever camping equipment we needed we just had*

*to carry. We started off with a few kids but over the years we must have taken thousands. Methodist rules applied and there was no alcohol. But some did drink, I'm afraid. Especially the grown-ups. We had to deal with the evidence so we dug deep holes to put the tins in. And sometimes we'd be digging and find that over the years other people had already buried their own tins in the same hole!*

Another, larger site at Rickmansworth was established and a programme of what might be called 'adventure holidays' was set up with the creation of the Stepney Children's Camping Association. Dan remembers his first camping trip with a group of young Bangladeshis in 1975: 'These lads turned up in impeccable green and purple suits. And then we went up to 'Ricky' in the mud.'

*Man Alive* was a BBC documentary series. One of the episodes from 1971 features four young East End boys who gave the film its title, *Vince, Paul, Lawrence and Richard*. They are up to all sorts: the commentary implying that they were on a fast track to hell — but who, as it turned out did all right for themselves in their different ways: their progress was tracked years later for a BBC archive project. Dan appears in the original film on one of the young people's trips, his hair as wild as the windswept countryside they all ran riot in. Watching the lads in the film, leaping and swinging through the trees, dangling off cliff sides on ropes, it occurred to me that they would never get away with it in the risk assessment culture of today.

There doesn't seem anything that the Basement Project didn't try at one time or another. One of the lads had a sound system, which led to the setting up of a weekly dance club night at St. Paul's Mission at the western end of Cable Street. Dan recalled, 'I think it ran on Friday nights and took place in almost complete darkness. We'd get a hundred and fifty, maybe two hundred kids that would come. The music was very *very* loud and some of the dancers were brilliant. There would be the odd bit of trouble and fights and the police used to hang around outside.' I had heard about the club but had never known how it came by its name: The Kwango Club. Now I had the opportunity to ask Dan: 'That's easy, Johnny Kwango was a very popular black British wrestler at around that time. He was a heroic figure to the kids.' The project was also quick to respond to the area's shifting cultural landscape, introducing mother-tongue teaching classes and opening up a Bengali children's library in nearby Cannon Street Road.

## The Shadwell Basin Project

The project continued to develop. Not always as planned. As Dan explained:

> *The Shadwell Basin Project started off almost by accident. The nearby docks were beginning to close and Shadwell Basin was a lovely stretch of water, unused by anybody. We were interested in the idea of a sailing or a canoeing project: sports about which we knew nothing at all. At first we tried to build our own fibreglass canoes; it was like they were made of concrete. But quite soon we found trained instructors who knew what they were doing and proper equipment. We got some funds and from complete scratch over the years it has developed into a wonderful watersports centre. A number of fine athletes emerged from the project who have competed at international level. I'm so proud of it. If I go to heaven — or hell — I'll be able to say that's at least one useful thing I helped to do.*

## Tony Crisp

Tony Crisp worked in the Basement over a number of years. Born in Bethnal Green, as a child he felt set apart from his friends; his house was the only one he knew that had any books in it: 'My first community venture was when I was six. I decided to create a lending library. I wish I could say I was responsible for those East Enders who subsequently grew into well-known literati and free-thinkers but instead I just got all my books nicked.' Tony came to teaching via his involvement with an experimental drama group in Aldgate, and his work at the Central School of Speech and Drama provided him with innovative ideas to help young Bangladeshis improve their English.

Tony doesn't remember being interviewed for his Basement job. It was more a case of being groomed for it. He had been spotted as someone sympathetic to the project ethos and found himself being invited to a series of apparently unrelated events. It would seem that in those days, people didn't apply for jobs at the Basement; it was more like being pressed into service. 'I later realised that these invitations were part of some process to see if I had the right credentials to be part of it. I would meet the workers as well as the kids who went there. It was like being checked out for entry into a very special club.'

Tony officially started working there as a teacher in 1978 but had become part of the team from the minute he was spotted. As with the other employees, it became his life. 'You had no concept of working hours. You were a Basement worker from the time you woke up to the point your head hit the pillow. Everything was connected.' Dan Jones was already working there. Tony told me, 'I spent several months trying to work out what his job actually was. Was he a social worker, youth worker, resident artist, community activist, trade unionist?' The lines were as blurred for Dan as they were for anyone else. 'Dan would sometimes need to do a painting urgently and come down to the Basement in the middle of the night to find a piece of wood. Once, he took home a large piece that had been lying around, unused, for several years. Then one day someone complained that the Basement kids had stolen the top of the camping trailer. Its whereabouts was brought up at a meeting. Dan admitted that it was on its way to Japan with a picture of the Shadwell Basin

Festival on it and that he had filled the strangely shaped hole in it with Polyfilla.'

The hothouse atmosphere of the Basement meant that employees — or almost anybody who happened to be standing around at the time — might find themselves fronting a project about something or other for which they had no previous experience. Tony recalls:

*It was either my first or the second meeting when I was given the job of organising the Shadwell Festival. I did it with another new worker, Roland Thomas, a sculptor and 3D artist who had worked with Bath Arts Workshop. The festival had to be organised in two weeks. I had a summer holiday — which meant that I was available! Being available was probably the greatest asset in the Basement. But it was a superb way of getting to know the local community and I couldn't have had a better induction and learning experience. I learnt that you could make primitive solar heating panels with recycled radiators, I learnt that you should always put an Irish band on at lunchtime and I learnt that a new group of local young hopefuls called Iron Maiden would work for beer. I also learnt that if you knew the right electrician, you could supply enough electricity for an entire festival from a single lamppost.*

In summing up, Tony said:

*The Basement was a loose assembly of individuals co-joined around an idea of activity rather than an employer. Things lasted as long as a particular activity and then moved on. One thing we organised that comes to mind is a page of the kids' writing that we got into a local newspaper* East End News. *That went on — with no actual editorial control over what they wrote — for over a year. It was a partnership of arts, social services and education, but the individuals concerned interchanged roles. There were few constants except constant flux. We had freedom in establishing our own working rules and practices. The point of commonality was a belief that creativity was the agent for change. Despite having respective bosses we didn't think of ourselves as being limited by them. We were all self-managers with a responsibility for each other in a community context.*

# Dan After the Basement

Dan Jones was associated with the Basement Project for seventeen years, after which he took a job with Amnesty International. In 2001, he received an MBE for services to international human rights: 'My work with Amnesty evolved in different stages, different sorts of work. I'm in the Campaigns Department. I have worked in more recent years in schools, primarily on human rights education. That's led to all sorts of wonderful adventures, meeting the most extraordinary people. I'm partly retired now, which is why I'm free to talk to you today.'

For people like me who knew Dan from when we were barely out of school, it's almost impossible to think of him ever retiring, partly or otherwise. Dan's beard is grey now but he is still throwing himself into new ventures. Before turning off the recorder and leaving the marvellous house of masks, we talked about his current project. The collecting of children's rhymes may not be new in itself; it has been a lifelong obsession, but he's about to start sifting through recordings he has made of well over a thousand contemporary playground rhymes to put them into a book. And with him now being a grandfather four times over it's likely that he will continue to be an influence on, and be influenced by, the voices of the young for some time to come.

# The Rosenberg Connection

## On Isaac Rosenberg

### Returning, We Hear the Larks

Sombre the night is:
And though we have our lives, we know
What sinister threat lurks there.

Dragging these anguished limbs, we only know
This poison-blasted track opens on our camp –
On a little safe sleep.

But hark! Joy — joy — strange joy.
Lo! Heights of night ringing with unseen larks:
Music showering on our upturned list'ning faces.

Death could drop from the dark
As easily as song –
But song only dropped,
Like a blind man's dreams on the sand
By dangerous tides;
Like a girl's dark hair, for she dreams no ruin lies there,
Or her kisses where a serpent hides.

— *Isaac Rosenberg*

## The Life

Isaac Rosenberg's parents, as had many others, fled the
Pogroms of Lithuania to seek refuge in Britain, initially
in Bristol, where Isaac was born in 1890, before gravitating towards the natural Jewish stronghold of East

London when he was seven. The family home was one room at number 47 Cable Street at the back of a rag and bone shop. The poet and artist stayed in the area for most of his short life, but his tombstone is situated just outside Arras in France.

When I interviewed Chris Searle about the genesis of the Basement Writers, we also talked about the inspiration he gained from the work of Isaac Rosenberg: Chris told me:

*I was born in Romford during the war in 1944. I grew up there and didn't really have much to do with East London until I came to teach here. And the reason I came here was because of Isaac Rosenberg. I was fascinated by him and his poetry. I went to Leeds University to study English and I became deeply involved in his work. I studied his poetry and found out about his time in Stepney and Whitechapel. I emigrated to Canada after university but never really wanted to stay there. I wanted to return and live and teach where Rosenberg had grown up. So that's what I did.*

*At that time, Rosenberg was seen as a lesser poet compared with people like Wilfred Owen. I mean, Wilfred Owen is a great poet. But when I was young he was considered to be the only real powerful poet of the First World War. Another, Siegfried Sassoon was seen more as a propagandist and polemicist. And there was Rupert Brooke, whose works were superficial patriotic rants. But the really complex poet actually, if you look at his language and his use of words, is Rosenberg. He was a working class boy, bilingual, who grew up round here and spent a lot of his time wandering the streets, falling in with that school of young Jewish men, including Joseph Leftwich, Stephen Winsten and John Rodker who later became known as 'The Whitechapel Boys'. They all gathered at the Whitechapel Library, which was the nucleus of intellectual activity in the area. It was the only place with the resources and the quietude where they could study and write.*

*A lot of Rosenberg's images come from the Hebraic tradition. He grew up speaking Yiddish and studying the Torah and going to the synagogue. What always struck me was that his experience must be somewhat similar to the life of a Bangladeshi child growing up in East London now. He transferred into the English tongue a lot of images and stories and myths and traditions that he'd learnt through his first tongue. And I think that's often what makes some of his poetry, especially some of the longer ones that he wrote before he died, difficult to get to grips with. The images are profoundly un-English. Others you can read and grasp immediately, such as* Break of Day in the Trenches. *And Rosenberg was, of course, also a very fine artist. He saw himself as both a poet and painter. He was one of a profoundly talented generation, with very little exposure to all the privileges of the more elitist artists' sects of the period.*

Rosenberg seems to have become permanently frustrated and bitter about not being taken seriously enough by the arts establishment, despite winning several prizes for his visual work at Birkbeck College evening classes. But he became sufficiently well-known to attract the attention of Jewish patrons who paid his fees at the Slade School of Art. Like Joseph Leftwich and many others in Stepney, Rosenberg became a member of the Young Socialist League, although, by all accounts, not a very active one. Some found his manner awkward, unskilled in the social graces. Nevertheless, in 1913, Rosenberg was pulled into the orbit of Edward Marsh, a monied supporter of up-and-coming artists, who introduced him to the heady Bohemian world of painters and writers. This circle included the poet Ezra Pound, who even when recommending him to a magazine editor, confided that the young Jew had: '... something in him, horribly rough ...' and put it down bluntly to the effect of: 'Stepney, East'.

# The Death

Among the number of recent books on Rosenberg, I was particularly drawn to a small volume by Shaun Levin, *Isaac Rosenberg's Journey to Arras: a Meditation*, published by Cecil Woolf as part of their War Poets series.

Not quite a biography, not quite a fiction. And as fascinated as Chris Searle is by Rosenberg's life, Shaun Levin is fascinated by his death. The story begins as Levin's Eurostar pulls out of Waterloo Station, picking up speed past 'the Pink Floyd chimneys of Battersea' towards Lille in France. His quest is to visit the poet's grave. The real start of his journey however had begun in South Africa in 1975, laying in bed and listening to Rosenberg's work on 'Poets and Poetry' on the radio and realising, 'that you could be a Jew and you could be an artist and you could be talked about on the BBC's World Service.'

In 1916, the enlisted Rosenberg set off for France from Southampton, fighting during the day and writing poems at night. Levin ponders the reasons for Rosenberg's decision to sign up: 'He wasn't selling paintings, wasn't shifting copies of his books, he'd had enough of working as an apprentice and looking for a job. So he enlisted. It was a way to be fed, looked after, stripped of the need to make decisions. War was an escape. He expected he'd have time to write, to put together a new collection. The trench poems would set him free.' Rosenberg lost his life during a German raiding-party at the dawn of April Fool's Day, 1918. He was twenty-seven years old.

Levin's account of his own journey to Arras is interlaced with memories of his failed affair with another man; his sojourn in the surrounds of the French graveyard is punctuated with estimations as to whether he will be able to get off with this or that other. But he eventually finds his way to the poet's headstone: the only Jew in the cemetery. There are ten pebbles on the tomb, to which he adds his own. Shaun Levin's homage is, in fact, a personal *Kaddish* for the death of his own relationship and of the hopes and personal ambition of the war dead. It is a pebble amongst the stones that have been accumulating around the reputation of the once-disregarded East London artist.

# Afterlife

As indicated by Chris Searle, the slight Private Rosenberg had initially been overshadowed by the officer-class poets. But over several decades, his work has risen in prominence. A major re-evaluation is taking place as biographers have been busily excavating his life. Chris, however, is able to claim a link with Rosenberg not available to most of those now charting his early years:

> *I tried to find out about Rosenberg's life, where he lived and who his friends were. And I found out that his best friend, Joseph Leftwich, was still alive. This was in the mid 1970s, I suppose. So I wrote to him and told him that I was a teacher and loved Rosenberg's poetry and he said* — Come over and see me. *So I went over to Highgate where he lived and spent the day with him. He was a lovely man, a really friendly bloke. Leftwich was also a poet and a translator. He produced an anthology of Yiddish poetry in English translation:* The Golden Peacock. *He spoke a lot about Rosenberg and his friendship with him and what they used to do together. So for me, this was wonderful. I was actually speaking to Rosenberg's best friend! This man whose life fascinated me and whose poetry I loved; here I was speaking to someone who had grown up with him! It was amazing. I think that Joseph Leftwich died in 1984 but I was lucky enough to talk to him and record his words.*

Some of those words, featured in an article by Chris in *Race & Class* in 1986, attest to Leftwich's friendship and understanding of Rosenberg's artistic impulse:

> *[Rosenberg] tried to rise to inaccessible heights in his language, but he worked to be understood and he worked to be appreciated. All his articulacy came out in his poetry. He was not a speaker at all, he was a mumbler, a fumbler and he needed poetry to articulate himself. I can't remember him once speaking at a public meeting, yet the rest of us always did. He would sit next to us and listen and the ideas would go in, as everything else did and everything*

*would come out in his poetry. But read him. Read* A Snake Fed on the Heart of Corinth *or* Returning, We Hear the Larks. *Those are jewels of English poetry.*

# The Basement Writers

## Lightning Strikes

In 2006, teacher Chris Searle was described as 'old-fashioned and unpopular'. That these epithets, spoken by his publisher, Andy Croft of Smokestack Books at the launch of an anthology of his poetry, *Lightning of Your Eyes,* at the Marx Memorial Library in London, were actually intended as praise, says as much about the times we live in as they do about Chris Searle. He is old-fashioned, it was explained, in that he retains his belief that only socialism can save the world. And unpopular in that he has travelled the globe trying to bring it about. I first met Chris in the mid 1970s, his six-foot-five frame towering above everybody else in the vault-like rooms beneath St. George's Town Hall in Cable Street. Seeking an outlet for my own creative work I had come to join a group called the Basement Writers. At that time, Chris was front-page news. And, according to who you listened to, was either a champion of children's free speech or a sinister pied piper.

## The Children of Blake

I interviewed Chris Searle for this book in the summer of 2010 and we wandered the East London streets together. It had been some time since he had visited his old haunts. I hadn't realised until then that he used to live off Commercial Road, just around the corner to where I live now. In 1970, aged twenty-four, he had arrived at Sir John Cass School in Stepney Way as a probationary teacher, having previously taught in Tobago, encouraging black youths to put on plays about rebel slaves — so his new employers should have had some idea of what they were letting themselves in for.

Chris Searle urged his pupils to write poems about themselves and their locale. And he marvelled at their efforts. To him they were the children of William Blake, the eighteenth century visionary artist and poet. Student writing, using slang and the words of everyday speech, would, for a time, become a teaching tool in liberal class-rooms. But liberal wasn't a word that could have been used about Sir John Cass in the 1970s. It was an old City Foundation school, run like a 'Victorian compound'. Amongst the school governors — and even the staff — was a clutch of old-fashioned churchmen and ex-military. The ensuing battle of ideologies that occurred now seems inevitable.

Passing his old house, Chris said, 'I lived just up the road to the school so I used to see the children around the streets and we'd joke and muck about. I'd say, let's go out tomorrow and we'll write some poetry. They'd laugh and take the piss but they loved poetry actually. I took them out in the streets and parks and they'd write about Stepney and the people who lived here. You'd think they'd go barmy but they behaved and enjoyed them-selves. I found it all very moving.' We had a copy of one of Chris's pupils' poems with us, *Autumn Morning in Stepney Churchyard*, written by Lesley Samuels. Chris paused to read it aloud; although it seems that even after all these years he can virtually recite it from memory. His delivery is deeply respectful, even sonorous. Towards the end of it there is a phrase, 'the ever-lay leaves', which we both got stuck on, repeating it to ourselves over and over. Chris said, 'I thought, where did they get such wonderful language? The poems reminded me of Blake's *Garden of Love*. Blake had said that streets were the ideas of his imagination and I thought, well, that's the same with these children.'

At the same time as Chris was coaxing poetry out of his class, he approached photographer Ron McCormick, whose exhibition of local photos he had stumbled across in the Whitechapel Art Gallery. He saw a direct link in the pictures that McCormick had taken of Stepney street life and the pictures being told in words by his students. He invited the photographer to the school to display his work and talk with the children. Some of them even wrote new poems, inspired by Ron's images of the old men and street markets that were part of their everyday lives. And from this, the idea of a book, incorporating words and images, was born. The title would be: *Stepney Words*.

## Stepney Words

Although the Headmaster of Sir John Cass was initially receptive to the idea of the book being sponsored by the school, the governors were less amenable. The poems in the proposed anthology were 'drab' they thought: the selection on the whole 'unbalanced'. 'They wanted the "light" side of local life,' wrote Chris Searle in his 1973 book, *This New Season*, 'they wanted the cockney sparrow to chirp and sing cheerfully from his cage'. Even today, it would be considered a pretty gritty gathering of work: abusive parents, football hooliganism, slum housing, street corner drunks. But Chris Searle has a different take on it. 'You can read Shakespeare and you can read Ibsen and you can see it all put on the stage but these poems inspired me more than anything'.

Chris, showing the lack of compromise that was to epitomise his career, refused point blank to censor the anthology. So he decided to publish it himself with his own money plus contributions from a supportive local community. But Chris's enthusiasm failed to win over the governors. They told him that the anthology could not be produced under any terms. In May 1971, three days after editions of *Stepney Words* were slapped down on the desks of every head teacher and every councillor in the area, and poems and photos from it had appeared in the then left-leaning daily national, *The Sun,* under the headline: 'The Astonishing World Of These East End Kids', Chris Searle was accused of 'flagrant disobedience' and sacked.

This, however, was only the start of the *Stepney Words* saga.


## 'We hate the Governors — Oh yes we do...'

Back at the school, a huge storm was brewing.

Chris had no part in the organisation of what happened next. He told me, 'Really, when I was getting kicked about, the children saw it as them getting kicked about. So they organised and launched a strike. I've always seen it as a strike that they waged on behalf of *their* own poetry, *their* own language, *their* own artistic talent. I was the bloke in the middle so they identified with me.'

Even so, there is a definite cult of the personality about Chris. He is, without doubt, a charismatic speaker and his style at John Cass must have been a welcome relief from the orthodox attitude that reigned there. The Chairman of Governors, who was the local Anglican vicar, had told Chris, 'You have to remember that they are all fallen children, that they are all in a state of sin.' Chris Searle was described in a 1997 *Guardian* article by Andy Beckett, as looking like a 'vast and gaunt George Best' in the photos after his sacking. But it is another, more spiritual, long-haired and bearded major player who springs to my mind when looking at the pictures of Chris amongst his flock during the schoolyard protest.

The strike had begun to be organised the day after his sacking became known. The *Guardian* article identified one of its leading lights: 'That afternoon, his class heard the news. Then they told their friends and decided what to do. Zeinaida de la Cruz, a fifth-former from Gibraltar with a fierce stare and very few cares, took charge: "We arranged groups, for everyone to tell each class ... From there, it didn't need to be organised — it just didn't seem fair that a teacher everyone enjoyed and liked was being thrown out.'"

And there really was a cloudburst over Stepney.

Chris Searle arrived at school that rainy morning with trepidation, sensing that things were about to happen that were beyond the school's, the governors', or even his control. What he found was all the school's eight hundred pupils outside the gates, singing, shouting and chanting: '*We hate the governors, oh yes we do*' ...amongst other things. Zeinaida, who if there is any justice in the world should have gone on to work as a top publicist, had already tipped off the local *East London Advertiser* (the journalist they sent along incidentally, was a certain Steve Harley, prior to exchanging his cub reporter's notebook for a guitar

and forming the 1970s chart group Cockney Rebel) and the scene was set for a media event the like of which has not been seen since. The cleaning ladies at the school refused to expunge the 'Don't Sack Searle' graffiti from the walls in support of the children, the national press turned up in time to see the school fence collapse and by early evening, television presenter Eamonn Andrews was asking one of the pupils on the *Today* programme why they were striking. She answered, 'What else could we do?'

Things moved up a notch the next day.

According to Alan Gilbey, one of the striking pupils, the children's march to Trafalgar Square was organised pretty much on the spur of the moment, although photos of it as it made its way along the Embankment reveal them hoisting up a ready prepared banner and with a police escort in attendance. Despite this, teenage shyness seems to have overcome them once they reached the Square. In the absence of Chris Searle (possibly trying to stave off the 'Pied Piper' label which inevitably became attached to him) nobody wanted to make a speech so they all went home again. Back at the school, the Head was shooing away concerned parents. Concerned, and almost certainly baffled that this entire crisis had been bought about by their kids' *poetry,* of all things. The school was finally saved by the bell — or at least by the Whitsun holiday weekend, the day after the Trafalgar Square march — and the protest petered out.

But the poems continued to attract attention. Poet Adrian Mitchell became a friend of some of the young poets and invited them to a performance of his William Blake play, *Tyger,* calling them onto the stage at the end. They also read their work at 'Poetry International 72' at the ICA and the Young Vic, alongside such writers as John Betjeman, Seamus Heaney, Germaine Greer and Adrian Henri. The event is documented in Chris's book, *None But Our Words,* where he observes: 'Ironically, the most prestigious voice of the event was that of the, by that time, very aged W.H. Auden — who, we remember, wrote that "poetry makes nothing happen". *Stepney Words* had told another story.'

*The front cover image from Stepney Words*

# After the Strike

A further volume of *Stepney Words* was published by Chris Searle during his exile beyond the school gates and a joint publication by Centreprise of both went on to sell more than 15,000 copies, which must have put the Sir John Cass students right up there with the nation's most-read poets, although I doubt they were included in any bestseller lists. Chris was eventually reinstated by the Education Secretary (yes, it was Margaret Thatcher) in May 1973, following pressure from the National Union of Teachers, the Inner London Education Authority and a High Court case. But it was a pyrrhic victory in a way. Chris felt alienated from both school management and staff; was denied a class of his own and after just over a year he left to take a teaching post at another school in Limehouse.

For many of us who knew Chris from his East London years, and who gathered again for the *Lightning of Your*

*Eyes* book launch, he will always be the bearded radical teacher who caused an almighty rumpus. But although the *Stepney Words* saga was a major event in his life, I also realised during the course of the reading that this was just one amongst many others in his career: in Mozambique, in Grenada and latterly in Sheffield, where he became a head teacher of the Earl Marshal School. He got sacked from that job as well, in 1995, when Sheffield MP, David Blunkett, brought claims to the Department of Education of low GCSE pass rates and a non-exclusion policy.

# The Boxer Poet

Even before the formation of The Basement Writers, Chris Searle had compiled several books. *Elders*, published by Reality Press in 1972, was a collection of writing by older people. One of the contributors was an ex-boxer called Stephen 'Johnny' Hicks, born in Stepney in 1906. It was through Chris that his pupils and ex-pupils began to visit Stephen in his small tenement flat. He was housebound by then, suffering with a badly ulcerated leg for which he refused to get proper treatment, fearing amputation. They befriended him, listened to his 1930s boxing stories and painted his flat. Chris told me, 'He was a hero to them. Through him they realised the struggles of older people and wanted to support him.'

In October 1973, the Basement Writers were formed. On Chris's suggestion, he and his ex-pupils met together every Tuesday to continue their sessions (extra-curricular this time) exploring their lives through their writing. Meeting, as they did, in a low-ceilinged, concrete room of the Basement Project, they couldn't really have had any other name. 'I was lucky to just walk into a ready-made situation, as the basement of St George's Town Hall in Cable Street had been turned over to young people's activities. It was accessible only down a row of steps on the street. The first few meetings we followed a karate and judo club. They'd be there with all their gear on. They would finish at seven and then we'd take over the space for poetry. It didn't seem strange at all. The instructor taking the class was really welcoming.'

I asked Chris if the famous Battle of 1936 had any impact on the group. They were certainly aware of it:

> *The sense of history, of having a poetry group in that particular street, Cable Street, I'm not sure we thought much about. But it was there, it was instilled. It was imbued in every word that was written. You were writing in a site of great historical significance where people had fought like hell against racism and fascism — and been successful! It was partly due to* Stepney Words *that the group had the idea of putting books out themselves. In fact we used the money from that to publish the first one. It was very selfless. We said, whose poetry shall we publish first. And they weren't saying* — Me! No me! No me! *They said unanimously* — Let's publish Stephen Hicks' poetry.

The book was entitled *The Boxer Speaks*. In Stephen's autobiography, *Sparring For Luck*, published posthumously in 1982, he wrote of that moment: 'Just imagine, a book solely devoted to one thing — my poetry. It was hardly believable, the first one of a whole collection of anthologies by authors of the Basement Writers.... The group consisted at first mainly of Chris's pupils and ex-pupils who wanted to continue their writing activities outside of school. The group soon grew though to include writers of all ages from the surrounding area.'

On that point, during our interview, Chris said, 'The group became an amalgamation of generations and to me that was its most enduring quality. It's much easier to get hold of a group of young people and get them writing poetry than it is to bring generations together who are initially quite hostile to each other and have them working together and producing things jointly.'

100

# Words from the Basement

I have vivid memories of my first meeting partly due to the presence of Chris Searle and partly because, maybe as some form of initiation, I was locked in a store cupboard by one of the other members. An outsider myself (born and bred in the adjoining borough of Hackney), I was intrigued to find as disparate bunch of people as would ever be found in a single room. Amongst those there that night were Leslie Mildiner and Bill House, who although still being in their teens, had co-written an autobiographical novel, *The Gates*, published by Centerprise in 1974, which told of their plight as 'school refusers' — or even 'school phobics' — as they had labelled themselves. It had been praised by people such as educationalist Leila Berg and like *Stepney Words*, it had caused a sensation all of its own. Because of its unique nature it attracted much media attention. There were newspaper articles and yet more teatime news interviews.

Another, seemingly mute, member of the group was Kim McGee, who had also been at Sir John Cass School. Encouraged to come along by Chris Searle, she had been too shy to make it on her own. So she brought her mother, Gladys, along for support. But it was Gladys who did all the talking. One of her early, short poems *'Please Read...'* became almost a group motto:

Please read my poetry —
  Don't let me write in vain...
  Because it is only in the last few years
  I found I had a brain.

# The Bard of Stepney

Born in Wapping in 1917, Gladys could only have been in her late fifties at the time she joined the Basement Writers. But with a stooped walk and severely wrinkled skin she looked much older. There was nothing frail about her however: between puffs on a cigarette, she would veer between matey jokiness and fierce verbal eruptions. It was Alan Gilbey who first dubbed her 'The Bard of Stepney' ('barred from pubs and betting shops throughout the borough,' he would announce at public readings). She was never *really* barred from anywhere — but it was sometimes a close thing. Gladys was always the star when it came to live performances. With a second-hand gold lamé trouser suit hanging on her tiny frame, constantly adjusting her spectacles, she would throw her arms about and yell out her poetry. But it wasn't all loud. Quiet introspective pieces about regret and loss were mingled with angry diatribes against injustices in society.

In the pub after my first meeting, Gladys let me leaf through the folder that she kept her poetry in. I was intrigued to see that it also contained various clippings about the Lindsay Anderson film *If....* made in 1968. I suppose it was condescending of me to wonder why the aging East Ender was so gripped by this biting allegorical fantasy of armed rebellion at a boys' public school. I found out that her other daughter had a small but crucial part in the film. If you've seen it, you'll remember Christine Noonan as 'the girl' (as she is credited) who has an erotic scrap with rebel toff Malcolm McDowell in the café where she works and who joins him in the iconic final reel as the boys shower the schoolmasters with machine gun fire from the rooftops. It is Christine who produces a revolver and plugs the headmaster square in the middle of his forehead.

Even in her seventies Gladys could dance into the early hours at parties, but ill health and accidents dogged her final years. She could take it though. She had, after all, entitled one of her collections *Old Age Ain't No Place For Sissies*. Gladys died in March 1999, surrounded by her family, including daughters Kim and Christine.

# Kim McGee

I asked Kim McGee about Chris Searle, and her mother:

*I was one of Chris Searle's pupils. He inspired me. We would have lessons where he would move all the tables and chairs out of the way and we'd just sit scattered around the room. He would say, 'Just call me Chris.' And we'd say, 'Is that allowed?' I was one of the school strikers and I went on the march to Trafalgar Square. I only went so far because I was a bit nervous. But when I came home, Gladys said, 'You should have bloody well gone all the way!' She met Chris when he came round the house to ask if she minded having one of my poems put into* Stepney Words, *even though it didn't have the blessing of the school. She said, no problem. And they became great friends after that.*

*Gladys lived in the East End all her life. When she was young she lived on the top floor of these old dwellings in Glamis Road with her sisters and two brothers. She had rickets and had to wear irons on her legs. If she was out and her mum and dad were too busy to come and get her she'd have to shuffle all the way up the stairs on her bum. She would have been in her twenties during the war. My Aunt Doris said to her, 'Oh, Glad, let's join the war effort. We could join up. We could travel!' So they joined the Land Army and got posted to Rygate where they had to cook and serve food for the officers. So she didn't really travel anywhere! She met Christine's dad who was in the Canadian Air Force. She must have met him at a dance and they formed a relationship. But she brought Christine up on her own. She met my dad when they both worked at the public baths. As an unmarried mum she'd had it really hard; in those days people looked down on you. If you wanted to rent a television or buy things on tap you weren't allowed to because there wasn't no mister. Life was easier with a ring on your finger. She said she did love him but these days she wouldn't have to get married. She encouraged Christine when she said she wanted to be an actress. I think that her and Gladys went to a Methodist Church in Cable Street where there was an amateur group and then later Christine went to drama school.*

*Money was tight when I was little. My dad liked a drink and Gladys was always trying to make some money by having a little bet. It frustrated the life out of me. There'd be*

103

him in the pub and her in the betting office. I'd stand outside and say, 'Mum, when are you coming home?' She'd be
looking at the racing pages, pulling the glass frame over to
her weak eye and studying the form of the horses. She'd roll
her eyes and say, 'Fucking hell, do you want the door key?'
And I'd say, 'No. I just want you to come home.' She'd say,
'I'll stay just ten more minutes, I've got to listen to this race.'
She loved it. But she wanted to get the money for us all
really.

When Chris Searle told me about the Basement Writers I
told Gladys that I wanted to go but was too nervous. She
said, 'Oh, Kim, don't be ridiculous. Just go. It's only over the
road.' So I said, 'Right, I'm going.' Got dressed up, got to
Cable Street, got to the bottom of the stairs and thought —
Oh no, I can't go in on my own! And I'd come up the stairs
and go all the way home again. Gladys said, 'Did you go?' I
said, 'No, I didn't, I'm too shy!' She said, 'Oh, for fuck's
sake, Kim!' I said, 'Can't you come with me?' And she said,
'I don't want to be down there, do I? It's for youngsters.' But
when Gladys finally did come she broke the ice. She had the
gift of the gab. She was the first non-young person to join
the Basement Writers. After my dad died, she started to
write poetry and I think that reading them out in the group
gave her a whole new lease of life really. She'd eff and blind
at the politicians on the radio — this was in the Maggie
Thatcher days — and write poems about various issues.
She got on really well with Chris Searle because they would
talk about politics together.

I'm still in touch with Chris Searle. Which is pretty good
going after all those years. I do storytelling for children
now. I read some folk tales and rearrange them a bit and
make puppets of the characters. For a basically shy person
you wouldn't think I'd be up there doing it. It's funny when
you look back and think this is where I am and that's where
I was then. I think that it's having people who believed in
you when you were a kid, giving you respect you never imagined having.

## Spreading the Word

The very first Basement Writers publications were not
books. They were posters, plastered up on billboards, on
hoardings and on the corrugated iron sheets that sur-

rounded the rubble-strewn building sites of the time. The poems included works on local, national and international themes. These were followed by a comic, *Up the Docks* by Alan Gilbey, highlighting what he felt to be the liberties taken in the redevelopment of dockland. Published output was prodigious: micro-books and pamphlets were typed up, illustrated and printed within an afternoon, half the content written the day before. *Sometimes You Can Hear The Birds Sing* was a collection of poems by Leslie Mildiner, *Inkslinging* by Alan Gilbey, *Bed Written* by Debbie Carnegie, *Living In the City*, a collection of song lyrics by Dave Swift, *Paper Talk* by Sally Flood, *Tall Thoughts* by young Asian poet Depak Kalha and many, many more.

In a 2009 special edition of the quarterly journal *Race & Class*, celebrating the work of Chris Searle, another original group member, Tony Harcup, makes the observation: 'The Basement Writers had a do-it-yourself aesthetic a good three years before punk, a decade or so before 'desktop publishing' and more than twenty years before the advent of the worldwide web'. There were radio features, poetry spots in the local press and contributions of work to local campaigns. The fading painted message *George Davies is Innocent* can still be seen on walls in the East End. Davies, fitted up for a crime he didn't commit, was eventually given a royal pardon. A Basement poem, written about this miscarriage of justice was praised by one of the campaigners: 'This poem is like forging a key for Georgie.'

# Alan Gilbey

Alan Gilbey was one of those present on the night of my first visit to the Basement Writers. My recollection was that he would always sit slightly apart from the main group, not saying anything but speaking through the brilliant cartoons that he would scratch onto a pad at a furious rate throughout the evening. There was the occasional poem as well, of course. At Sir John Cass, he had

Chris Searle for drama and has a vivid memory of the class being taken out to the churchyard opposite the school where there are mass graves of victims of the Great Plague to re-enact the catastrophe. 'There were all these children laying on the gravestones groaning and I was a donkey pulling a cart full of dead people.'

The enlarged Basement Writers soon began to perform their work in the black box theatre of the Half Moon, a converted synagogue in nearby Alie Street. Alan remembers their very laidback attitude. 'They'd hand us the key, giving us access to the entire space and its thousands of pounds worth of equipment and just asked us to drop the key back through the letter-box when we left!' Despite his shyness, Alan threw himself fully into the more theatrical side of the readings. They featured poetry, song and knockabout comedy (this was where Gladys McGee first donned her glitter suit), and no matter that the performers sometimes outnumbered the audience. It was apparent from the off that some of the group, including Alan, were naturals, whereas some of us, myself included, would just shuffle onto the stage, read a few bits and pieces and shuffle off again. I remember the rehearsals as intense and frantic — but the shows always seemed to come together at the last moment.

An occasional guest singer and musician at the shows was the willowy and somewhat ethereal Stephen Delft, who had a guitar-making workshop on Cable Street, where he lived with another friend of the Basement Writers, Judith Piepe. Judith, a German refugee (invariably described as 'motherly' in biographies) had been a central figure in the London folk scene of the early 1960s, giving guidance — and a home — to young musicians and lost souls in general. She was particularly influential in getting American singer-songwriter Paul Simon's career off the ground when he dossed in the workshop in 1965.

The haphazard experience of the Half Moon shows pointed out a new direction for some Basement Writers members. Alan split off to form Controlled Attack, a

106

punk-inspired theatre group with fellow Basement Writers Leslie Mildiner and his brother Harvey, an ex-soldier, straddling the no man's land between agit-prop, the fledgling alternative comedy club scene and pure lunacy. It was also the growing network of small-scale, informal London venues to which Alan brought a solo stand-up comedy act. Later, as a community drama worker on the Isle of Dogs, he devised a series of site-specific plays, including *A View of the River*, which looked at attitudes and stories surrounding the 'Enterprise Zone' land-rush in dockland during the early 1980s. Later, he inevitably tackled the story of the Battle of Cable Street: the story is detailed in the 'Art of Cable Street' section of this book. Alan still lives in East London. His quirky street tours with Steve Wells, *The Back Passages of Spitalfields*, have attained a cult status, herding locals and tourists alike through the dark and dank alleys of the East End and telling its stories in a theatrical fashion; a welcome alternative to the endless Jack the Ripper walks. Alan is also now a successful screenwriter and script consultant, working particularly in the world of animation, utilising his lifelong love of cartoons.

**After Chris Searle**

In 1976, Chris Searle exchanged the glowering skies of Stepney for sunny Mozambique, where he went to seek new challenges as a teacher. He had already begun to ease himself from his Basement role, not wanting to be seen as the figurehead of what was by then a self-run group. It was due to his inclusive example and democratic nature that the group continued to flourish. All the time, personnel was constantly changing. As original members moved on, two women in particular became prominent in keeping the Basement ideal alive. One of them was Sally Flood. Sally would write her poems while working as an embroidery machinist during the day and read us the results later in the evening. As another middle-aged woman, Gladys initially saw her as something of a rival. Gladys confided to her later that her first thought was, 'Oh, I've got competition here.' But Sally became a Basement regular and the two women forged a friendship which they maintained until Gladys's death.


## Liz Thompson

Another stalwart was Liz Thompson. When Liz first came along to the group I was immediately struck by her quirky, offbeat writing style. She wrote poems, mainly humorous, and reams upon reams of prose, handwritten on the backs of old leaflets and council-generated mailouts. I was also interested in Liz because she was one of the few members to live in Wapping. That may sound strange to outsiders: you can walk from Wapping to Cable Street in a few minutes. But a divide had existed for generations. Liz explained to me, 'In the old days, you had to go up to Cannon Street Road to encounter the Jewish community. Below that it was pretty much Irish. Jewish people didn't really come to Wapping and we didn't migrate north of Cable Street much either. We'd get on the tube and go further afield without touching down anywhere else on the way. It sounds a bit odd but that's how it used to work'. But there were other divisions much closer to home: Liz explained:

*I grew up in Wapping and spent my time gravitating between there and my grandparents in Bermondsey. My family were representative of the great Catholic and Protestant divide. Wapping was like an Irish village in a way. My dad's family were Irish Catholic and my mum's family were Protestant Londoners. It caused quite a lot of difficulties. They didn't see eye-to-eye in their various ways. My maternal granddad was against the marriage and my dad used to refer to my mum's family as the Bermondsey Mafia. It was thought to be a very dodgy thing to marry someone from south of the Thames in the first place. So there were two big divides — the river and religion.*

*For generations, my mum's family were 'toshers' or sewer hunters. They would go and look for anything valuable that had got lost down the drains or flushed out onto the foreshore of the river. But they weren't squeamish and weird though it sounds, they used to make quite a good living out of it. Tosh was the name of the copper that was used to encase the keel of a ship so that the shipworms couldn't get in and rot the timber. And any of that which fell into the river was about the most valuable type of metal that could be found. Later on they invested their money in things like property to rent and booze to sell.*

Up to this point in my interview with Liz I had assumed she was talking about her grandparents, until she mentioned how things became more difficult for her family of toshers when restrictions were brought in during the 1840s. Her family are unique in my own experience in their ability to conjure stories from generations long gone. And it was some of these folk memories that fed her fiction:

*It all got more secretive and there were less people toshing. Only a hardcore of people kept going because there were bigger risks involved — apart from the natural hazards that were associated with it in the first place. Within some of my family it carried on sort of unofficially to about 1900 but most of them found other things to do. They worked onwards and upwards, which is one reason why they weren't very happy about my dad's lot. They thought that anyone who worked as a docker had to be an idiot. It was ironic really, that they were two of the most dangerous jobs that you can think of, yet they looked down on each other. I took along a bit of family history to my first night at the Basement. They thought it was a bit weird but they were intrigued. It was something that not many people's families had been involved in. Not only that, I was a woman writing about an almost exclusively male-orientated way of making a living.*

*I used to be a tosher myself, but not in a subterranean way, just on the foreshore with a metal detector — the twentieth century version. I found this and that; it wasn't bad. But there's a limited resource because there's less happening on the river, so gradually there was less to be found. None of my family are based in Wapping anymore. They've moved on, scattered to the four winds.*

Like others in the Basement Writers, it was local issues that inspired Liz to make her work public:

*I did poetry about the docklands being demolished and the people's geography being wiped out and local people being squeezed out. Private developers were using loopholes in the law to cut off access to the riverside, which was actually a fire hazard because if anything happened to one of the buildings the river would have been the nearest source of water — and they were barricading it up! I wrote a poem with the line, 'Come back Alf Garnett, all is forgiven'. But it was ironical. I didn't mean that people should be prejudiced and inward looking, it was to do with the fact that people felt disconnected from what was happening around them and that they were losing control of their lives. Everything that used to be familiar was being demolished and uprooted and was outside people's sphere of influence — it was going to happen anyway.*

And then one day, a long time after I'd stopped being a member, the Basement Writers had to clear out of Cable Street when for whatever reason the room became no longer available. Meetings resumed in other venues and the group remained strong, continuing to perform and publish. But with Sally and Liz increasingly affected by ill-health (Liz eventually moving out of the area entirely) meetings became less frequent and then stopped altogether. Interestingly, when I spoke to Liz in 2010 for this book, she still saw a flickering of the Basement Writers flame. 'There are still people who are in contact with each other. Things have changed. People are able to do more on the internet, so there isn't that need quite so much to meet face-to-face anymore. Although it's nice to do so. But people can be in touch with each other by means which weren't around a few years ago.'

110

# THAP!

## The Tower Hamlets Arts Project

In 1974, Thames Television launched the 'Eyesites' scheme. Their idea was that with a budget of £10,000 (channelled through the Greater London Arts Association) professional artists would be invited to submit artworks that would be made into giant posters and pasted up on various temporary hoardings around Tower Hamlets. But as with other such philanthropic brainwaves to brighten up the borough the plan was thrown back in their faces by the people of the East End. It emerged that over half the budget for the scheme — inevitably tagged 'Eyesores' by its critics — had been set aside for the hiring of the hoardings alone. Also, any benefits gained from gazing at rain-lashed, mud-spattered roadside designs would be very short term. It was thought that the money could be used in other, much better ways. Rumblings from the Basement Project and elsewhere worked its way up to a full-throated roar from the existing arts workers of the area.

A public meeting in February 1975, backed the suggestion for a collaborative scheme that would bring together activities in drama, photography, painting, film, music, writing and publishing under a coordinating body that would be called the Tower Hamlets Arts Project, known universally as THAP. The Basement Writers were involved from the very start, with Alan Gilbey, their resident cartoonist, supplying the distinctive *Batman* inspired splat that became the THAP logo. After some initial eye-rolling and wearied frowns, Thames TV eventually saw the sense of the argument. The borough's contribution to the initiative was the appointment of an Arts Officer to support and manage the scheme, creating a precedent for the post. This came in the form of Phil Shepherd, a flame-haired whirlwind of activity who had blown in from the 'alternative' scene of the Bath Arts Workshop, and a programme was put into action.

THAP was launched at the start of 1976 and finished a year later with a month-long programme of events, capturing the work undertaken during that time. The celebrations took place at the Whitechapel Art Gallery and critics recorded their bemusement at finding this international venue, which had premiered the work of Picasso, Rothko and Frida Kahlo, now awash with rock bands, truanting schoolkids, local poets, and friends of Phil performing surreal theatre pieces in the spit and sawdust bar that had been set up in one of the backrooms. The nearest thing to a Jackson Pollock original was a paint overspill from the silkscreen workshop. Another innovation was a bookstall which ran for the whole month. Based on the model of the Saturday market stalls run by Stepney Books it proved to be a success and strengthened the long-term ambition of creating a permanent bookshop in East London.

After that first year, with the Thames money gone, there was a concerted effort to continue. THAP became an independent organisation, working alongside the council arts department. But there was a need for a headquarters — and, some wondered, might that not be combined with the dream of establishing a bookselling outlet? With the support of the Greater London Arts Association, the THAP bookshop opened in Watney Street (usually referred to as Watney Market) in April 1977, in a crumbling, mice-ridden building in a semi-derelict row of shops. At the opening event, with music and street theatre, the supportive Leader of the Council, Paul Beasley, even managed a song. Although operating as a collective, made up of volunteers and partners, the project took on its first paid employees, including Alice Bigelow, Alan Gilbey and me. As with the Basement Project workers, the job became our lives; there was no

112

real distinction between what we did in working hours and what we did outside them. And at last, East London had a bookshop.

## More From the Lost Library

It couldn't be said that everything always ran smoothly in the bookshop. The concept being so new, we were constantly being asked if it was a library and if we had read all the books. Kids nicked stock, there were break-ins, outsiders and drunks came to seek solace and every day brought a new financial crisis. There was a strong commitment to collective working and an exploration of what arts in a 'community' context actually meant — about how the way we worked would impact on an end product. We made it up as we went along. Weekly planning sessions, starting in the middle of Friday afternoons above the shop would go on for so long that we sometimes had to leg it down the road to make it for last orders in the local pub.

Alongside the wide range of events being organised, with the input of Denise Jones from Stepney Books, we created our own publishing unit. It turned out that Tony Harcup's view of the small-scale book production being done by the Basement Writers as a sort of proto-punk enterprise wasn't so far off the mark. It was here that local publishing and punk collided. In 1978, the THAP Bookshop was visited by a member of the Desperate Bicycles, personally hawking their shoestring budget single, *The Medium Was Tedium*. Although not having a record section, we gladly stocked it. With its exhortation to just 'go and do it', how could we not? Later, THAP also published a collection, *Poems*, by acoustic punk Patrik Fitzgerald, who went on to attract a loyal, cult following. We were also on the organising committee, and ran a bookstall, for the massive Rock Against Racism carnival in Victoria Park in April 1978, featuring groups such as

X-Ray Spex, the Tom Robinson Band and the Clash. The publishing wing of THAP continued to follow the pattern of pushing out biographies and anthologies of local writing, at the same time making some imaginative forays into the contemporary landscape. *Ben's Bunker Book,* for instance. Ben Hayden took it upon himself to spend two weeks in a hole in Limehouse, in line with government advice in the event of a nuclear strike, laying bare the lunacy behind it.

I suspect that the most enduring THAP publication will be *Across Seven Seas and Thirteen Rivers: life stories of pioneer Sylhetti settlers in Britain,* by youth worker Caroline Adams. Published in 1987, it charts the most recent wave of mass immigration to East London; and which, though starting as a trickle would eventually transform the cultural make-up of the area. The author states that the steady stream of migration after the war led to a Sylheti population in Britain of some five thousand by the mid-sixties. At the time of publication the figure had risen to 200,000, with 35,000 settlers in East London. The book features a collection of interviews conducted with men who, as Caroline states: '...were born early this century, the sons of peasants in villages in Sylhet District in what is now Bangladesh but was then Assam, in the north-eastern part of British India.' And who, in the storm in which they lived their lives, would eventually be washed up on Britain's not always welcoming shores. As on previous occasions, it was left to a community publisher to shed light on a largely unexplored history.

Through its publishing work and writers' workshops, THAP became an early member of the Federation of Worker Writers and Community Publishers, a national network linking dozens of like-minded groups. Mad minibus journeys to various parts of the country brought them together for a yearly conference. THAP eventually moved from Watney Street to Whitechapel near to the London Hospital, where it was renamed Eastside, and is now — as The Brick Lane Bookshop — located in the street of that name.

Although I have included this account in the section on the Basement Project, it wouldn't be entirely accurate to claim THAP as one of its offshoots — there were too many other influences and individuals from elsewhere who made it all happen. But its influence was crucial. Such was the movement of people between projects and the sharing of resources it wasn't always easy to work out where one initiative ended and another began: there was a generosity of spirit and a trust in letting people get on with it. Even those initiatives based in the Basement itself were able to operate on a fairly autonomous basis, groups such as the Basement Film Project, which is looked at in the next section.

# 5. Cable Street on Film
## The 'Cable'

## 'The Cable Street Casting Agency'

Cable Street is not usually associated in people's minds with film but there are significant connections. I had heard tales that in the 1930s and 40s, Black and Asian people had been whisked off the streets of East London in order to supply colour for this or that stirring imperialist romance filmed at Shepperton or Pinewood or some gung-ho jungle adventure film. Cable Street as a sort of casting agency. In my imagination I see a Cable Streeter sitting in the Troxy Cinema in Commercial Road, nudging his friend beside him — '*Oi, that bloke standing behind Stewart Granger by the mud hut. That's Ali, isn't it? The bloke who serves the tea in that café by Christian Street. Can't be, can it? Looks like him though, doesn't it?*' But I'd begun to think of it as an urban myth. Until there came written confirmation in film director Michael Powell's 1986 autobiography *A Life in Movies*. He is talking about the filming of *Black Narcissus*, released in 1947, an odd tale of madness and repressed sexuality amongst a group of Anglican nuns, set in the Himalayas (filmed at Pinewood). The cast included Deborah Kerr, David Farrar and Sabu, the 'Indian boy from the Maharajah's elephant stable who had become a film actor':

> *In those days, when the war was just over, there was an immense floating population of Asians around London Docks, and we had no difficulty in building up a list of extras for the crowd scenes: Malays, Indians, Gurkhas, Nepalese, Hindus, Pakistanis, hundreds of them. We formed groups of different castes and races, and each group had a leader. We began to notice how clever the art department were being about the handling of these people. The costume department would encourage them to bring their own costumes or to pick out props and costumes for themselves from the common store.*

116

I don't know of any accounts by those extras themselves. So I'm left with my imagination... A cold morning when a Rolls Royce draws up outside a café. Want to earn some money? A chauffeured ride to the studio. A day pretending to be a character with your own approximate skin colour. Cash in hand. The train ride home. Back in the café: *'I met that Jean Simmons today, lovely lady.' 'Sure you did, Ali, sure you did. Just pour the tea, eh?'*

\* \* \*

The Cable Picture Palace, at 101 Cable Street, is remembered today only by the oldest of East Enders. I'm glad to be able to include here what is surely the definitive account. Jim Wolveridge, an avid film-goer, often spoke to me of his visits there. He wrote the following, previously unpublished, account of his youthful cinema-going days, which ends on page 122:

# 'The Acme of Imperfection'

Stepney in the inter-war years was often a depressing place. Many of its inhabitants lacked jobs, decent homes, proper food and the money to buy it. One of the few ways to escape, if a temporary one, was the picture palace. Whatever else the area lacked, it was well endowed with movie houses — more than a score of them ranging in size and scope from the tiny Cable to the giant Troxy, and encompassing the exotic Palaseum, and the specialist Classic. At one time or another, I had been in all of them.

It was at the Cable that I served my apprenticeship as a cinemagoer — an apprenticeship that began when I was no more than a babe in arms. At this stage of my career I was too young to go unaccompanied, but nature provided me with a doting grandfather, and Joe (the Cable's owner), with free seats (Joe, in addition to owning the Cable, also had property in the area, and my granddad was one of his tenants. They were also personal friends — hence the Buckshee tickets).

117

We enjoyed Joe's hospitality for a few years, and might have continued to do so, but Joe, due to advancing age, decided to sell out, and the new owner also called Joe, wanted payment for admission. My grandfather who earned a precarious living as a costermonger could not afford to buy tickets for the pictures, so henceforth the Cable was denied to him. After the old boy was expelled from Eden, my father gained possession of his rightful heir, and he being reasonably solvent at the time, took me to the pictures with him. Before this happened though, my parents told me that I had been granddad's constant companion, and that whenever they wanted me, they

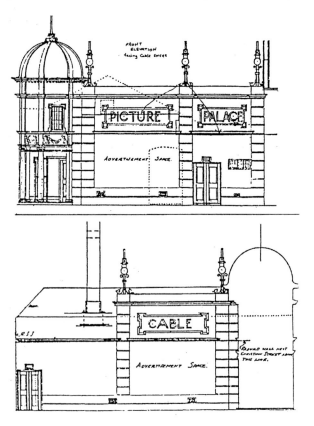

would go into the Cable and find me on his lap, fast asleep and snoring my head off. I seem to have been a film critic quite early in life. I didn't remain one though, and soon learned to love the cinema and all its works.

The Cable, bless its heart, was the most loved and the most uncomfortable cinema in the whole of Stepney. Why was it loved? I'm not sure, but loved it was! Mention the place to any of the area's old timers and just watch their eyes light up with pleasure and affection. What made it uncomfortable? That's far easier to answer. It was stifling in summer and freezing in winter, and its seats were hard enough to cause corns in unmentionable places. It was small too! So small that whenever one of its customers left their seat to go to the toilet, his or her shadow would appear on the screen. This didn't worry the case-hardened, who'd grown immune to cat calls, but sensitive people with weak bladders must have suffered agonies. The musical accompaniment to the films being shown was on a miniature scale too. Anything larger than a trio would have left no room for an audience, so the music was provided by a solitary pianist. He, the joanna-player, was a man of limited repertoire. Whenever Tom Mix came galloping to the rescue — a thing Tom frequently did in the kind of films I liked, the maestro would break into the *William Tell Overture*. Sometimes to show his versatility he would vary it with the *Light Cavalry*, but William Tell remained his favourite.

The Cable was not exactly overstaffed. Apart from the pianist, the projectionist who remained anonymous, and Joe, who very wisely took charge of the pay-box and takings, Ginger did all the work around the place. What were his duties? Many and multifarious. He was the doorman, the ticket collector, the usher, and, the Cable not running to glamour girls, the ice-cream seller. The ice-cream did not come from a regular supplier but from a man who kept an ice-cream barrow outside the cinema. He had an arrangement with Joe whereby Ginger would come and collect a tray of wafers in the intervals, and pay for what was sold

119

later. Those wafers were whacking great things! Almost two inches thick, practically solid ice, and barely flavoured with a little lemon or strawberry essence, they nevertheless provided a good, big mouthful for a halfpenny. Ginger's tray was the lid off a biscuit tin, which was often full of holes, and which in any other establishment might have led to a little awkwardness. Once inside with his cargo, Ginger didn't stand in the aisles looking pretty — we had no time for such fripperies, but in response to calls of 'Oi, over here', the tray would be passed hand to hand along the row of seats. Melting ice dripping through the holes in the tray would soak the knees of the customers' trousers, but this didn't worry us — we were a hardy breed in the Cable.

Ginger was in charge of sanitation too. On a hot day he would walk along the aisles spraying the place with perfumed disinfectant. He was very lavish with his use of the spray, and sometimes the patrons would find themselves being fumigated too — but on a hot day... maybe we needed it.

In the twenties, and to a lesser extent in the thirties, in order to advertise an extra special feature, it was customary for attendants to dress in costumes that fitted in with the type of film being shown, and Ginger who was expected to be industrious, would have to get dolled up too. Sometimes he would appear in the guise of a pirate, sometimes Tommy Atkins, and quite frequently a Foreign Legionnaire. Attendants at the large picture palaces were men of commanding presence — they had to be in order to justify the uniform, but Ginger had no presence at all. He was a squat, tubby man with the battered face of an ex-boxer, and while it was true that he had the right kind of swagger, the perisher didn't shave that often, and I felt that a Foreign Legionnaire with ginger bristles took all the romance out of things.

Ginger was also the chucker-out — what a rich full life that man led! He had very little trouble with the adults, who on the whole were an amiable bunch, but the kids tended to lead him a dance — especially at the Saturday matinees. The matinees started at ten in the morning and the price of admission was two pence. When the show ended at one o'clock, we were expected to leave and make room for the adults, who were charged four pence for their pleasures. We youngsters though wanted more than our money's worth and would try to sit through the show at least twice. The standard dodge was to lock ourselves in the lavatory, and when Ginger had grown tired of banging on the door and bawling 'Come out, I know you're in there', we would come out of hiding and re-seat ourselves. Ginger soon learned to deal with this. He lurked unobtrusively at the back of the hall, and then when we had been lulled into a false sense of security, he would suddenly emerge from the shadows, pounce, and demand to see our tickets. If we had a tuppeny ticket, or claimed that we had paid four pence but had lost the evidence, then Ginger, deaf to pleas and threats of 'I'll tell my dad on you', would, to put it politely, evict us.

Our busy bee was also in charge of security, and locking up the premises entailed quite a lot of work. The Cable had no front door that could be padlocked and Ginger had to go through quite a complicated process of erecting a series of metal grilles and securing them with chains, which took quite a time. When his day's work was finally over he would mount his bike and ride off no doubt saying what most of Stepney's toilers said at locking up time: 'Shut the shop and bugger the customers'. He would arrive back at work the next day, dismantle the barricade, and put up the frames containing stills of the current attractions.

By the end of 1929, most of the area's other cinemas were changing over to sound, and the Cable should have followed suit, but it didn't. Joe could not afford the cost of the new-fangled equipment, so the Cable's stars kept quiet and let action speak louder than words, and stayed quiet right up to the middle of 1931. This made no difference to the cinema's trade. It had a loyal clientele, most of whom would not desert the old place. Its seats were cheap — an important factor in those hard-up days, and being so small it was easy to fill. Silent films too were a good deal livelier than the rather static early sound films, and once the novelty of sound had worn off there was still quite a large audience for the silent drama.

The Cable would have gone right on showing silent movies had the supply not run out and forced the place to be modernised. Even though I would never again hear William Tell within the precincts I welcomed the change, and with productions like *King Kong, I Was a Spy*, *Drums of Jeopardy* and *Beast of the City*, it was not surprising.

By the time I was sixteen, my visits to the little place on the corner of Christian Street began to become very infrequent. By now I was going to the posher and more comfortable places like the Troxy and the Palaseum, and the Cable was taking a back seat. There was probably a mild element of snobbery in this; I, like any lordly teenager, wanted to be seen in all the best places. This though was not a major consideration — I would still go to a bug hutch if it was showing the kind of films I wanted to see, but the Cable showed attractions that I'd sat through at the Troxy or Palaseum a few weeks previous. That being the case, my old home from home was deprived of my custom. One day in 1938 I did pay what was to be my final visit, to the place that employed Ginger. It wasn't out of nostalgia, I'm afraid. The film that day was *The Sun Never Sets*, which somehow or other I'd missed seeing. Apart from Ginger not asking to see my ticket, nothing had changed — I still had to avoid a spray of disinfectant. *The Sun Never Sets* turned out to be a far from prophetic title. The sun set for the Cable the first day of the blitz when it received a direct hit. Now a garage occupies the site, and there is nothing to show the place ever existed. True it still lives on in memory, but I think something more substantial should be added — a plaque perhaps. I shall have to talk to the Council about this.

# To Sir, With Love

## The Book or the Film?

*To Sir, With Love*. Are you thinking of the book by E.R. Braithwaite? The film? The mega-selling Lulu rendition of the theme song? You might indeed be thinking of all three — understandably, as they have all become tightly entwined in the public mind. Until fairly recently the Coronet edition of the book still featured a photograph of the film's star, Sidney Poitier, on the cover. Customers picking it up in the shop might not even have been aware of its autobiographical nature. The block capital blurb on the back simply stated: THE BEST-SELLING STORY OF A NEGRO TEACHER IN A TOUGH SCHOOL IN LONDON'S EAST END.

Having purchased that edition, the reader would have noted that the author shares a surname with its main character — although he is mainly referred to as 'Ricky' — establishing it as a 'true' story. The character was renamed as 'Mark Thackeray' for the screen. But for anybody coming from the book to the film there would have been a more striking difference. The story in the book is set in the pallid dawn of the 1950s whereas the action in the film takes place against a brightly coloured swinging sixties backdrop in line with the year it was released, 1967 (publicity tagline: 'A story as fresh as the girls in their minis'). The filmed update called for some necessary adjustments. For instance, black faces on the streets of London were no longer so unusual by the mid-sixties. Therefore, episodes from the book with Braithwaite being openly insulted in restaurants and refused lodgings didn't find their way into the script.

Otherwise, the film, directed by James Clavell, remains fairly faithful to its source. We first catch sight of Ricky

aboard a double-decker bus perusing the 'earthy char-
women' (who remind him of 'peasants in a book by
Steinbeck') returning to East London from early morning
cleaning jobs in the City. He hops off along Commercial
Road and makes his way along New Road, still ravaged by
Second World War bombing raids. And although Cable
Street doesn't get a name check, this is where he ends up.
He is about to experience his first day as a teacher at what
in the book is called Greenslade Secondary Modern School
(and which is given yet another name, North Quay, for the
film) but which, in real life was actually St George's-in-the-
East. He immediately gets on with the headmaster, but not
so with the rest of the teaching staff. In the book,
Braithwaite is very clear about his disappointment at being
denied a job in his chosen profession of engineering, due to
undoubted racism, and comes to teaching out of necessity.
He is an ex-RAF man and a traditionalist; he's not going to
take any nonsense from his class of cocky cockneys. He has
sympathy with them, however, comparing his own childhood days in sunny Guyana and the depressing school
building in poverty-stricken East London.

From then on, both book and movie progress along firmly
established lines — from the American 'social commentary'
movie *Blackboard Jungle* (which incidentally features a
young hoodlum Sidney Poitier), through the sooty black
and white realism of the British *Spare the Rod* (unfairly
neglected, I suspect, due to the fact that its star is none
other than middle-of-the-road East End entertainer Max
Bygraves) to the somewhat less gritty popular telly sit-com
*Please Sir*; initial disinterest from the pupils, transmuted
into gratitude and love, and a growing respect from his
peers who come to recognise his aptitude and steely deter-
mination. And no wonder he wins the kids over, risking
trips to museums, good-naturedly taking a tap on the chin
during a boxing match and dispensing advice to mothers on
how to deal with their wayward daughters.

Just how deeply racism is ingrained in his pupils'
psyche is illustrated to him when the mother of a mixed-

race boy dies. Although the kids organise a collection for a wreath, none of them are willing to take it to the doorstep of the family's house. In the book, Braithwaite is understandably disgusted but is moved to tears on the day of the funeral when they all turn up outside the house in their best clothes. 'Oh God, forgive me for my hateful thoughts, because I love them, these brutal, disarming bastards, I love them…' The book also has a muted love interest, with a white female teacher, which is even more muted in the film, with little indication of much going on between Poitier and a strikingly blonde Suzy Kendall beyond sharing a cuppa by the staffroom tea urn.

In the book, it is his girlfriend who gets angry about racial slights on Braithwaite's behalf, criticising him for running away from the problem rather than confront it. The only time he really gets angry is when the school is stitched up by a newspaper. The unnamed rag is invited in by the headmaster in the hope that it will counter negative publicity that the school had been getting: one of the boys had been involved in a stabbing. The hacks descend with flashbulbs popping and inevitably the photos all feature girls swirling their skirts at a dance session and boys with fags dangling out of their mouths. This episode is omitted from the screen version. There is a significant addition however. Poitier causes hilarity amongst the pupils by demonstrating a little of his homeland patois. Braithwaite would certainly have been familiar with this way of speaking, although I find it doubtful that in real life this son of Oxford-educated parents and the product of the prestigious Queen's College in what was then British Guiana, would have been proud to display it in the classroom.

Otherwise, the adaptation is pretty faithful right up to the end. With those updates. In the book, at the end-of-term party, he dances a 'Ladies' Excuse-me Foxtrot' with a girl who has had a crush on him, while in the film, Poitier engages in an (interminably long) energetic disco workout with actress Judy Geeson after being serenaded with the title song by Lulu and an incredibly competent fifth-form band (in reality, the Mindbenders). Considering that they are saddled with a fairly mushy script, the cast, including television battleaxe Rita Webb and the more refined future Hyacinth Bucket *Keeping Up Appearances* star, Patricia Routledge, do a remarkably good job (my personal favourites: the aforementioned Scots rocker Lulu and a kohl-eyed Adrienne Posta as a couple of spud-faced scrubbers).

But, as I have discovered, there is yet another version of the story. That is, those of the kids at the school. And the discrepancy is far greater than those in both the book and the film.

## Alf Gardner

Alf Gardner is the only contributor to this book who tracked me down rather than vice-versa. A few years ago I started to receive telephone calls at (for me anyway) unearthly hours on Saturday mornings. The mystery caller at the other end of the line announced that he was writing a memoir. He knew that I had been involved in publishing at the Tower Hamlets Arts Project and wondered if I could be of any help. I explained that I was having enough trouble getting my own work published but that I would take a look at his manuscript. And I was very glad that I did. Alf eventually published the book himself, *An East End Story — 'a tale of Friendship'*, which came to feature a brief introduction by me. After reading many dozens of manuscripts about East London family life, I found his loner's tales of riverside haunts in Wapping, and experiences in the red-light clubs of Cable Street engrossing. When I came to write this section up, I recalled that he had also mentioned in his book that he had been a pupil at St George's-in-the-East School. And that the 'humourless' E.R. Braithwaite had been one of his teachers there.

126

One overcast morning in the summer of 2010 I met up with Alf at the site of his old school. As mentioned, Cable Street is not referred to by name in Braithwaite's book, and people are generally unaware that it is the location of the story. It may be because the building is almost invisible from the street, tucked away behind the row of Georgian houses that stretch between the Town Hall and Cannon Street Road. People don't know it's there! An iron gate bars access, and has been permanently bolted since the building closed as a school. That day we were lucky. The old schoolhouse is being converted into flats and the gate was open for the arrival of vehicles bringing in building material. We wandered in, our shoes muddied in the dirty track sown by the trucks.

Ignoring the curious stares of the builders, Alf told me:

*St. George's-in-the-East wasn't a large school. There were never more than a hundred and fifty pupils, divided into just eight classes. In my older sister Mary's class there were only about a dozen children. Alex Bloom, the headmaster, was extremely popular with the pupils and teachers. Throughout the four years I was there I had just two, but excellent, teachers: Mrs Dymphna Porter who specialized in creative writing and Mrs Rose Gamble, who taught mainly art. It was a well disciplined little school. I witnessed no hooliganism or bullying whatsoever. We even had a 'student voice': the pupils had an opportunity to say how the school was run through various pupil-teacher committees. Our weekly review was extremely popular — every Friday morning pupils were encouraged to write about their previous week's attendance. We could say if we thought a particular lesson was relevant, interesting or boring and give our opinions on the ability and effectiveness of teachers.*

*E. R. Braithwaite began to teach at St George's in 1953. As a strict disciplinarian, he favoured corporal punishment. Fortunately for us boys, Alex Bloom had banned all use of it. When Braithwaite came he couldn't understand it. But the ban didn't prevent him from hurling keys, chalk or wooden-handled blackboard dusters at any boy he thought wasn't paying attention. It was obvious to me that Braithwaite was disliked by the boys, but not by the*

*girls. They probably liked him because he was very
lenient towards them. In Braithwaite's book he implies
that he was there for about eight years, which is a fallacy.
He was at our school for about six to nine months. He
actually taught in the East End for about nine years. So
it seemed to me that he had also included in his book various incidents and episodes that he had experienced in
those other schools.*

*There were no facilities for metal and woodwork at our
school so we went to a couple of neighbouring schools for
those lessons. One day I returned from one of the other
schools late in the afternoon to be told that Alex Bloom
had collapsed in his office and had been taken to the
London Hospital in Whitechapel. The next morning we
were told the sad news that he had died. A week later in
the rain, Alex Bloom's funeral procession stopped outside
the school. A reporter from the* Daily Mirror *took photos
and recorded the event. I left school at fifteen with no
qualifications. Many of the children who attended St.
George's came from poor backgrounds. There was never
enough money for food, coal or clothing. The majority of
my friends just wanted to work and earn money.*

Alf bought the book *To Sir, With Love* when it came out
in 1959. 'I thought — what's this?' In our conversation he
tactfully described himself as 'extremely disappointed' at
the way he felt that Braithwaite had misrepresented the
situation at his old school. If anything, the film interpretation seemed to him even more outrageous. 'During the
summer of 1966, I was working as a stock cutter at a
dress factory in Cavell Street. At lunchtime I would
wander down the nearby Watney Street Market and buy
fruit and sandwiches. On one of these visits I saw the
actor Sidney Poitier there filming the screen version of *To
Sir, With Love.*' Alf saw the finished product when it came
out. When he talks about it, it's as if he takes the film as
a personal slight. 'Total rubbish,' he said. 'The pupils in
the film were portrayed as unruly, nasty teenagers,
which is the opposite of the truth.' Like the book, Alf feels
that the film has turned the truth on its head, depicting
the head teacher as weak and ineffectual with no control

over his school, whereas he clearly believes that it was Braithwaite's presence that was disruptive.

Eventually we left the builders in peace and Alf bid farewell once more to his old school. I hadn't quite finished with him yet however and he appears again later in this book, talking about another aspect of Cable Street's history: its period as a red-light district in the 1950s and 60s.

## Dominoes

The main problem with compiling this book was not a worry about a lack of material. But rather, dealing with a surfeit of it. Not only that, in almost every instance, one piece of research revealed a link with something else that wasn't part of my original plan. You see my problem? Think of me as a bloke sitting at a keyboard squeezed into the corner of a tiny room. Behind me are a selection of books, including autobiographies, biographies, novels, poetry collections and learned histories; there are photos, pamphlets, slides, rolled-up and framed posters, flyers, newspaper clippings, tapes, CDs, DVDs and videos. All of them indicating various paths I might explore. I soon started to think of the whole enterprise as not so much a book but as a set of dominoes.

The *To Sir, With Love*, section is a good example. Conveniently, to illustrate my point, on one shelf, the original E.R. Braithwaite book has fallen against an old video of the film version, which has fallen onto a CD containing Lulu's rendition of the film's theme song, which has fallen onto another video, a homage to the movie, entitled *Sidney's Chair*. More about that, shortly.

## Reel Streets

Have you ever whiled away a rainy Sunday afternoon in front of the telly, watching an old British movie? A

British movie in black and white or in colour, which is not particularly gripping, and yet you continue to watch avidly? A movie which has been filmed on location in London and which has given you a secret thrill when recognising a particular street or building? A street long since washed away by mass demolition? Or a surviving building, floating alone in a sea of unsympathetic redevelopment? And even if you have never seen that building before, which is in a part of London in which you have not trodden, what is it that you still find so thrilling?

The *Reel Streets* website, which seeks to identify and display locations used in British movies, is the brainchild of John Tunstill, who at a young age realised the power of the moving image. One of his early memories, from the Coronation in New Southgate, is of the engine of a passing V1 flying bomb cutting out close to the cinema and exploding nearby. The audience, emerging from under the seats, however, continued to be mesmerised by the George Formby feature that was playing out on the screen. Such is the hypnotic effect of the cinema is that it makes us nostalgic for things that we never personally experienced, and which perhaps didn't actually exist in the first place. The website is interactive in that subscribers will offer a still from a film with an indication of its location, or, if they don't know it, invite others to do so. It wasn't so long ago, before DVDs and videos, that scenes in a film would speed by with no opportunity to stop or pause. So while some might see *Reel Streets* as an example of a service devised by geeks for the edification of geeks, I see it as a new form of local history publishing.

A pre-*Carry On* Barbara Windsor, with a hairstyle to challenge the emerging high-rises, her heels stabbing at the cobblestones as she trots through Wapping in stills from *Sparrows Can't Sing*. A pre-Bond Sean Connery, up to no good in Cable Street in the wide-boy military comedy *On the Fiddle*, and the tall, imposing dock walls of *The Pool of London*, prior to the destruction of dockland. All of these black and white beauties are available to view. Yet the more recent street scenes from *To Sir, With Love*, are in a way more evocative than the others. They capture the moment when Britain switched from black and white to colour. What we gained during those years of the mid-sixties was a pop-orientated artistic renaissance and a richer cultural mix, and what we lost — particularly in East London — was acres of housing stock and the tight supportive communities that lived in them. Many of the streets in *To Sir, With Love* were demolished almost as the film reached the cinemas. The rows of little houses appear as concrete versions of The Small Faces' song *Lazy Sunday Afternoon*, unaware of plans already being made on their behalf to bring in the wrecking-ball and package out the contents to Dagenham and Barking.

*To Sir, With Love*, set in one Cable Street school, was actually filmed in another: Johnson Road School, further eastwards. Many local people still remember the day when the cameras rolled in. And for one person who was too young to remember it, the effect was profound.

## Roberto Bangura

In Lulu's 2002 autobiography, *I Don't Want to Fight*, it documents, all too briefly, her work on the film, *To Sir, With Love*. Her experiences of the USA — UK divide are fascinating. On the shoot, Lulu found the star, Sidney Poitier, to be distant and stand-offish. The Hollywood actor was horrified at the eating habits of the British cast and crew — unaware that during the 1960s, on this side of the Atlantic, standard fare for both pop star and prole alike was a plate of egg and chips. Approaching him for a friendly chat, she puts her foot in it by accidentally mixing up Poitier's wife with a past lover. Any chance of her expected behind-the-camera camaraderie was lost from that point on. When I interviewed Roberto Bangura, I was interested to hear that he had also had an encounter with Sidney Poitier.

Roberto Bangura's father was a West African seaman who had taken up residence in Cable Street as a teenager in 1945. And it was in the street itself that he was thrown together with Roberto's mother, an Italian au-pair, on a blind date. A marriage followed in 1951. Roberto was one of that generation born in the 1960s who first encountered *To Sir, With Love* on television. He told me, 'I was probably about eleven years old. What was surprising about it was that it looked and felt like a Hollywood film and yet the background and milieu were so familiar that it gave it a somewhat surreal quality. Seeing that huge, glamorous *Columbia Pictures* logo at the start and then finding ourselves in Wapping, of all places, was very strange. Mind you, somebody should have told poor Sidney to get off the bus before it went all the way to St Paul's Cathedral via Tower Bridge and then back to Wapping. Ah well, I guess he *was* new to the area.'

The film was instrumental in Roberto's realisation that the distance between Stepney and the silver screen was not as distant as he had supposed. It also led him to the book, and the awareness that what had been left out of the film was more interesting than what had been put in. Roberto later met up with the daughter of a cast member, who told him that the love scenes that appeared in the book between the main character and his young, white female colleague *had* been filmed but were cut from the finished movie so as not to unsettle the US market. And throughout his subsequent career, the film has continued to follow Roberto, who has frequently met up with people closely connected to it.

The connections were even closer than Roberto imagined. In Wapping, he got into a conversation with one of the parents who attended a mums and toddlers club that he was working at. 'She said that she had gotten Sidney Poitier's autograph when she was a kid, not five hundred yards from where we were standing. It turned out that *everybody* in Stepney had turned up to watch the filming of *To Sir, With Love*, including my own mother and,

132

during the shooting of a scene in Watney Market, even me! But I was much too young to remember it.'

On becoming a student at the National Film and Television School, Roberto began his search for a vehicle that could transport his thoughts on inter-racial relationships and the mixed-race experience on to the screen. But he kept coming up with what he admits were 'dull ideas'.

'I wanted to explore how us multi-racial kids learned to grow up in a world where there were no precedents. Our parents didn't have the language to deal with the intricacies and nuances of our experience. Pointing out how great Cassius Clay was fell somewhat short if you didn't want to be a boxer.' In fact, the story into which he could weave these themes had been staring him in the face almost his entire life.

## Sidney's Chair

*Sidney's Chair* became Roberto's second year project, shot and scripted by him in 1993 but not finished until two years later. This lean, twenty-one minute fantasy is set around the *To Sir, With Love* shoot in Shadwell. Local twelve-year old Ricci Owobe and his white friend Mina make a nuisance of themselves as they try to move into the orbit of the movie star. They end up pinching Poitier's personalised chair — one of those collapsible wood and canvas jobs with a name imprinted on the back strip — and hiding it. After being disturbed by Gabriel, the neighbourhood black tramp, Ricci takes the chair home where it is discovered by his white mother and black father. After being sent to bed for his crime, Ricci confides to his mother that despite being in awe of Sidney Poitier he is troubled by his own and his father's dark skin. But later, after almost being run over by a driver who racially abuses him, he is defended by his father, who he now begins to see as a hero. Ricci and Mina finally return Sidney's chair and get his autograph, only for the famous chair to be stolen again, this time by Gabriel.

The film opened doors for Roberto. It was shown at festivals throughout the world and led to a career that has included directing feature films and episodes of major television series such as *Casualty* and *The Lakes*. But *To Sir, With Love* was never very far away. In 1997, Roberto was at the Toronto Film Festival promoting his low-budget production *The Girl With Brains In Her Feet*. Finding himself at a swanky open-air freebie amongst hot-dog munching movie stars, Roberto was reduced from filmmaker to fan on seeing the tall, still handsome, Sidney Poitier making his way through the throng. He plucked up his courage and introduced himself. Roberto recalls the conversation and the outcome: 'I said, "I, um, just wanted to say, um, I'm a huge fan and, um, in a way I think you're responsible for me being here today," He smiled somewhat quizzically and looked at his minder who in turn looked at me rather benignly, guessing that I was probably a harmless idiot.' Poitier was graciousness itself, murmuring thanks and shaking hands and the script that Roberto had spent decades rehearsing in his mind in the eventuality of this exact occasion — about growing up in East London, seeing *To Sir, With Love* and how he fashioned *Sidney's Chair* on the back of it — was lost. There were no opportunities for retakes. Roberto was palmed off to Poitier's daughter who indulged him in polite small-talk as the actor disappeared back into the crowd.

# Tunde's Film

## Cable Street Cameos

Just around the corner from Cable Street, at the southern end of Cannon Street Road, is where gangster Harold Shand's mum nearly comes a cropper in the seminal 1979 British crime movie *The Long Good Friday*. Luckily, she is already at prayer inside St George's-in-the-East church when a bomb, a calling card from the IRA, rips apart the chauffeured limo waiting for her in the courtyard outside. The film is located mainly in Wapping and features the antics of crooks, councillors and the American Mafia in the emerging Docklands Klondike. In a later film, actor Bob Hoskins, who had played Harold in *The Long Good Friday*, makes an appearance in Cable Street itself while visiting St George's Town Hall. This time Hoskins plays a character called Sam Garcia in a scene from the 1992 spy thriller *Blue Ice*, a perilously thin homage to the Len Deighton inspired films of the 1960s, beginning with *The Ipcress File*, starring Michael Caine as secret agent Harry Palmer (comparisons are inevitable, given that *Blue Ice* also stars Michael Caine as a secret agent called Harry). Further west, St Paul's Church House in Wellclose Square, played an important role in the 1943 World War Two film, *Fires Were Started*. Director Humphrey Jennings created his 'camera poems' for the GPO Film Unit and Crown Film Unit. Now we would call them docu-dramas. The action takes place over a twenty-four hour period, dramatising the work of real fire-fighters in the Auxiliary Fire Unit. The story concerns the dousing of a flaming riverside warehouse, threatening an anchored ammunitions ship, and the fire-fighters' base is St. Paul's Church House.

All the above films, like *To Sir, With Love*, feature Cable Street and its environs in what amounts to a cameo role, shot by visiting directors, cast and crew. But there is a film that was conceived entirely in the lower depths of the aforementioned town hall, created and performed by local youths and filmed in Cable Street; a product born of The Basement Film Project: *Tunde's Film*.

## 'I'd rather be a loser, than live a life of fear'

*Tunde's Film*, released in 1973, opens with a slow pan across a Dan Jones canvas, a bright playful street scene where Orthodox Jews rub shoulders with Hell's Angel bikers, girls play weddings with netting swiped from a market stall and mums push prams past garish open shop-fronts with all manner of bulging fruit and vegetables on display. Marvellous though this colourful portrayal is, it is at odds with the sparse street life that appears in the actual film, shot exclusively under grey, overcast skies and largely by night.

A surprise for anybody watching the film today is that the main theme song is co-written by Saint Kitts born, Birmingham-raised, Joan Armatrading, later to become a major artist worldwide, and sung by her collaborator, Pam Nestor. The lyrics set the tone: *'I'd rather be a loser, than live a life of fear'*. It's a sharp score and the opening chords betray a distinctive Isaac Hayes *Shaft* influence. That influence extends to the very first scene of the film where we see a lone black youth walking down Leman Street, which, in a steely twilight could easily be taken for New York. Also, throughout the forty-minute or so feature, Tunde's multi-race crew sport the long coats and highly-teased afros worn by *Shaft* actor Richard Rowntree in the 1971 blockbuster.

The loner exchanges nods with Tunde (all the main characters retain the performers' names) and his friends in Cable Street who are entering the Kwango Club. Here, energetic youths in tank tops and tam o'shanters perform a sort of proto-break dance to a ska beat, while the lank-haired girls, in time-honoured fashion, dance with each other. At this point, a bearded, shaggy-haired youth worker, convincingly played by Dan Jones, announces that it's time to go, but as they shuffle out into the night, a police van pulls to a halt. Abuse is exchanged, a bottle is broken against a wall and a fight ensues. When police reinforcements arrive, all but two of the group are bundled into the back of the van while the two escapees, Taploe and Harry, retreat to Dan's Cable Street abode. They are full of stories of beatings in police station cells and concern about the fate of their friends, while Dan is more worried that they'll wake the baby. The seeds of revenge are sown in the young men's minds.

Tunde and his friends gather at Dinah's Café on the corner of Cable Street and Ensign Street for a lunchtime meeting. Anger brews across the Formica-topped table as, between sips of tea, tales of intimidation are passed around with the sugar bowl. All the talk is about getting back at the police and the racism that they feel is stopping them getting work. The camera trails behind Tunde as he tours the garment factories. We catch sight of some Asian people here — then still a small minority in the borough — toiling alongside the elderly Jews who they would soon usurp in the East London rag trade. Shortly after, Tunde and a friend are once again stopped by the police. They immediately leg it. There follows an exhilarating chase through the rainy streets as the two effortlessly scale brick walls and put their knowledge of local geography to use, laughing as they run the cops ragged in the backstreets.

A summit at Taploe's place. And further talk of revenge. *'Well, we could always rob a bank,'* somebody suggests. They quickly decide on the Co-Op Bank off Leman Street because of its close proximity to the police station. *'It'll be a right show up for the Old Bill.'* After a short interlude where one of the black youths meets up with his white girlfriend (mother from balcony: *'Tell the wog to piss off!'*), the action shifts to Bigland Green. As a kids' football match kicks off, Tunde and Taploe talk with two older black men who have access to firearms and after a further gang meeting by a burnt-out car it's settled that the robbery will go ahead.

Dan has heard rumours that something is in the air and pleads with Taploe to let him know what's going on. But what's going on, unknown to him, is a shotgun handover in the Ship pub further up Cable Street. During the evening, a dodgy, moustachioed character takes one of the gang into the gents' toilet to hand over the long, string and brown paper parcel — shielded inside one of those ever-present long coats — which is then transferred into Taploe's holdall the next day at Dinah's. Things are coming to a head. In the few short scenes that follow we see the police pounding on a number of doors until one of them is opened by a member of Tunde's circle. The police enter and we assume an imminent betrayal.

The day of the bank job. The parcel is unwrapped and the getaway car moves off. It makes its way along Cable Street and moves into Leman Street. Then, with the bank in sight, a police car screeches to a halt in front of them. The gang evacuate the car and flee. The final image in the film is of a helpless and stricken Tunde, trapped in the same street where the film started. As sirens wail on the soundtrack, the image freezes. Tunde has nowhere to go. All that's left is a brief reprise of the Joan Armatrading theme song, *'I'm not sure that I am brave, but I am ready'.*

But how the film came to be made, and the making of it, is easily as interesting as anything that appears on the screen.

# Tunde Ikoli

Tunde Ikoli was born in East London in 1955, the offspring of a Nigerian father and a Cornish mother. His mother had arrived in East London via Holborn after having bitten the hand of a hostel manager there who had been showing her too much attention. Tunde's father was already established as a Cable Street habitué, having done some travelling since his departure from Nigeria and somehow tipping up at the West India Docks. They met in one of the Cable Street cafés and in the space of six years they had five children together, Tunde being the oldest. He told me:

*My parents didn't stay together long. By the age of four, me and my brothers were put into children's homes. Two of us were sent to one place, the other two to somewhere else. I never saw the other two brothers for ten years. I was with a foster parent in Lowestoft, a Miss Scott. There's no way it would happen now — a black kid and a single white woman! I loved that woman. By the time I was eleven I was speaking French and playing the violin. I was there until 1964 when they took me to Hornchurch, a massive children's home. It was only a bus ride away from the East End and I began seeing my mum on a regular basis, and sometimes my dad.*

Tunde was sent to Sir John Cass School and was slapped down by his fellow classmates on his very first day for revealing a knowledge of the language during a French lesson. 'And from that moment I dropped all pretence about education. I tried to be the hard boy, I hung around with the people who fought, the people who cheated. I didn't bother with any kind of schooling.' Things didn't get any better. By then the oldest of seven, he acquired the responsibility of getting the whole brood up and ready for school, regularly making himself late as a consequence. His dreams of being a professional footballer were shattered when he fell through a skylight on the school roof whilst attempting to retrieve a wayward ball; his leg was ripped apart and the gash required eighty-eight stitches. Later, a grudge fight with a teacher led to a caning from the headmaster and his resolve that he would leave as soon as possible at the age of fifteen.

*I got a job as a tailor's cutter, cutting slacks and skirts for seven pound ten shillings a week, looking up at the steam on the barred windows. I hated it. My only release was the movies. On a Saturday from twelve o'clock in the afternoon until four o'clock in the morning I would go to the West End and see five or six different movies. I was in a different world. In the front seat with a big screen in front of me I could forget all about whatever. And in 1972 I saw* The Godfather *and I thought to myself, you know, I want to be an actor. I want to be like Marlon Brando. That film changed my life in a way that nobody will ever understand.*

One of Tunde's best friends was Taploe Johnson, another mixed-race youth, who lived in the same buildings and who Tunde admits helped ease his passage from children's homes into the East End. 'We were part of a crew, the Cannon Street Mob; we used to hang around on the corner. I hate the phrase but it was multi-cultural in the best sense. Amongst us lot there were whites of Irish background, mixed-race Africans, Somalis, there were Bengalis. You would go to work and you would then go down to Cable Street to hang out. You think it's going to last forever. But it's not because you all grow up and do different things.' Taploe introduced Tunde to Dan Jones and the Kwango Club. Dan, in turn, took them all up west to see *Shaft* and told them the history of the gangs of New York, feeding Tunde books about the lives of other young black kids in other cities.

Dan also directed Tunde to an amateur dramatic group at Aldgate's Toynbee Hall. 'But it was full of City people,' he told me, laughing at the memory. 'I played a schoolteacher in a production of *The Prime of Miss Jean Brodie*. A cockney black guy! Nowadays that's all well and good because of positive casting but at the time I felt — *this just ain't right!*' Tunde decided to write his own play and present it to the group, a wishful fantasy titled *The Singing Window Cleaner*, written with himself in the starring role. Its inevitable rejection by the other players caused him to leave in a huff.

'I told Dan that what I really wanted to do was make a film about my experiences in the East End. Dan was always enthusiastic, he'd give you confidence. He introduced us to Maggie Pinhorn.'

# Maggie Pinhorn

Maggie Pinhorn already had a strong East London connection through a family business. She told me, 'They were a temperance family and their major involvement was in housing for the poor. They worked with the Peabody Trust and became estate managers.' As a little girl she'd visit her grandfather's office in Commercial Road and with the old fella would help collect the tenement rents and be an honoured guest at the Limehouse restaurants in what was then still Chinatown. Perhaps that was what gave her a taste for the big city. 'I grew up in the countryside but I always wanted to come to London. As soon as I could I left home and came to art school here at Central Saint Martin's. From then on this was the place I wanted to be. I loved it.'

Student London in the 1960s must have been an enlightening place and time to be. Maggie did more than her share of waiting on café tables but there were perks. The Rediffusion Television Studios were just up the road to the school, where they shot the legendary *Ready Steady Go* music programme. A financial butterfly net was used to scoop up the bright young artists early on Friday evenings for when the show went out live. It must have been beyond most young people's dreams at the time: to be lured in to jump around in front of the Animals and the Rolling Stones and to be paid for the pleasure of doing it.

Maggie studied theatre design but her real interest was in film. While still at school she was always being told off for ignoring her homework in favour of bunking off to the local flicks. After doing four years at art school however she found she had no money to go on to do a film course. 'That was a great shame in a way but brilliant in others because it meant that I had to go and find a job in the film industry.' Quickly sussing where the real power lay in the film world, Maggie made contact with publicist Theo Cowan and was soon being escorted around various studios. 'There were all these generous, lovely, paternalistic Jewish gentlemen, all of whom looked at this *goy* gal thinking, "Why shouldn't I give her a chance?" I finally met up with Ken Adam, who designed the sets for the James Bond movies. He's a very black and white man; he draws everything in black and white. And he said to me, "What I really need is someone who can work with colour. You can do that. And because you've done theatre design you know how to build models". So I got the job: building the set models and bringing colour into them for the film.'

Maggie worked on James Bond's Japanese adventure, *You Only Live Twice*, the four-wheeled children's fantasy *Chitty Chitty Bang Bang*, the Swinging London spoof-thriller *Otley*, starring Tom Courtney and, with perhaps fate playing a hand in directing Maggie back eastwards, the big screen incarnation of top telly hit *Till Death Us Do Part*, the story of Wapping racist bigot, Alf Garnett. But she felt constrained in the art department, eager to create her own work and happier collapsing onto mattresses in subterranean cinemas to watch experimental European films flickering on a wall through a haze of cigarette smoke.

'I started Alternative Arts and produced a film with director Stephen Dwoskin in the early 1970s called *Dynamo*. It was made in basement strip clubs in Soho. It's all about the myth, the mask, how you present your persona to the world. The stripping is a metaphor for what's left. It was made with really good actresses like Linda Marlowe and Jenny Runacre.' But it wouldn't be long before Maggie would be working in a different sort of basement in a different part of town. And that was largely due to Dan Jones.

# When Maggie Met Tunde

Maggie told me:

*Dan Jones had got this idea about how these kids he was working with could make a film but he didn't know how to go about it. It so happened he knew my dad, who was still working locally in property, and had found out through a review of* Dynamo *that I was working in film. So I went and talked to him. I said, 'Yeah, I'd be interested in doing that'. I had some money left over from when I was working in the industry and basically I was funding myself to do the things I really wanted to do. Firstly, I had to be checked out by the Inner London Education Authority to see that I was a suitable person. And actually, that became increasingly useful later on. Because when I had to go down to Leman Street police station to bail out members of the cast I could show I didn't have a police record. Dan arranged for me to meet the group at the Basement and said he'd come with me. I said, 'Please don't,' because I'd observed that when you were with Dan everybody related to him and they didn't relate to me. He wasn't the sort of character who could be on the sidelines. So I asked him not to be in the room. But I knew he was worried because some of them might be armed.*

The assembled company of East End lads sat around the long, oblong table in the Basement room: all staring down at the petite, pretty, blonde middle-class girl at the end of it. Maggie didn't waste time with any small talk. 'I understand that some of you guys might be armed,' she announced by way of an opener. 'If so, I'd rather have whatever you've got in full sight on the table.' It can only be imagined what a protective Dan, hovering just outside the door, was thinking at this point, hearing a loud metallic crash as various weapons duly gouged the tabletop.

When I mentioned Maggie's story of the meeting to Tunde, he looked slightly wary, as if I was trying to put one over on him, reverting to stereotypical images: East End Boys & West End Girls. Tunde conceded that they were 'a rough lot', but that people didn't regularly carry weapons. He never did himself. 'There were people who did have blades and stuff and there might have been occasions when people did stuff to frighten people or wind them up. But I didn't like all that. The thing was that when Maggie came down to the Basement it was a big cultural clash. It was like she was from another world. And on one level people were interested in Maggie because she was a pretty girl.'

Maggie says of that first meeting, after the weapons were laid out:

> *A huge debate ensued: about whether you should be armed or not armed, who you should and shouldn't nick from. Out of this, we got on like a house on fire. There was no pretence of them trying to be like me or me trying to be like them. I found out that Tunde was the scribe. Tunde was the one who really wanted to make the film and he wanted his friends to make it with him. He would write stuff down and I would take it away and translate it into script form; I'd break it down into scenes. And I think that's probably the strength of the film even today — it was written. That doesn't mean that within sequences conversations weren't improvised, which was fine, as it became apparent that some people in the group couldn't read.*

Tunde backs this up: 'Maggie did a brilliant job. The script was a basis, a starting point, rather than everybody remembering what was written. Nowadays, you'd say it was more like a Mike Leigh thing. The budget, I think, was about two thousand pounds and Maggie was able to bring in a top-notch cameraman, crew and film processing people.'

Maggie explained, 'We went all round the neighbourhood and decided that Cable Street was going to be the basis of the film. Cable Street, Watney Street and Leman Street — we weren't going to move out of that square. One thing I'd learnt about making independent films was about staying in one place. Make a film about peeling an orange. Learn to be observant. And everything Tunde wrote about took place there anyway.'

144

# Making Tunde's Film

Maggie went on:

> *Jonathan Power, who had made a film about an adventure playground in Islington, was sent along by The Rowntree Trust to talk about what I wanted to do and they came up with the funding. Also, a journalist called Linda Christmas wrote an article for* The Guardian *about what was going on. And from that a lot of people came out of the woodwork: sound engineers, cameramen, editor, a guy who did the soundtrack. They all said they wanted to help. Some things we had free but we had to buy film stock. I was using all my film industry connections at that point. We found a studio to develop the film and all that kind of stuff. It was incredible.*

Despite that, Maggie remembers it as a tough shoot. 'We had a week to make it in with minimal resources, shooting on 16mm film. Everyone was supposed to turn up at nine o'clock in the morning and by twelve o'clock, they did. So you can imagine, the crew were sitting around for three hours.' Although co-directed by Maggie and Tunde, Maggie was most able to use her behind the camera skills. She remembers particularly the conversation around the table in Dinah's Café, reminding the cast about the topics they'd devised, getting the camera to chase the lines of interweaving chatter. 'I had to be firing on all cylinders at that time.' And once it was all in the can: 'We put it all together for weeks after in the cutting room in Soho. I was very concerned that they were all involved in the whole process. I can't remember exactly how Joan Armatrading got involved but I remember her and Pam Nestor recording the title track in the basement of the London Film School, written especially for the film.'

# East End Channel One

At the time, it must have seemed to both Maggie and Tunde's crew that almost anything was possible, likely even. 'While we were editing the film,' said Maggie, 'the BBC started the Community Programmes Unit. They invited a dozen or so independent filmmakers to make programmes for *Open Door* about various communities. They asked if I'd like to make one and I said I'd be happy to do it with the kids I'd worked with on the film. We sat down and talked about it and we decided we'd make our own television station called East End Channel One. It included Taploe giving the weather report, complete with wet sponges for clouds and cotton wool for snow, improvisations, filmed inserts and spoof commercials. Clive James did a review of the rough-cut we'd given him of *Tunde's Film* — and it was all going out live in the studio at about half past eleven at night! Through her *Till Death* connection, Maggie dragged along scriptwriter Johnny Speight to sit in with the lads alongside fellow East Ender, Marty Feldman, the scriptwriter and comedian. 'Other people like jazz musician Benny Green and actor David Kossoff called up and they took the calls live on air.

I was in the control room throughout the programme. Doing live TV is *phew*! It's like live football — you can't miss the ball. In those days they didn't stop the programme; they just let it run. It was quite unusual, ordinary people weren't usually on TV, especially a bunch of working class kids from the East End.'

# The Premiere

'For some reason,' Tunde told me, 'when *Tunde's Film* was released, it went mega. Not in the sense that anybody made any money from it, but more like it being shown at festivals and getting press coverage.' The first showing was a local one, in the concrete hulk of the Berner Estate Tenants' Hall. Maggie explained:

> We showed it there so all the mums and dads and everybody else could come and see it. And, of course, Joan Littlewood comes because this is a proper working class thing happening. I was thrilled because I'd studied her work and seen Oh What A Lovely War and that whole series of plays she'd directed at The Theatre Royal in Stratford. She was an absolute heroine of mine. The acoustics in the hall were appalling; you couldn't hear what was going on. It was mayhem! But throughout the entire film people were cheering. They completely loved it. At the end, Joan came up to me and said, 'Maggie, that was fucking great, mate'. Those were her exact words. And I thought — Yes! It was the best pat on the back I've ever had.

When Maggie bunged all the kids into the back of a transit van and took them and the film up to the Edinburgh Festival, it was the first time many of them had been out of the area, let alone London. She said:

> We found a huge old flat for them that was empty except for some mattresses to sleep on. There were lots of rooms but they all chose to sleep in one together. They kept complaining that they didn't like it but when I found out for

147

*them where the nearest discos were they were happy. The festival organisers were worried that if they were invited to the party they would wreck it! I said, 'What? They'll wear their best clothes and they'll be as good as gold.' I can remember George Melly being there, who was writing film criticism for* The Observer. *I had some great chats with him and he knew exactly what I meant. And, sure enough, they all turned up, dressed up, and everybody went —* Wow.

Tunde remembers the Edinburgh trip, 'mainly for watching a lot of weird films and having steak diane. Steak and chips was something you didn't usually have. Also, the group was starting to split up a bit. Some of them felt that my head was up my arse a bit. After all, it was called *Tunde's Film.* So they locked me out of the hotel room one night.'

# 'I'm not sure that I am brave, but I am ready.'

Tunde told me about the aftermath:

*After the film came out I decided that I was going to be a writer, a director and a producer. But my wife was pregnant and I couldn't even find a place to live. I'd phone up somewhere and because I had a cockney accent they'd say come round and you'd knock on the door and somebody would open the window and say, 'What do you want?' I'd say, 'We're here about the flat. I was on the phone half an hour ago.' 'Sorry, mate. Flat's gone.' The Royal Court in Sloane Square were casting* Play Mas *by Mustapha Matura. So, of course, I've got a black face and a big afro and they're all white middle-class and they assume we're all the same. They had seen a clip from my film and sent me a telegram. I thought, yeah this is what I've been waiting for! But when I look at the script, it's written in dialect. And I'm thinking, is that* three *or is it* tree, *because it's written t'ree. I'm thinking, this man can't write! What's going on? So I started to read it: 'DE MAN*

*WENT DOWN DE ROAD.' I'm a cockney, my dad's African. What do I know about a West Indian accent? I read about two lines and the woman auditioning me asked, 'Tunde, do you have any other plans besides wanting to be an actor?'*

Despite failing the audition, the theatre were keen to encourage Tunde. He was introduced to its legendary manager Oscar Lewenstein who offered him a playwriting commission and arranged to pay him to basically hang around. Sometimes he turned up for work and sometimes he didn't. Then one day, while bunking off at home, another telegram arrived instructing him to present himself at Boreham Wood Studios first thing in the morning to work as director Lindsay Anderson's personal assistant on the film of David Storey's play, *In Celebration*. 'I had met Lindsay at the theatre and sent him a note asking if he would like a co-director or a tea-boy. I never thought anything of it. I had the best six weeks of my life. There wasn't much for me to do. I realise now I was a bit of a trophy. Lindsay made work for me. I would get his tea and put a little bit of whisky in it and in the evening he would get his car home and drop me at Finchley.' More jobs came up at the Royal Court; Tunde became an assistant director for this and that, sharing foot-long cigars with Albert Finney and being verbally abused by a drunken John Osborne. 'A great time,' says Tunde. It occurs to me that it must also have been a strange time, hanging out with key players in British theatre and film by day and with your mates on a Stepney street corner by night. A play he had written, *Short Sleeves in Summer*, was put on in the upstairs theatre and commissions from all over followed. Sometime he wrote the plays and sometimes he didn't.

Tunde talks today about his tendency at the time to disappear at various intervals in his life, not really sure at how to take advantage of the opportunities he was being offered. Having said that, he received acclaim for his play,

*Scrape Off the Black*, produced at the Riverside Studios, became writer-in-residence at the Theatre Royal in Stratford, and wrote and directed two television films, *Elphida*, in 1987, and *Smack and Thistle*, in 1991, the latter produced by Working Title and sporting a strong cast which included Patrick Malahide, Connie Booth and Geoffrey Palmer. The story of that one revolves around Abel, a drug-addict determined to go straight — after that final heist, of course. In breaking into a wealthy household, he stumbles across Elizabeth, who is suffering from an overdose. He saves her life but as a consequence becomes embroiled in a drugs conspiracy spanning East London and the Houses of Parliament. Again, the film was well received.

Even so, Tunde says during the interview, 'I don't know why, I just drifted away from things. It's because I never saw myself as a writer, I always felt that the stuff I'd written was accepted more because of what I was rather than for the quality of the work itself. So on one level, I've had a really good career and on another level I could have had an even better career if I had concentrated more.'

## Alternative Arts

Tunde Ikoli currently lives in Limehouse while Maggie Pinhorn is based a mile or two away in Spitalfields. She told me, 'I have a studio on the roof of the Montefiore Centre, which is an old school. Alternative Arts today is about giving support to new artists, we've never dealt with celebrities. We run an Alternative Fashion Week for young designers, Wisewords, which is a programme of events performed by women, and Photomonth, which is a real labour of love. Photography really is the East End's art form. It has grown from fifteen to over two hundred exhibitions and events.' Lots of other stuff too, including a horticultural show. Maggie is always talking about future challenges. It's me who keeps dragging her back to

*Tunde's Film*. She said, 'What I learned most of all is that when you're working with young people on a project like that the thing is to give them experiences. Not objects, not things, but experiences. So they had the experience of making the movie, the experience of showing it, the experience of going to the festivals. You learnt by doing and learning by doing was the absolute ethos of the Basement.'

# 6. The Art of the Battle
# The Cable Street Mural

## 'I'd like to be able to do a picture.'
Julie Gershon, Battle veteran.

Somebody *did* do a picture. A giant mural was painted on the exterior wall of St. George's Town Hall in Cable Street. It was completed in 1983 and has provided a focal point for events and commemorations ever since. It has become almost obligatory for prospective local politicos to have their picture taken in front of it, eager to associate themselves with the dynamic street action it portrays. And the dwindling number of Battle veterans are invariably wheeled out (sometimes literally) to the site to provide an accompanying image for an interview. It's even been known for old Blackshirts to pay it a visit. And it was paid a particularly disastrous visit by the BUF's 1980s contemporaries, which nearly scuppered the entire project. The idea of a mural to commemorate the victory of local people at the Battle of Cable Street was first proposed in 1976 by the Tower Hamlets Arts Project, before it had paid staff, before it had a bookshop, when it was a sprawl of people with an endless stack of ideas, many of which fell into the categories of the impossible or near impossible. The idea of a mural fell into the latter category.

## David Savage

David Savage, who was known as Dave Binnington until the 1980s, was born in Yorkshire in 1949, going to Ruskin College at Oxford before coming to London to do a post-graduate course at the Royal Academy in 1971. There, David met Desmond Rochfort, and together they formed

the Public Art Workshop. Both had studied the murals of Mexican artists David Alfaro Siqueiros and Diego Rivera, and that influence is apparent in the Paddington Murals which they painted under the Westway Flyover. When Dan Jones found out about their work it seemed that here was a chance that the dream of a Cable Street mural might become a reality, and David was taken on to undertake the task.

The proposed wall, on the west-facing wall of the town hall, was huge: sixty-three feet wide and fifty-four feet high. Given the location and the free and easy nature of the Basement Project it was natural that the artist be based there. Basement worker Tony Crisp remembers David Savage's arrival: 'The first thing that you noticed about Dave was his stutter, which was physically exhausting for both Dave and anyone he was communicating with. Despite the stutter or perhaps because of it,

153

he chose words very carefully. He would put so much energy into a conversation that it really had to be worth it.' Maggie Pinhorn, also working there, recalls: 'There was a cupboard under the stairs that was quite big so Dave made that into his studio. He was an incredibly neat and brilliant woodworker and he made himself these long shelves. The kids absolutely adored him because he was working with all these hammers and nails and saws. So right away there was a really good connection between them and him and the mural.' The original funding applications were sent out in the name of the Public Art Workshop, while later letter-headed notepaper and other publicity material, dated from May 1978, has the name Cable Street Mural Project at the top with the words: 'In Co-operation with Public Art Workshop', in smaller type underneath. So at some point there was a happy merging of the two projects. Things got less happy later on however and because of the manner of his leaving I was cautious about approaching David Savage for an interview. I had known him when he worked on the mural; I had interviewed Battle veterans to help with his research. But I hadn't had any contact with him in something like twenty-eight years. And as far as I am aware, he had never spoken about the mural on the record in all that time either.

# A Meeting in Bloomsbury

I met David Savage in the plush surroundings of a Bloomsbury hotel where he was staying in London on business, up from Devon, which has been his home since 1983. With his new name came a new, flourishing business. He tells me that he makes, 'very modern furniture. Probably quite expensive furniture. It's usually one of a kind and made for relatively wealthy people. But it's expressive. I run a workshop and I've got staff, a team of six people. We sell it all over the world.' A glance at his website confirms the work to be that of a brilliant and accomplished artist. But it is his time on the Cable Street Mural that I had come here to talk about. Speaking of the Basement, David said, 'Somebody eventually took pity on me. I came out of this cupboard which had once been used for camping equipment and into a bigger office where I set up a studio. But the thing took so long to get off the ground. The wall was in a poor state of repair. I was promised it would be rendered quickly but it didn't happen for nearly two years. I was waiting and waiting, but this gave me an awful lot of time to interview people and ask about what had actually happened.'

As well as interviewing surviving veterans, David studied books, films and photographs of the event and incorporated what he found into the mural design, including, as described in the Cable Street Group 'Battle' book: '...the dramatic uniforms of the BUF, the eggs, milk bottles, tools and the contents of chamber pots coming from the upper windows of houses, the mounted police "Cossacks" with long weighted clubs surging through the crowd, the use of marbles and ball bearings against police horses, the overturned lorry, and the chairs, mattresses and household junk that formed the barricade.' All of this overseen by a depiction of the new-fangled police autogiro circling overhead. He also spoke to contemporary local characters and residents, including them in his design. This was then made into a slide which was projected on to the wall itself and carefully drawn in.

Through his extensive research, David started to draw his own conclusions:

*The conventional wisdom was that the Battle was an event basically organised by political parties, who all seemed to want to claim credibility from it. But the more I dug around I understood that none of them can claim any real credit for it. There were people who were members of the Communist Party, the Independent Labour Party and whatever who were on that street moving people around but it was a very spontaneous thing that picked up the concept of No Pasaran*

*— They Shall Not Pass, from the Spanish Civil War. It was a concept that had gone viral. It was something that was very violent and very unpleasant but a very glorious thing to have done. We organised an event. All sorts of people came who had been there but had never actually met before. It was like a celebration. They were telling us stuff that was absolutely new and very authentic. That fundamentally changed the image I wanted to show. And that was difficult because you couldn't be schematic and have red flags and banners, and I got the distinct feeling that I lost an awful lot of support as a consequence of that. I think because it was partly sponsored and funded from the Council they wanted accreditation. Nothing was ever said but from the moment I made it clear that I was not going to do that I didn't get any of the help that I needed. I may be imagining it but I felt that the warmth and support that I received at the start of the project evaporated when I started to wave my arms and said —* This didn't happen this way!

# Enter Paul Butler

'The design of the mural was about energy,' David Savage stated emphatically when I met him. 'And about violence. And about movement. About human beings caught up and scared. Put yourself near a police horse and feel how scared you are when it starts to move. They are big, terrifying animals. That was what I wanted to convey, all these people in a narrow space and a lot happening. But one of the things that I was struggling with was the narrative. I wanted the painting to be a bit more abstract, so I needed something that would tell the story. Historically, the way that was achieved was in what is called a praedella, a line of small paintings at the bottom — a bit like a strip cartoon.'

Paul Butler's work had already been featured in shows such as Arts for Society at the Whitechapel Gallery but his growing interest in murals led to him write to David Savage (then Dave Binnington) and Desmond Rochfort after reading an article detailing their work under the

Westway Flyover. 'Then, one day,' Paul told me, 'Dave called out of the blue asking if I would be interested in a new project in Cable Street. He explained that he wanted me to paint some panels along the bottom of the wall. It was a Herculean job he'd taken on. It's hugely physical, too much for any single individual.'

In my interview with David Savage, he said:

> *I was up on the scaffolding working on the wall probably about eighteen months to two years. Entirely on my own. This was a project that was planned to be done by three people. I was supposed to have a couple of assistants but there was never the money for that to happen. For a short while I had a guy who was on Community Service but he nicked my paints and my radio! It was terribly lonely up there in the rain and the cold. It got to me in the end. As for the mural, I had started at the top of the wall and worked down to about half way. Those parts were pretty well finished. We'd already had phone calls, physical threats. But I'm a big bloke and I didn't take much notice of it. Then one day someone called me up to tell me the news. I suppose I thought* — Well, it was going to happen sometime.

## The Mural Defaced

It was inevitable that the mural would attract the attention of the supporters of far-right political groups active in the area. In 1980, the scaffold which was used to carry out the work also acted as the device by which fascists would deface it. Graffiti was daubed across it in bold six-foot high letters. The damage was immense. There is a variance however in the separate accounts given to me as to what happened next.

David Savage said, 'When I saw the amount of damage that had been done, I thought, I can't clean that off on my own. I left at that moment. I remember Tony Crisp and Maggie Pinhorn trying to talk me into staying but I was physically exhausted by it. And apart from the people in the Basement I felt completely unsupported. I left then. I didn't go back. There weren't any other options. Paul Butler was there but at that time he was only just getting involved with the project.'

Paul's account however implies that a crisis meeting had been set up, which would mean that David's exit might not have been quite as immediate as he remembered. Paul says, 'Dave had started drawing out the elements of the design, some of the buildings, which come curving over at the top, the pliers flying through the air, the egg and some of the figures. And then I heard that the mural had been attacked and had graffiti daubed right across it. BRITISH NATIONALISM NOT COMMUNISM and RIGHTS FOR WHITES or something like that. I went over to talk with Dave and Vivien Lovell who was the Visual Arts Officer for Tower Hamlets. The borough were funding it, along with the Greater London Arts Association, the Gulbenkian Foundation and The Edward Austin Abbey Fund. At the meeting, Dave was pretty agitated and upset. I can't remember it all in detail but he said he couldn't go on with the project. Vivien and I were trying to persuade him not to go but at some point he upped and left and we followed him out and he got on his motorbike. We were saying, 'Don't go, Dave.' It was as dramatic as that. But he got on his bike and roared off. Vivien was in tears. And that was the last I heard or saw anything of him. I was left holding the proverbial baby. I got in touch with Desmond Rochfort and said, 'I've got this huge project. Can you help?'

# The Rescue Attempt

Vivien Lovell has memories of a period between the defacement of the mural and the meeting where David made his departure: 'I remember going to the Basement with my then boss, Peter Conway, the Principal Arts Officer, and commiserating with Dave.' Vivien phoned the Keimfarben factory in Germany where the paint had been produced and spoke to a 'Herr Doktor': 'He recommended a chemical formula to apply to the graffiti, which I managed to source at the Chemistry Faculty at Queen Mary College in Mile End Road. Gallons of the stuff were prepared. I collected it in my ancient VW Beetle, with all the chemicals sloshing about in plastic bottles in the boot. All probably highly illegal and dangerous. We mustered a team of a dozen or so volunteers who scrubbed away over a weekend, to no avail — it was the right formula but the chemicals just vaporised in the open air. The only other option was to sandblast it off — tragically losing most of the artwork that Dave had carried out.' It was after this, Vivien recalls, that the meeting took place where David resigned from the project.

# Enter Desmond Rochfort and Ray Walker

Desmond Rochfort had painted several large-scale works at community centres in London before Paul Butler commandeered him for the Cable Street project. Rochfort's research in Mexico and the United States, and the stream of books he has produced on the Mexican muralists, have since established him as a world authority. Rochfort came to the mural with a knowledge of the Keim paint system, having used it while working with David Savage. 'But,' Paul concedes, 'it was a steep learning curve nevertheless. The technology goes back to the late nineteenth or early twentieth century: a kind of fresco technique. The paint was basically pure mineral pigment which you painted on to a porous base which was then sprayed with a silicate solution. It was very permanent but also very vulnerable to any oil-based material because it would soak right in. So because of the damage to the mural, the brick of the wall had to be re-rendered and we had to wait a long time for that to happen so we could get started again.'

Paul thinks that it was Desmond Rochfort who then put him in contact with Ray Walker. Ray was born in Toxteth in 1945 and studied at Liverpool Art School. I got to know Ray more than I did any of the other artists, regularly having a drink with him on Friday evenings when he'd collect his wages for another mural he was painting in Chicksand Square for the Tower Hamlets Arts Project. I was intrigued about his involvement in the Mersey Beat scene, playing in bands at the Cavern and regularly meeting up with the Beatles. But what he always really wanted to do was paint. His work, influenced by the surrealist movement, got him into the Royal College of Art in London. In 1974 he met his wife-to-be, Anna, also a painter, and in 1976 they moved to the 'bleak and austere concrete jungle' — as he put it — of East London. During this period Ray began to pick up commissions for large-scale exterior works, mainly on crumbling, knackered walls on the sides of community centres. *The Promised Land,* on a huge wall in Chicksand Square, off Brick Lane in 1979, was the most ambitious. Giant figures dominated the picture, bringing together various modern archetypes, including skinheads and bowler-hatted businessmen. It was perfectly placed here: an area of dire poverty just a stones throw away from the wealth and privilege of the City's Square Mile.

Ray's large-scale work increasingly reflected political themes. In 1981 he was given a free hand to paint a triptych at the Imperial War Museum, *Army Recruitment.* His research included talking to young squaddies, just months ahead of the Falkland Islands conflict, causing him to reflect that some of these raw-faced recruits might have been amongst its casualties. It now seems inevitable that he would become part of the team that would complete the Cable Street Mural. Ray died suddenly in 1984, after the mural was completed.

## The Work Resumes

Paul Butler says, 'We started again at the beginning of 1982. Me, Des and Ray met up and talked about what needed to be done. In some ways I relished it. It was a great opportunity. I was pretty inexperienced and I was probably biting off far more than I could chew. But in the end, I think I managed to chew it. We had to renegotiate the whole project because the lower part of the mural, two thirds or three quarters of it, had to be completely re-rendered at enormous cost.'

When work began once more a new working method was devised. Those images on the upper part of the mural that had already been sketched in were repaired collectively. But the lower two thirds were re-designed and re-drawn. While incorporating certain elements of the 'Binnington' design such as the arc of the central horse's neck, they undertook their own research into the subject matter and images. Each of the three artists took control of a third of the lower part of the picture. Ray Walker focused on the left hand section, Paul Butler on the middle section and Desmond Rochfort on the right. Paul says, 'We drew up each section and then brought our drawings together and incorporated them into an overall design.' It was the first time that Paul had worked on a collaborative basis. He found the process stimulating if sometimes slightly unnerving, certainly in relation to the physical working conditions:

*The scaffolding was very high and right up against the wall — you had about six floors, or lifts, of scaffolding going up — so when you were working on it you never really saw the bloody thing. You knew what you wanted but you had to climb all the way down the scaffold and walk a distance away to see if the diagonal needed to tilt a little bit more over to the left, then you'd have to go all the way back up, redraw it, come all the way back down and have another look. So it didn't half keep you fit, battling the wind on the top of the scaffolding, your paint flying off, splattering all over for miles. We never used ladders, we used to go straight up the outside, grabbing hold of the scaffolding poles like a monkey. We all made a huge contribution towards the mural but none of us claimed ownership of it. We were extremely proud and extremely pleased with it. It was a fantastic time: a great moment in our lives and a hell of an achievement.*

The mural was completed in 1983. Amongst the speakers at the opening ceremony in May was Jack Jones, General Secretary of the Transport and General Workers Union and veteran of the Spanish Civil War, and local MPs Peter Shore and Ian Mikardo. But the years since the mural was finished have been as turbulent as those of its creation, with continued attacks by vandals

# Back on the Scaffold

Paul Butler recalls:

*I worked on the mural again after the third wave of vandalism in 1994. It had been paint-bombed, which did terrible damage. The British National Party was standing for election at the time. When I was working on it, I went down the road and when I came back I found that my car, parked near the mural, had white gloss paint poured all over it and all the tyres slashed. Then someone phoned the local paper and claimed to be from an organisation called Combat 18 who were a right-wing paramilitary organisation and said something like —* We punctured his tyres and we would have punctured his lungs if he had been there. *So we had a police guard after that, this copper stood at the bottom of the scaffolding for a bit. He was there for a day or two but then he disappeared. Sometimes, myself and a colleague who I roped in would be at the top of the scaffolding tower. We'd look down and see these blokes in bomber jackets and think —* Shit! They're going to shake the tower and we'll fall off like bloody apples out of the tree. *And then one day we saw this smart looking geezer in a pinstripe suit turn up with three or four burly minders so I climbed down to see who they were. The guy was having his photograph taken in front of the mural and it turned out that it was one of Oswald Mosley's bodyguards. He must have been in his eighties. The irony of that was just priceless.*

162

*When I was restoring it, people in the street would make suggestions. I loved that aspect. People would turn up from South Africa, Sweden, Australia, Canada. They came from all over with their backpacks just to see the mural. So I was very pleased with the mural as an art-work and also because of its symbolic value. I loved the interaction.*

# Dave Binnington and David Savage

While I was interviewing David Savage there were several things that I was hesitant about asking him. One was his opinion of the finished mural, completed after his departure. He told me that he can still see elements of his original design in the finished artwork and parts of the upper section. 'There was a cartoon that could have been followed,' he said with a shrug, 'but it wasn't. That was okay, fine. I wasn't there and people were doing it in a different way.' But he added, 'I'm as mad as hell that the Independent Labour Party banner is back on the wall after all my bloody work. It's there and it shouldn't be. It's a lie. Everybody wants to claim the Battle for themselves.'

The other two things I wanted to ask him about were why the man I used to know as Dave Binnington is now called David Savage, and where did his pronounced stammer go? It emerged that the two issues were related. 'Binnington is not a word that a person with a stammer can say. It's right on the front of the lips. Stammerers block and when they block everything jams up; it's like you've gobbled a sandwich too fast. When I moved out of London in 1983, my partner was called Jan Savage and I found I could say her name. It was a key to enable me to speak. It's immensely liberating to be able to say who you are. So from that point I used that name. If you can't say who you are then you don't exist.'

# The Ghosts of Cable Street

## Arnold Wesker

At the time of writing, a new production has just brought
Arnold Wesker's *Chicken Soup with Barley* back to the
Royal Court Theatre, where it was first introduced to
London audiences. The reviews have been uniform in
their praise. It's a solidly theatrical three-act play, over
half a century old, mainly concerning issues that started
over twenty years before that. On its debut, the critic
Kenneth Tynan wrote that: 'Mr Wesker confronts us, as
sanely as the theatre has ever done, with a fundamental
issue: is there a viable middle course between welfare
socialism and communism? He has written a fair, accurate and intensely exciting play.' And today, even though
its political discourse may be unfamiliar to younger the-
atregoers, it still excites.

Arnold Wesker was born in Bethnal Green in 1932. His
father was a Russian refugee, his mother from Hungary.
Both were Jewish and had arrived in East London as a
consequence of the anti-Semitic pogroms in Eastern
Europe. They were also both members of the Communist
Party, as are the parents in *Chicken Soup with Barley*.
Young Arnold, by all accounts, was a bit of a handful,
being expelled (temporarily) from school at fifteen. He
probably wasn't best pleased when, having passed the
entrance exam for the Royal Academy for the Dramatic
Arts, he failed to get a grant from the London County
Council. Two years of National Service in the RAF interrupted a variety of jobs working in bookshops or carrying
spanners for people. While working as a kitchen porter in
Norfolk he met his wife-to-be, Dusty, and, with her,
returned to London. All the while he was sending off
poems and stories to various publishers, and inspired by

a production of John Osborne's incendiary *Look Back In Anger* he also started to write for the stage. He had already written one play, *The Kitchen*, before sending *Chicken Soup with Barley* (written in just six weeks) to Lindsay Anderson, then a director at the Royal Court Theatre. In the run-up to the new production newspapers have claimed that the play has returned to its birthplace. But it actually premiered at the Belgrade Theatre in Coventry in June 1958, before transferring to the Royal Court the same year. What is clearly remembered however is that it created an immediate sensation.

## Chicken Soup with Barley

The first act of *Chicken Soup with Barley* takes place on the day of the Battle of Cable Street, October the 4th, 1936: although due to the realist nature of the play, all of the action in the street (apart from a bit of shouting and argy-bargy in the wings) necessarily takes place off stage. We meet the play's characters inside the family house: Sarah Kahn (somewhere in her mid-thirties at the outset), her husband Harry and their two children: fourteen year old Ada and five year old Ronnie. The boy (who I think we can safely assume to be a portrayal of Wesker himself) is only glimpsed towards the end of the first act. Sarah has been battling with the world long before the added opportunity of the Cable Street conflict, not least with Harry, a bit of a waster who is not beyond dipping into her purse for the odd ten bob note. We also get to meet various friends and relatives (including Dave, a volunteer against fascism in Spain) rushing on and off stage bearing banners and bringing dispatches from the frontline. Although the fascists have been sent packing the mood, which should be triumphant, is soured at the end of Act One with a row between Sarah and Harry over his recalcitrant ways.

The second act takes place ten years later. The war is over and the Kahns have moved to a block of flats in

Hackney. Harry is as shiftless as ever, not even being able to make it through a full week of his latest job. While Sarah berates him we discover that the teenage Ronnie is out delivering some May Day leaflets and that Ada, now married to Dave, is on her way round for a chicken and barley soup supper — the Jewish penicillin. It only seems to dawn on poor Ronnie when he returns to the house that his father and sister have lost the (communist) faith. Not only that, Ada is talking about leaving London when Dave (who is waiting to be demobbed) returns. The bedrock of the family's earlier beliefs has started to crack. One year on, Ronnie, now a 'socialist poet', is working in a bookshop, Harry, despite his deteriorating health, is employed as a store-keeper and Ada and Dave, now with a baby, have made good on their promise to leave London, with 'no more political activity'. Sarah, however, remains as radical as ever, still a Party member and off to a branch meeting that evening.

By the time we reach the third act, set in 1955, Harry has suffered from a number of strokes and is physically incapable of working rather than merely unwilling. He and Sarah are looking forward to reuniting with a fellow Cable Street veteran, Monty, who brings along his snooty wife to the Hackney flat. When they get to talking, it seems that Monty has also left the Party and settled down as a greengrocer. Ronnie is absent and despite his literary ambitions, is reported to be working as a cook in Paris. Monty's wife begrudges all the talk of old-time politics and there's a fair bit of niggling going on. By the time that Harry soils himself the reunion is pretty much at an end. In the final scene, another year on, Ronnie returns to the family home — but not in time to meet the group of first act vets who had been awaiting his arrival — and Harry too has gone to bed before he makes his entrance. Even before Sarah can make him a cup of tea however her despairing son is accusing her: how can she remain a member of the Party given the recent Soviet suppression of the Hungarian Freedom

Fighters? But he is also accusing himself: of losing the faith, of not caring, of turning into another Harry. Only Sarah remains steadfast in her beliefs. The last words of the play are: 'Ronnie, if you don't care you'll die'. Her attitude might be interpreted as that of someone who won't adjust their black and white political views in an ever-changing world. But we're on her side. The play is the first part of a trilogy. The other two being *Roots*, which is permeated by Ronnie's character (although he doesn't actually appear) and *I'm Talking About Jerusalem* which brings us into 1959, and up to date on several of the *Chicken Soup* characters (and news of Harry's death).

Arnold Wesker's career is too long and varied to examine here. But with over forty plays, several volumes of short stories, poetry and essays, journalism and work for television and radio under his belt, he is far more than the writer of 'kitchen sink' drama, that slightly derogatory category in which critics lumped together those of his generation who dared to write about real life. Wesker received a knighthood in 2006, for services to drama.

# All Singing, All Dancing Fascists

The Battle has, apart from historical accounts and autobiography, been recorded in drama more than other art forms. But unlike the Cable Street Mural, which is able to represent the furious energy of the day, stage-bound works have been saddled with a realist setting telling, mostly in dialogue, of the events. In October 1996, the Light 'n' Shade Theatre Company performed *The Battle of Cable Street* by Simon Blumenfeld at the Hackney Empire Studio Theatre. Simon Blumenfeld had the distinction of having been a bestselling author even before the Battle. His novels, *Jew Boy* (1935) and *Phineas Kahn* (1937) chart the lives of the Jewish community in East London. His Cable Street play is set mostly in a café, where the characters lead us through the story in a clear chronological order. Apart from the proprietor and his wife there is a young male firebrand and a female student — who are involved in a romance — and a number of others, including an elderly Jewish tailor and an Irish docker, representing the differing attitudes towards Mosley's threatened march. In the Hackney production, one of the young activists was played by a black actor and the play successfully conjures up the spirit of unity as described by Charlie Goodman in an issue of *Contemp - orary Record,* in 1994 '... it was not just a question of Jews being there on 4th October, the most amazing thing was to see a silk-coated Orthodox Jew standing next to an Irish docker with a grappling iron. This was absolutely unbelievable.'

The Battle also featured in the play *No Pasaran!* by David Holman, written for the M6 Theatre Company in the 1970s. This version followed the fictional journey of a young Jewish boxer who witnesses first-hand the rise of fascism in Germany and who, on travelling to England, sees its shadow fall over East London.

Alan Gilbey, the Chris Searle school striker and Basement Writer, who formed the theatre group Controlled Attack, also worked for a time as a community drama worker on the Isle of Dogs. It was during this period that he took on the Battle of Cable Street. In fact, Alan tackled it three times in all. A previous no-budget version featured a lot of chair-throwing in a local youth club production. The second, *You Should Have Been There*, with the amateur Dramatic Events Company in 1986, was a one-hour promenade performance, using bold verbal and visual statements. The image of an actor play- ing the ghost of Oswald Mosley, stomping around the former synagogue in Princelet Street, Spitalfields, where it was staged, was a provocative one. The third and final incarnation, *Shattersongs*, was performed with an enlarged group, now called WOOF! Theatre Company, at the New Half Moon Theatre in Mile End in the late

168

1980s. This version used cabaret-style songs, comedy and striking semi-surreal images to represent not just the Battle but contemporary anti-fascist activity. Alan was particularly pleased that they had managed to acquire a real lorry to represent the one turned over in 1936. The production presented a much less triumphal view of the conflict. At one stage, a character steps out of a frozen human tableau to question his role in a propaganda poster. And in one of the songs, *The Art of Glazing*, the point is made that perhaps fascism in all its forms will never be fully defeated and that constant vigilance and resistance is essential.

# 'Yes indeed; in Merry England'

Lazar Shrensky was one of those young Jewish writers who found solace from dull workdays by attending the Whitechapel Library, meeting up with other novelists such as Simon Blumenfeld and Ashley Smith, (whose house and lifestyle he felt to be 'somewhat Bohemian'). In his autobiographical, *Twelve A Penny*, Shrensky describes his own household where the large sideboard in the parlour was crammed full of his notes for a novel, written on scraps of paper and on the back of envelopes. After having his first manuscript rejected, a subsequent attempt, *King Sol*, was published by Chatto & Windus in 1939. The story concerns a Jewish man and his frustrations in life — and inevitably — love: the main character here being a young East London boxer. The book has been out of print for donkey's years, but if you go rooting around in second-hand bookshops to find one (you'll be lucky if you do) don't go looking for it under the name of Shrensky, as his publishers persuaded him to adopt the *nom de plume*, Barnett Sheridan, their reason being that if readers assumed the book was written by a 'foreigner', it might be detrimental to sales figures. The book features an early example of the Battle being incorporated into a fictional text. The author was there on the day, and through Sol's eyes describes a scene that: 'Never in England would he have believed possible'. He concludes: 'Yes indeed; in Merry England; in the dirty, straggling, snobbish, slum-ridden centre of the world, the barricades were up.' He describes the event as a multi-ethnic one, cataloguing: 'The black men; the Chinese; Indians; the white foreign sailors; the Catholics from Prescot Street; the Jews; men without permanent address from ninepence-a-night houses; painted women from the shady cafés; the broad shouldered dockers; tramp-looking newspaper men; young, serious-looking men and women; coster men from Petticoat Lane — all crowded the narrow, smelly slum that tore up the road for a barricade.'

## Cable Street Beat

The Battle has been recorded frequently in poetry, most famously by the 'Tramp Poet', an ex-serviceman who had lost a leg and an arm. Although not referred to by that name, he is featured in Leslie Shepard's 1962 book *The Broadside Ballad: A Study in Origins and Meaning*. He is named there as Mr J. Smith, then over sixty-five years old. He wrote broadsheet poems, such as *The Battle of Cable Street*, which he sold in Oxford Street. The event has been threaded into several novels, including one in the 'family saga' genre: *All Shadows Fly Away* by Audrey Willshire. Various artefacts surrounding the Battle include a sixtieth anniversary plate, produced by a group of ex-miners, and banners, postcards, posters and badges. The phrase, 'They Shall Not Pass', has been adopted by other causes down the years. Not all with serious intent. It crops up in a 1998 Christmas edition of the long-running telly soap, *Coronation Street*. A barricade is erected at the door of the Rover's Return and the phrase yelled out during a protest against something or other that the new publican has been getting up to. And it crops up in the Beatles' 1965 film *Help!* during a comic fight sequence. In 'Corrie' the line has doubtless been smuggled into the script as an in-joke while in the fab four's energetic romp it looks suspiciously like a knowing ad-lib from Jewish comedy actor John Bluthal.

Rock Against Racism (RAR) emerged in 1976, a roots level group which in noting the rise of the National Front sought to enlist the new punk bands that were coming to prominence to the anti-racist cause. It worked a treat: the high-spot being the now legendary East London Victoria Park 'Carnival' in April 1978, organised in conjunction with the Anti-Nazi League. Some 80,000 people attended to watch a roll-call of New Wave performers. The memory of the Battle itself was evoked during the late 1980s for a further series of anti-racist concerts. Cable Street Beat was formed to counter the rise of performances by rock groups allied to extreme right-wing organisations. Like RAR, Cable Street Beat had their own logo and slogan 'Music Against Fascism'. One of the most memorable anti-fascist bands, to my mind, were The Men They Couldn't Hang, with their rousing (although at some points historically dubious) 1986 anthem, *Ghosts of Cable Street*.

*Listen to the sound of marching feet*
*And the voices of the ghosts of Cable Street*
*Fists, stones, batons and the gun*
*With courage we shall beat those Blackshirts down.*

## Battle Echoes

Although the rise of the English right featured in novels, such as *King Sol*, it was largely ignored by the cinema of the time. And, in fact, pretty much since. But it is threaded into the tapestry of David Lean's, *This Happy Breed*, based on a play by Noël Coward. Although seen as a bit cosy now, and an obvious piece of wartime propaganda (it was released in 1944) it documents, through the experiences of an ordinary suburban family, the changing face of Britain between the wars. So we get old men's tales of World War One bravado, the advent of the 'talkies' filtering in from across the Atlantic, the General Strike of 1926 and the stirrings of revolt from the younger cast members in both the political and personal arenas. There are off-screen and unspecified rumbles in Whitechapel and, in one scene, a ranting Blackshirt. Frank and Ethel Gibbons, played by Robert Newton and Celia Johnson, are having a day in town. At Speakers' Corner in Hyde Park they pause to listen to a black-clad, Mosley-like soapbox orator. There is no comment on this apart from Ethel pulling a face and suggesting that she and Frank go for a cup of tea. The film is impressive in its scope and the set pieces largely successful. It is rare in that it was filmed in colour, stock being difficult to obtain at the time. But its palette is curiously flat (at least in the prints that are available today), like the film itself: the characters never really rising above caricatures.

Was it the Rock Against Racism movement and the backward glance at the Battle of Cable Street that led to the fascist threat becoming a subject of Rock 'n' Roll iconography? Alan Parker's 1982 film adaptation of Pink Floyd's *The Wall*, imagines a contemporary Blackshirt army, led by a leather-coated Bob Geldoff, yelling incomprehensively through a megaphone. While in 1986, the musical box-office bomb that was *Absolute Beginners*, based on the writings of Colin MacInnes, features Steven Berkoff as a character billed as 'The Fanatic', an obvious take on the late 1950s Oswald Mosley at the time of the Notting Hill riots.

A depiction of Oswald Mosley as a character in a film or television drama didn't occur until 1998, when the Jewish television writers Laurence Marks and Maurice Gran (previously responsible for prime-time sit-coms such as *Goodnight Sweetheart* and *Birds of a Feather*)

172

authored a four-part Channel 4 production. *Mosley* played up the idea of the BUF leader as some sort of wayward matinee idol. 'A great man destroyed by unbridled ambition', according to the blurb on the boxed video release. It's difficult, I know: you've got this actor in the shape of Jonathan Cake, and he's carrying four hours of big-budget television drama. You can't make him out to be a total bastard because the audience need to have *some* sympathy with him. So here he is presented as a charismatic dreamer carried along by events. The Battle of Cable Street makes little more than a cameo appearance in the final segment. It flies by in moments, a major event broken down into a series of short, impressionistic shots. Finally, our television Mosley appears to regret the anti-Semitism he has inflamed (which is hardly borne out by the facts) but in the final minutes the messages are mixed. When, under defence regulations in 1940, Mosley is interned in Holloway Prison, he is verbally abused by one guard while being saluted by others.

The events in the East End of London all those years ago seem to be actually gaining prominence even as they recede from living memory. As noted, over the past thirty years especially, there have been a number of arts activities relating to the Battle, and several major festivals have commemorated it, each one bigger than the last. The publication of this book coincides with a full programme of concerts, exhibitions, film presentations and discussion groups at Wilton's Theatre and elsewhere to mark its seventy-fifth anniversary. And there will be plenty for the arts community, as well as the historians, to mull over for many years to come, I'll bet.

# The Art Collector of Cable Street

## 'The brave people'

I have quoted Louis Collin before in the section on pre-war Cable Street dwellers, from an interview conducted by the Cable Street Group. He was born in 1908, moved to Cable Street in 1910 and lived there until 1933; a pattern established in other stories. So why set this account here, so far away from his neighbours? Partly, length: he had much to say and proved to be a natural raconteur — and partly because the tale of his father's passion for collecting art and antiques was so unique. I recognised something of myself in Mr Collin's father. A magpie. While he sought to collect treasures I collect memories, snapping up every loose pearl and bauble in sight. Speaking in his home, fiddling with a small sandstone pipe in his hand, Louis Collin told us:

> As a child, these people came through who I used to call 'the brave people'. You know why? Because they could go into a shop and command attention. They were probably educated people. I'd never met them before. They had about them an air of confidence that I wanted. I used to hear them speak so beautifully. I never heard them swear. And when I was a child I made my mind up that I would never use bad language. I've never used it since because I felt that what's come from the gutter should be left in the gutter.
>
> In the family there were four girls and three boys. We lived in Wellclose Square just off Cable Street. It was an old sea captain's house and the only one in the district with a bath. It had twelve rooms and every window had inside wooden shutters. My father paid thirty-five shillings a week for it. We had two tenants upstairs. They paid four shillings a week for two rooms. My father was an outdoor ladies' tailor. He had a little workshop at the back of the house. He was the first man in London — and that has ever been since — who could take a piece of

174

brown paper and mark out the design of a garment and cut it out of the brown paper and give it in to be made. He used to say to me, 'When you learn to do this on paper, and you can visualise how it's going to look, how it's going to finish and how it's going to be made then you've accomplished something.' He said he learnt it from a Frenchman who came over here. At that time the tailors were making linens and pinning them on stands to get the shape of the garment. My father got a job in Artillery Lane and was very well-paid for his time. He had artistic intent but was unable to write. He came over in 1885 or 1886 when he was about sixteen years of age. My mother's parents came from Budapest but she was born here so consequently my father had to speak English so we never used Yiddish at all.

# 'A unique man in his way'

*My father was a unique man in his way. In his cutting room he had a bird to listen to. He came from the country near Warsaw and it reminded him. He had to have a little canary in his office and we had a cockatoo in the house. A cockatoo! It used to scream when you went to bed. Wonderful things he brought. Next door to us in Ship Alley lived a Roman Catholic family called Miller, a family of six sons and one daughter. They were all ginger-haired and used to go to church on Sunday mornings for Mass. The man used to sell second-hand furniture. His sons used to take a horse and cart and travel the country for a whole week, sleeping in the van, and come back from buying stuff from all the houses: lots of antiques. I was about three or four years of age then. He got friendly with my father. They were very close — a Roman Catholic man! They lived in an old disused public house. There was a fireplace there and a chair that was for my father. Every Saturday, I used to have to go and call him to get him away. He taught my father about china, about silver, about paintings. Over the years, my father brought Dresden china, two Hogarth paintings, Turner paintings for a half a crown and five shillings. And that was in the East End of London! My sister used to play the piano and he brought a grand piano to play on. He wanted her to be a concert pianist and every Sunday we used to sit as a*

175

*family round the piano and my sister would play. A friend of hers used to play the violin and there was a girl opposite who used to sing with them. It was all most unusual for the East End, all the children sitting around and listening to my sister playing Beethoven. My father even brought us portfolios of Shakespeare's plays in foot-length volumes, leather-bound with gold trimmings and every play had pictures in it.*

*We had a dinner service of a hundred and forty-four pieces. I see those plates today hung up in antique shops. This friend of my father used to smoke a small cigar in a pipe and my father loved that so he went out and bought my father a pipe. Here is the pipe. It's made of sandstone, hand-carved. It's just over a hundred years old. The man himself used to smoke one with the head of a man with a high hat. It was very unusual. He brought my father cigars from different places. He'd be sitting by the fire and he'd take a piece of china, tell my father what it was, show him how to read the date, how to read the markings, how to read the silver. And my father collected them and paid so much per week. I remember that if my father hadn't paid him for a few weeks he used to come round — I always remember he had a red beard — he'd look at me and say, 'I'm mad! I let him have all this! I'm mad! I'm mad!' and marched himself out.*

*Over twenty years my father bought two Louis the Fifteenth china cabinets, ormolu — brass mixed with gold — trimmed around. In it was set glasses, cut glass. Sometimes he used to take them out and touch them and they used to ring, they were so finely cut. And he collected all this. We had a black stand with a head cut in marble — I don't know who it was — in the corner of the room. And we had a glass case fitted with the most exotic birds you've ever seen. He had a bedroom suite that was inlaid with different woods. We had an octagonal table: in the centre was a piece of Dresden china. It was covered in petals, small tiny flowers. And if you looked through the petals you saw a bird in the centre.*

*Just before I moved out to get married my father bought a little leasehold house in Forest Gate. It was a double-fronted house so he could set out the grand piano, all the furniture, the cabinets and all the articles he'd bought. And in 1941, the night before the last night of the bombings, the all-clear sounded. There were four trees out in the front of the house and when they came out of the shelter at the back they didn't know there was a land-mine hanging in one of these trees. My sisters and my brother went up to bed and my mother and my father were having a cup of tea in their armchairs. There was a long oak sideboard and the top blew off and landed on top of these two armchairs and the stuff fell on this board. Their shoulders and arms were injured but they were saved. I heard it and rushed around there. We looked for my two sisters and we dug them out of the debris. It was too late to do anything. One was seventeen and the other twenty-eight. It was funny, another sister was sleeping next to her in the same room and never got hurt. And my brother who was sleeping at the back of the house managed to scramble out unhurt. My mother and father were in hospital for a while. Everything in the house had gone. This pipe you see he had in his pocket. Everything else had gone. I couldn't find a trace of anything, it was all blown to pieces. The pictures, the paintings, the china, everything, completely gone. And the Wellclose Square House was still all right! Ironical, isn't it? It took him twenty years to collect and it was all destroyed in a flash of a second.*

*After the war my father had a stroke. He could walk with a stick. He had a limp. I was running a factory in the City and doing quite well. I had a car and he asked me to take him down to Wellclose Square. I always remember this scene. He got out of the car — old man Miller had died during the war — and his eldest son, Jack, was standing on the corner with all the furniture outside and he saw me and my father walking down the street. I always remember this. He was a big hulking fellow and I can see him running towards my father with all his worth. And he flung his arms round my father and kissed him on both cheeks and started to cry. Can you imagine?*

# 7. 'The Ponces Move In'
# The Shadow of Ruins

## East London Through a Lens

The overwhelming perception of Cable Street after the Second World War is that of a hive of immigration and prostitution, the two being inextricably entwined (partly due to sensationalist newspaper reports) in people's minds. Yet the area had a history of harbouring stranded seaman dating back to the start of the eighteenth century, and the Cable Street Group interviews confirmed that prostitution was an everyday hindrance for those living there long before the bombs started falling. But perhaps the withdrawal from the area by so many Jewish families during the war laid that other world bare, and their absence allowed for its expansion. Bernard Kops returned from evacuation during the conflict to find East London already transformed. In his 1963 autobiography, *The World is a Wedding*, he wrote: 'There were great gaps of jagged space where houses once stood.... Now I was no longer worried about my future but more about day-to-day survival. No longer did I collect shrapnel but leapt for shelter as soon as the sirens went. A taste of salt came into my mouth and fear made my eyes twitch. All feeling of community had completely faded. We were all withdrawn into ourselves.... The Jewish community, the family, the spirit had died.' In these great gaps other things flourished, which became of great interest to social observers.

Nigel Henderson came out of the RAF at the end of the war with nerves 'stripped like wires' to bury himself in that 'cathedral of black bones': London. Based in Bethnal Green he trudged the East End pavements with his camera, recording everyday street scenes whilst conducting more experimental work in a makeshift studio in his house. Henderson's photography, and the diary entries of his sociologist wife, Judith, encapsulate the atmosphere of the post-war years: a stocky, headscarved woman stands on a bombsite with a shaggy-haired child in tow, selling second-hand comics from a battered trestle table; a bespectacled short-trousered boy lounges about in the shadow of ruins; cotton frocks made from parachutes; the Relieving Office and American Red Cross clothing; rationing; fuel cuts; a two-hour queue for two pounds of potatoes; borrowing a spoonful of this and begging a cup of that. And people riven with serious ill-health who 'did not care whether the world stopped.' But signs of life still: *Huckleberry Finn* from the library; 'Kendo' — the bare-chested strongman — performing his street act for the benefit of three bemused onlookers while framed pictures of former glories hang crookedly on the fence behind him; nylon stocking forests and wig-stalls in Petticoat Lane, where the heads of dummies are skewed atop poles in imitation of those which once adorned the spikes on Tower Bridge; and Bert Smith, portable knife-grinder, touring every corner of the borough on his customised ice-cream tricycle, much puzzled at the man with the lawnmower in Cable Street, where there are no lawns but who had, Bert later discovered, laid one out on his outhouse roof.

## 'Red-Light' Cable Street

I introduced you to Alf Gardner in the section about *To Sir, With Love*, the ex-pupil who brought E.R. Braithwaite to book in his self-published autobiography, *An East End Story*. But Alf's schooldays make up only a part of it. Much of it is about his friendship with Burmese-born Dave Upson and the experiences they had together in the notorious cafés and clubs of Cable Street. I had been talking to Alf that rainy day outside his old school and with the recorder still running we began to make our way towards the western end of the street. He told me:

*I first met Dave during the summer of 1959. I'd been to an evening class and was walking home along Commercial Road when I noticed a woman stretched out motionless on the pavement outside the Nelson Head. I thought, blimey, what's happened? Is she ill? Is she dead? I immediately ran across the road to a phone booth to call an ambulance but I was beaten to it by David, who had also seen the woman. We went back across the road to stay with her until the police and an ambulance arrived, then we went into the pub for a drink. From this meeting we were to share a warm, platonic, friendship that was to last for thirty-seven years.*

Whenever I have heard Alf recount the story, I note that he always inserts the word 'platonic' into it, just in case people get the wrong idea. To hammer the point home, he added, 'In the pub we started chatting and discovered we had a lot in common — women mainly.'

I've always found it hard to equate the softly spoken and slightly formal pensioner with the eighteen-year old thrill-seeker that he was. '1959 was a glorious year, weather-wise,' he continued. 'One of the great post-war summers: it went on and on and on. I would often meet Dave in the evenings and wander around and go on pub tours. He knew a hell of a lot of women. He was about fourteen years older than me, so through him I was meeting lots of them too. Our conversation seemed to be restricted to females. But I was determined to join the Merchant Navy so I was equally enthralled by the exciting stories of his fourteen years at sea.'

Alf often found himself in the Brown Bear pub near the Seaman's Mission Hostel in Dock Street, used mainly by West African seamen. One of the prostitutes was Dolly, an overweight fifty-year old in semi-retirement after thirty years on the game. Dolly was a regular source of embarrassment, always grabbing him in a bear hug and telling everyone in the bar how much he looks like her son. But Alf seems to have drifted along, wandering in and out of the down-at-heel cafés and low dives with an almost detached air, unflummoxed and unsullied by events. In all, the perfect social observer, I suppose.

'Coming up here,' Alf informed me as we approached the Wellclose Square end of Cable Street, 'is where it started getting a bit rough.'

## Café Society in Cable Street

Much of the roughness was connected with the cafés. I also spoke to the Reverend Ken Leech about them, although as you will hear later, he made their acquaintance for quite different reasons. The Reverend is still able to catalogue the different communities that they served: Bruno's, the Valetta and St. George's (for the Maltese); the Rainbow (Sierra Leone and the Gambia); the Tequila Club (West African); the Rio and Abdullah cafés in Ensign Street (Somali); Mr Howard's (Nigerian) and the self-explanatory Yugoslavia Café. I am particularly taken by the Green Parrot Club in Grace's Alley, run by Billy Olu Sholenke, who had a special insurance policy to accommodate his wife Pat's performances as a fire eater. Alf Gardner was familiar with these places, some of them even before he'd left school. 'Lots and lots of clubs and brothels,' he told me on our wander. 'The brother of a friend of mine got stabbed to death in a Maltese café here in Pell Street. He was half-Maltese. He was on leave from the army and he and a pal got into an argument with somebody and this man got a knife from the kitchen and he stabbed both of them. I remember in 1953 when me and another boy, Alfie Garrels, went around the school for money towards a wreath and Alex Bloom, the headmaster, allowed us to take it to the service.'

## 'An East End Story'

Alf Gardner and his drinking pal, Dave Upson, although never setting out to look for trouble, always seemed to find it. One adventure in the Cable Street area, included in Alf's book comes about as a consequence of Dave's attempts to impress a new lady friend, Eileen, with his tales of life on the wild side. Even Alf is uncharacteristically dramatic on this occasion: when she asks him if it was as notorious as the scandal sheets made out, he replies: 'Much worse'. He refuses her plea to be given an escorted tour of the pubs and clubs. 'I explained that the area, like Soho, was a red-light district that respectable women avoided day or night.... Far from deterring Eileen, my deliberate discouraging description of Cable Street seemed to arouse her interest more, giving me the impression that she was keen to visit some of the bars at the earliest opportunity.' Alf and Dave were familiar with the scarily named Black Door, a wretched basement bar off Leman Street. The clientele seems to have been made up entirely of razor-slashed members of the underworld. On one of their visits a man at the bar produced a pistol, waving it around at the other customers. After he was ejected, Alf and Dave discreetly finished their drinks and left. Alf is understandably surprised therefore when Dave, finally giving in to Eileen, takes her there on a guided tour of the area. According to the story fed back to Alf, a couple of regulars got jealous as Dave smooched with his new girl at the bar and a fight ensued. 'A terrified Eileen fled from the club and disappeared and Dave with his two black eyes was left to stagger outside. His attempts to contact her again were unsuccessful. She refused to see him again or venture back to the East End.'

The weather was getting worse, curtailing our chat. We parted in the rain, Alf retreating back to his flat on the Isle of Dogs where he continues to write up the stories of his life. An expanded and revised version of *An East End Story* is in the offing. Written testimony is one of the links of this book. I realised early on that in researching this section I would be relying partly on retrieved works: the 'lost library' likely to yield more than an appeal for prostitutes and their pimps to get in touch.

# 'The East-Enders'

## Ashley Smith

Research sometimes happened by accident. One day, while browsing in a second-hand bookshop, my hand fell on a small-format, hardback volume. On the cover, in stark bold lettering, the title: THE EAST-ENDERS. Written by Ashley Smith and published by Secker & Warburg in 1961, it is part of what seems to be an interesting little series: *Britain Alive,* also featuring works by Dennis Potter, Mervyn Jones and Stuart Hall. The copy that I had stumbled on was a special one, an inscription on the inside cover revealing it to be a gift from East London historian Professor Bill Fishman to the writer Joseph Leftwich.

Ashley Smith was a Jewish East End writer who by the time he made his contribution to the *Britain Alive* series had an impressive list of well-received novels behind him, such as *The Brimming Lake* and its sequel *You Forget So Quickly*, both dealing with East End themes. He also wrote the experimental *A City Stirs*, published in 1939. There is no story in the conventional sense. It is an evocation, almost cinematic in concept, of a single day, peopled with a cast of thousands; all observed by the omnipresent author who hovers above them as they go about their tasks. There's a touch of the documentary in *The East-Enders* too, although by now the author's feet are firmly on the ground, pounding the pavements of his youth, rushing here and there to record the changes. What strikes him most are those structures which, as he suspected at the time, were to define the East London skyline for decades to come. And for which, as far as I'm aware, Ashley Smith has minted an entirely new word: he speaks of 'soarers'. In America they were shiny and glamorous and called skyscrapers. In England we settled for miserable, municipal, tower blocks, and somewhere in between there are high-rises. But for Ashley Smith they are soarers. His return begins with an inventory of the thoroughfares that mark the perimeters of his personal East London. He allows Cannon Street Road, 'Why a street *and* a road, a local Councillor asks me plaintively every time I see him', and Valance Road, 'included only because of its fish and chip shops.' He continues:

*In … calling attention to the East End, Cable Street for some years now has left all other competitors behind. Dope Peddler in Cable Street. Strip tease club in Cable Street. Vice rings in Cable Street. Razor gangs in Cable Street. People who stab you in the leg even while someone else is sitting on them — in Cable Street…. But what is not generally known, indeed hardly known at all, is that Cable Street has two, or rather, three faces, like Eve. The north-eastern end where Cable Street curves round to debouch into Commercial Road is a bulwark of stern industry, towering factories and Haulage Depots and Transport Yards: the central straight part, east and west of Glamis Road is … the very hub of the East End's indestructible gentility. Hardinge Street and Johnson Street are around, and ladder rungs of smaller streets where the doorsteps are smothered daily with whitestone and the profusion of pubs shows that men of principle are here, who keep any relaxation of morals only for Nights Out and Evenings In. They are indeed the kind of men who would write letters to* The Times *deploring the notoriety heaped upon their neighbourhood were it not that they never read the paper. In this well-tended stretch of street there are also the Stepney Town Hall and the St. George's Library, one of the intellectual centres of the East End for generations, irreparably bombed now and replaced on a smaller scale like a lollipop that has been sucked for a long while. Finally, there is the third section of Cable Street, which is the filthiest, dirtiest, most repellently odoured street in Christendom, an offence to the eye and nostril, a menace to the health and happiness of its unfortunate inhabitants, and a standing reproach of criminal dimensions to any authority which has the power to tear it down, burn the ground clear of its foulness, rehouse its*

*people in places fit for people — and doesn't, and hasn't,*
*even though intention has flirted with execution here for*
*more than thirty years — a longstanding engagement*
*with marriage, apparently, as far off as ever.*

It is to this third section of the street that the author
guides us. Here, he thumps on the rusted knocker of a
house and is guided up some stairs by a 'brittle-looking
Trinidadian' who in turn introduces him to a burly West
African 'with the usual piano teeth' and his wife. With
washing on an indoor line dangling round his ears and
his feet sticking to the grease-covered linoleum floor,
Ashley Smith chats politely with the unnamed man for
several pages while strange smells waft past his nostrils.
With a few well-placed words and snatches of dialogue,
the author uses the encounter to illustrate one of the
themes running through his book: the East End as a
place of constant change. The tone is foreboding and pep-
pered with vague innuendo, yet of a philosophical bent.
Maybe this lot are different to the last lot, he seems to
imply, but in the end they'll all just end up as East
Enders anyway.

After I had paid for the slightly battered second-hand
book at the till, I wandered towards a greasy spoon café.
And as I began to leaf through it over a mug of stewed tea
it served up yet another surprise. A small, yellowed newspaper clipping fluttered out from between its pages. It
was a review of the book, headed CHANGING SCENES
by another Jewish East London author with a prodigious
output, Emanuel Litvinoff. The review is short and with-
ering. The clipping isn't dated and there's no indication
which paper it appeared in, although there are some tantalising snippets of news on the back of it:

*The future of Jews' College was discussed at a brains*
*trust organised by the Junior Chapter and Verse of the*
*Brixton B'nai B'rith. Mr Morris Ledgerman, Chairman of*
*the College Council, said that the fact that the College*

*had no pupils and would soon have no staff was no argument against it. 'It's still got a building,' he said, 'and if we're going to start closing down buildings just because they're not being used, an awful lot of people will be put out of business.' Another speaker suggested that the College building should be converted into flats. 'It may have stopped producing ministers,' he said, 'but it may start producing a surplus.' To which Mr Janus Levy, another member of the panel added: 'Better a surplus than a surplice.'*

# Father Joe, Edith and Bertha

## Joseph Williamson

Another book documenting those years was the autobiography, *Father Joe*, by Joseph Williamson, published in 1963. The author lived the sort of life, from impoverished beginnings in Poplar to priestly scourge of Cable Street that should have ended up as a late Ealing Studios social commentary film. Preferably with Alec Guinness in the lead. But although no movie was forthcoming he did become a media figure in the national press as, with deft handling, he brought attention to a situation that he was passionate about.

Williamson became fatherless at age three in 1897. An old ship's boiler that was being broken up in the East India Docks fell apart, crushing his father in the mud. From then on, his mother struggled with a large family, taking in washing to make ends meet. Joe, because of his natural singing ability, joined the choir at the Church of St. Saviour's, where one day, a voice told him that he must make not only a spiritual leap, but also an almost unheard-of social vault, to enter the Anglican priesthood. He was taken under the wing of a priest, Father Lambert, and on being demobbed after the First World War, attended St. Augustine's College, Canterbury. But after four years, his own sense of inadequacy led him to conclude that he had only just scraped through. In his book, he lamented: '...every allowance must have been made for my upbringing.' Williamson married between the wars and then, after a stint as an Army chaplain, in 1952 came the message from a friend that he seems to have been waiting for all his life. It began: 'It's about time you returned to London...'

Williamson's destination, St. Paul's, was known as the Seamen's Church, complete with a ship's weathervane on the steeple. He found it in a bad state. But it was nothing to what he discovered beyond its walls. In Cable Street: '...you are at once in a world of crowded tenements, sordid cafés, bomb sites, and narrow alleys lined with buildings which should have been pulled down years ago... The area is the breeding ground for vice of every description, where in recent years evil and unscrupulous men have moved in with their all-night cafés and their brothels, making life hell for the decent people who have to bring up children in the midst of all these horrors.' To counter this he provided Christian teaching for children and led Good Friday processions through the 'worst parts' of Stepney. 'Drama forces the message home: I have found myself on my knees in the gutter of Cable Street, demonstrating how the Lord washed the dirty feet of His disciples. I have pleaded for mercy and forgiveness at the foot of the crude wooden cross which we carry'.

Before long he had become the father to three children and 'Father Joe' to the toughs who run the cafés. His popularity was due in part, he felt, to his tendency to put practicalities above prayer, trying to alleviate the suffering of his flock, including rolling up his sleeves to do the washing-up for a harassed housewife.

Although there were occasional raids on the brothels, with 'street waitresses' being carted away in the 'meat vans' (an expression that Father Joe took a while to understand the significance of) things just kept getting worse, with coachloads of sightseers turning up to watch the action. At this point Joseph Williamson embarked on the project that would make him a household name in East London and beyond. He decided to transform Church House, a dilapidated building in Wellclose Square into a refuge for prostitutes, opening in the summer of 1958 with a team of women workers — washing, scrubbing and taking the girls to the VD clinic. The girls sometimes stayed for weeks, sometimes for months at a time. They were free to come and go — within set times — but there were tales of girls bunking off down the fire escape in the middle of the night and of those who complained they felt like they were in prison.

The purpose of the refuge was to give the girls a breathing space before leaving their old life behind them. But with the cafés still in full swing just along the road — tempting his girls back into prostitution — he decided to organise some sightseeing tours of his own, inviting the great and the good to witness the depravity in Cable Street for themselves. Pamphlets were fired off in every direction. Even the London County Council (owners of some of the buildings used as brothels) got the message. As a row of the 'filthy hovels' were being demolished, Father Joe sank to his knees in the street and said a *Gloria*, a picture of which appeared in the next day's *Daily Mail*.

# Edith Ramsay and Bertha Sokoloff

*Edith and Stepney: The Life of Edith Ramsay* is a biography by Bertha Sokoloff, published by Stepney Books in 1987. Bertha was a Communist Party member when she first met Edith, on the Labour side of the Council Chamber in 1945. But she didn't really get to know her subject until the late 1960s.

Edith Ramsay was born in Highgate in 1895 to a middle-class Scots family which, although not wealthy (according to Edith), still had two maids to run the house. Her grandfather had worked at a foundry but her father arrived in London as a Presbyterian Minister. Edith came to teach in East London at the start of 1920, taking up residence in a tenement with a shared lavatory in Spitalfields. Not that hardship seemed to worry her. In writing a 1924 report, *The Derelict in Whitechapel,* she checked for herself the conditions for homeless women in 'Mother Nevill's', signing into the lodging house incognito and experiencing an airless room crammed with fifteen beds and spending the night under flea-infested bedsheets. The women, in 'moral peril', are broken down into categories including 'a varied type of repulsive, almost entirely animal woman'. By 1931, she was teaching at the Heckford Street Adult Institute. Her work in various institutes was to become her life work, acting as an unofficial social worker well into her eighties. There seems barely a committee that she didn't at some point sit on or a philanthropic venture that she was not part of. She set out to deliberately make a nuisance of herself, always pushing and prodding for more classes, more services.

Bertha Sokoloff dovetails her own story with that of her subject, contrasting her experience as a Stepney girl born and bred with that of outsider Edith. Bertha's testimony gives glimpses of her Jewish upbringing. Poverty, for many, was a way of life. But she also recalls visits to the Jewish Theatre and the singing of Yiddish songs which stayed with her always. Such was the extent of Jewish cultural life in Stepney that, during her childhood, she had little experience outside of it; during the 1930s, Jew and Gentile rarely mixed. Edith noted that barriers also existed elsewhere. Wapping, the 'dockland village', was still largely Catholic. Edith had been present in a house where two young sisters had died and the nurses there had refused to pray with the Proddie father. Edith herself had no qualms about such things, attending a Mass one day, a Jewish service the next. She entertained the Jewish poet Avram Stencl in her tiny flat and spoke of the synagogue luncheon club as 'our club'.

Throughout the war, Edith fought to keep the institutes open while Bertha became one of a clutch of Communist councillors under the leadership of Phil Piratin, who gained a parliamentary seat. Edith became a Labour Councillor but left the Labour Party (seemingly wearied by the shenanigans of party politics) and moved house. And this is where her interest in Cable Street seemed to start. Once installed in the district she was elected as an independent councillor in 1959, in the ward covering the west end of the street. One of the reasons for her success was the name she made for herself as a tireless campaigner. She was now able to help to bring national attention to a major cause for concern in her locality.

That cause of concern, Bertha Sokoloff writes: 'was the serious deterioration of the Cable Street area and the heavy concentration of all-night cafés, clubs and brothels, which sprouted in response to and in exploitation of the large numbers of single black men who were settling in the area'. She goes on to say: 'There were also many from the Mediterranean area, Cypriots and Maltese and some of the latter were particularly singled out because of their involvement in the exploitation and ensuing crime. There was the sufficient grain of truth to lend a little substance to the image of the Maltese as profiteer, exploiter and pimp.' In Edith's eyes however, her work was not to take the form of a racist or moral crusade but, in part, to improve the lot of those 'mysteries' who came from all parts of the country to be sold at the bargain basement level of prostitution.

At this point in Bertha's narrative, Father Joseph Williamson makes an appearance, becoming Edith's partner in visits to various dens of iniquity. But we get a slightly different picture of him here from the one he paints of himself in *Father Joe*. It is Williamson who is instrumental in bringing press attention to the area, becoming a media figure in his own right, but it is Edith who is inevitably dubbed the 'Florence Nightingale of the Brothels'. Edith even managed to get elected onto the 'committee' (which never met) of the Cosmopolitan Club, run by a Ghanaian called Sherriff who saw his recruitment of Edith as a mark of respectability. Bertha writes: 'One can imagine the scene: the tawdry room, the assorted black men and the white little tarts, and as Edith entered with Father Williamson Mr Sherriff would cry "A sandy for Miss Ramsden" — he meant a shandy of course. What, I wondered, did Father Williamson drink? Edith said he wasn't offered anything!' Edith was called as a witness when Mr Sherriff was seeking a bar licence and made the point that there are far worse clubs about.

She knew this because he had taken her in his car to see some *really* bad ones in South London. But Edith wasn't being taken completely for a ride since it gave her the opportunity to make acquaintance with the girls, encouraging them to attend dressmaking classes at her institute in Myrdle Street. Through her contacts she was able to reunite the runaways with their families and assist them in leaving their old life behind.

Bertha encouraged Edith to keep a diary in the 1970s of her still heavy voluntary workload. She joined her on walks around Spitalfields, investigating the changes brought by the Bengali incomers: changes to local politics, to schools, to housing policy. Their journeys together finished in the harsh winter of 1979 as mountainous piles of rubbish blocked entire streets and rats scurried across main roads during a series of strikes by public service workers. Even when she moved to sheltered accommodation, Edith remained active, still receiving visitors of all creeds, until her death aged eighty-eight. Edith's life in Stepney was a long one: her aura of otherness coming from the fact that she had sprung from a life and age that had long vanished. Since first encountering Edith on opposite benches of the council, Bertha had raised a family, and when asking her one-time political rival why she had never married, Edith told her, 'Every man I danced with in August 1914 was dead by 1916'.

Father Joe, Edith and Bertha have all passed on now. Unavailable for my prying questions. But I didn't just have to rely on the written word, as my interview with Alf Gardner demonstrated: I had a further contact, who had known just about everybody during Cable Street's notorious red-light years.

# Houses of Hospitality

## Kenneth Leech

I had often bumped into the Reverend Kenneth Leech — universally known as Ken — in his later East London days. Ken knew Father Joe, Edith Ramsay and seemingly half the people in the borough. But when I came to interview him I had to travel to Manchester, to where he retired a few years back. I especially wanted to talk to him because of his knowledge of Cable Street and about his memories of the seemingly endless procession of eccentric clergy who trod the pavements there. His career is unique, spanning the Cable Street of the late 1950s and the Brick Lane of the 1970s, where he was active in campaigning against fascist activity. A believer in the power of prayer, he also advocated earthly-bound action. He is the only reverend I'm aware of to receive a bloodied bullet through the post as a warning. I met and recorded my conversation with him in one of the rooms attached to the three-hundred-year-old St. Ann's Church, close to Manchester's huge steel and glass shopping centre.

Ken Leech was born in Ashton-under-Lyne and grew up in a cotton mill town; where the view from his window was 'like a Lowry painting.' The chimneys of twenty factories were in sight, his mother informing him that she had worked in each and every one of them. After attending school in Hyde, Ken got a scholarship to King's College London. 'It was 1958. I didn't know anything about London except that the Franciscans had a house in 84 Cable Street. So I ended up living there; it was a former brothel. I think it had been condemned about the time of the First World War. When you pulled the lavatory chain you felt the roof was going to fall in. It had rats and cockroaches and all sorts of creatures in there. And you couldn't really close the bedroom window because there was a gas leak,' Ken took off in the early 1960s to do a second degree at Trinity College. While for most people, the tranquillity of Oxford would have been a welcome change from the sound of mice gnawing the woodwork, Ken talks of 'escaping' back to Cable Street at the weekends.

Ken Leech got to know the area's movers and shakers; he was a friend of the Communist councillor Solly Kaye and of the fiercely anti-communist Edith Ramsay, who Ken remembers fondly as a 'kind of Lady Bountiful'. He recalls, 'One of the first things that someone said to me when I arrived in the East End was if you wanted anything done in Stepney, go to the three Communists or Miss Ramsay — but not both at the same time.'

Ken Leech told me, 'A key figure there was a Franciscan priest called Father Neville Palmer. He was a *sort* of Canadian. From Prince Edward Island, which I gather some people think isn't really part of Canada. He'd been in the area since 1943 so everybody knew him.' Father Groser is another name that is remembered even today. An active socialist, he was, according to Ken, very involved in the 1926 General Strike and was beaten up during it. 'He had a church that doesn't exist anymore called Christ Church in Watney Street. It was John Groser who arranged for the Franciscans to come to the area but he told Dennis Gidding, who was the curate of St. George's-in-the-East, that he hadn't anywhere for them to live. So Gidding said that the police had just closed a brothel at 84 Cable Street and that might be suitable. They called it the St. Francis House of Hospitality, which I thought was a bit unwise as all the houses around it were houses of hospitality.'

## 'A good way to stop a fight'

Ken Leech continued:

He was always known as Father Neville or Brother Neville. Most people didn't even know his second name. A lot of the Africans didn't know how to spell his name because they'd never seen it in print. We used to get letters from all over the world addressed to Father Nibble, Father Snivel, Father Navel and one posted in the Gambia addressed to Mister Fadernebble, Cable Street, England: and it arrived without any difficulty! He died in the mid-seventies. Later on, the Citizens' Advice Bureau phoned me and they said, 'We've got a Muslim gentleman here who's going through a divorce and he says that Father Neville is going to sort it all out but we can't work out who this Father Neville is.' I said, 'I can tell you who he was but he's been dead for some years.' I knew the Muslim gentleman, he used to sell peanuts in Petticoat Lane, and I realised that he meant me: Father Neville had become a generic name for all Christian clergy. He always wore a very bedraggled brown cassock; a very shy man who always understated everything.

I remember waking up at about three in the morning. I looked out of the window and there was a bottle and knife fight going on in Cable Street. I heard Father Neville go down and say to them, 'How are you these days?' I thought, that's a good way to stop a fight. In the morning, when I asked him about it, he brushed it off as just 'a little dispute'. Whereas, Joe Williamson exaggerated everything! For instance, he once said that there were a hundred prostitutes operating at the west end of Cable Street. So I measured it and thought that even if they were standing on each other's shoulders there was no way that many could have fitted in. The prostitute area basically ran from number 2 to number 90. It was a very small section of the street. He was threatened with libel action quite a few times. He described the London County Council as being the owners of a vast and shameful brothel. They had an all-night sitting to decide whether to sue him. Their legal advisors said, 'If you sue him you will win but we advise you not to because he'll use the Central Criminal Court as a campaigning ground and you could lose the next election.'

Some people accused Williamson of racism. I don't know that he was but he gave a lot of ammunition to racists because he always said that the Maltese and the blacks were in control of the brothels. And there was some truth in that. But they were not typical Maltese and they

195

*were not typical black people. The old British National Party, not the current one, used to praise him to the skies because they said that he was the only person who was drawing attention to the evils of Cable Street, which they saw as the evils of black people. Kathleen Wrsama was very critical of Williamson. She was my next door neighbour, Ethiopian by origin, I think. But she'd been brought up in Yorkshire and spoke with a Yorkshire accent. She was married to Solomon Wrsama, who was Somali, so all the Somalians thought she was Somalian. They referred to her as 'Mrs Solomon'. She founded the Stepney Coloured People's Association in the 1950s and ran their home as a Somali lodging house. She thought that Williamson was a racist. She once appeared on a television programme called* Surviving, *and talked about Williamson. She didn't name him but it was quite obvious who she was talking about. She never locked her door. All through her life her door was never locked. She said, 'I never know who wants to see me.'*

*I remember being with the Chief Superintendent at Leman Street the day after Joe had retired. He said to me, 'I breathed a sigh of relief when that man went.' And I asked him why. He said, 'Well, with most social activists, they played the game by the rules, they always took the police into their confidence. They marched, they demonstrated, they picketed but we knew how to deal with them. But with Joseph Williamson you never knew what he was going to do next.'*

# Soho and Brick Lane

If nobody knew what Father Joe was going to do next, it sometimes seemed that Ken Leech didn't know what he himself was going to do next either. He was in Soho for a period during the late 1960s, and when someone suggested the need for a night-time refuge for the area's homeless he volunteered to do it. Many of them were from Scotland and the north, lured by the Swinging London vision and increased work opportunities. Ken had already founded the Soho Drugs Group and watched the problem grow during his time there. He had just thirty quid in the bank but, perhaps utilising some of the chutzpah learnt from Joe Williamson, managed to secure a Dean Street basement to take in this crowd of economic migrants. The refuge was called Centerpoint, a mirror image of the tall, empty, Centre Point building nearby. The project grew in size to eventually service 5,000 young people a year.

In 1978, a local man called Altab Ali was killed in a racist attack in Whitechapel as National Front activity was growing in the mainly Asian Brick Lane. Ken Leech was vocal in his opposition to the violent and intimidating presence of their members, selling their newspapers and handing out leaflets. 'I received quite a few death threats because of it. And I did receive a bullet soaked in blood. There was a note that said, "Your next visitor will be your maker, Father." I released it to the press, which I thought was the best thing to do. Around that time, three men turned up at the door to warn me off. I had an Alsatian dog at the time called Rebel, who was the gentlest creature you could imagine. She had never been known to growl at anybody. But when these three appeared she went to the door and said, GRRRGH! And I've never seen people run so fast. She followed them round the corner to make sure they'd disappeared.'

At the end of the interview we both left at the same time, and passing through the church, I noticed Ken giving a short but firm nod in the direction of the altar: a bit like when passing an acquaintance in the street. Only then did I realise that I had asked Ken about almost everything but his faith, focusing exclusively on his social activities. And as we parted in the busy shopping mall, I realised that I wasn't now going to get the chance. It was probably for the best however — sparing him my ignorance of theological matters. A random glance through the titles of Ken's publications makes it plain however that he has always seen the spiritual and social as inextricably linked in his philosophy.

# Coming to Cable Street

## Explorers

Research for this book, although exhilarating, has had its downside; the slightly deflating realisation that I am just another of wave after wave of explorers who have landed on the same shore. Stan Hugill's *Sailortown*, published in 1967, was a sort of early 'Rough Guide' (to rough places): an exhaustive, and exhausting, account of the world's ports, which includes Cable Street. Roi Ottley's 1952 book *No Green Pastures* also brings us here. The author was the first African-American war correspondent to work for a major white USA newspaper. Harlem raised, he found that Britain's equivalent suffered in comparison. Instead of the exuberance he found in the 'roaring cafés' back home, he found here an atmosphere that 'resembled the Casbah in Algiers — mysterious, sinister, and heavily-laden with surreptitious violence.' Probably the most well known of these street-level investigations is *The Coloured Quarter* by Michael Banton, published in 1955 (and who I got to meet almost by chance as this book was going to press). It's inevitable that the same people appear as characters in several of these books. Phyllis Young, for instance, a welfare worker, appears in both the Banton and the Roi Ottley volume, slightly re-framed in each. Not all people coming to Cable Street were here for research purposes. An unexpected feature of café nightlife in Cable Street were the celebrities who would sometimes pop into them. At that hedonistic junction of the 1950s and 60s, traffic was intense. Tom Driberg, the left-wing Labour MP was often seen in joints like The Green Parrot. As Chairman of the Labour Party he combined a desire for social justice with other desires for which he was arrested more than once. Homosexuality was an offence in those less enlightened times but friends in high places always managed to keep the stories out of the newspapers. After his death, those stories started to filter through, to the point where he seemed to be accused of absolutely everything.

Another visitor was Colin MacInnes, remembered mainly as a vibrant chronicler of multi-cultural west London life in *City of Spades* and *Absolute Beginners*. But *Mr Love and Justice*, a tale of police and ponces, published in 1960, was set in the Cable Street area. MacInnes dropped into the cafés, fishing for storylines. 'In Cable Street,' he wrote, 'the castaways from Africa and the Caribbean perform a perpetual, melancholy, wryly humorous ballet of which they are themselves the only audience.' He is another whose reputation has had its ups and downs. Those people I spoke to who had actually met him however have positive memories. More than a decade after the clubs had folded, he still retained Cable Street connections. Basement Writer Leslie Mildiner, co-author of *The Gates*, told me, 'He came to talk to us about an article he was writing. He was eccentric, caustic, charming and inspiring. He showed us nothing but encouragement.'

Dan Farson, the journalist, loved the East End. He set up camp here in the early sixties, wrote stuff, bought a pub and filled it with slumming celebs. Alf Gardner used to sometimes bump into him in the clubs and described him as a nice man who got less nice the more he drank. I never met him in East London but I did literally once bump into him. During the 1980s, he was stumbling out of a Soho bar as I was stumbling in. I recognised him immediately from old book covers and half-remembered television appearances. 'I know who you are,' I blurted out, somewhat tongue-in-cheek. 'You are the great Dan Farson!' At this, his eyes moistened and he threw his huge arms around me, stating that I was probably the last person in the world who still knew who he was. I would have loved to talk to him about his East End days. But he then gestured to another stumbler alongside him.

199

'But do you realise,' he announced grandly, 'that you are also are in the presence of the world's greatest living artist?' He directed me towards his companion. 'Of course I know who you are,' I said. 'Francis Bacon'. The somewhat dishevelled artist pointed his finger at me. 'And I know who *you* are too!' he stated, in an accusatory manner, 'You're one of those kids off of *Grange Hill*!' He was wrong, of course (but ever since then I've been searching for biographical works which shed light on Bacon's hitherto unknown enthusiasm for the long-running teatime drama about the goings on at a fictional comprehensive school). The encounter was pretty much over after that. I never got around to asking Dan Farson about Cable Street.

## 'Cablestrasse'

To end this section on a positive note.

The trajectory of George Foulser's life, although remarkable, is not unique. He was born in 1920, died in 1975. That he was from a family of dockers, went to sea as a sixteen-year old on a sailing barge, that he became a member of the Communist Party, became a writer, stoked the boiler in Poplar Hospital, became a squatter and, from the late sixties on, distributed an irregular, hastily-stapled journal of his observations and ramblings entitled *The East London Speed Freak*, all makes him difficult to pigeonhole. But this join-the-dots sort of biography will be familiar to many. We've all known one. A working class drifter constantly trawling for ideas and ideologies that he was perhaps never wholly convinced of, infuriating fellow crew members when he inevitably jumped ship. He was one of those people who never managed to fit in anywhere because he was always somewhere else at the time.

Cablestrasse. *Cablestrasse.* CABLESTRASSE. The word has a ring to it, doesn't it? Certain associations. Pictures form in our heads. In his 1960 *Observer* article of that title, George Foulser claims it to be the local nickname for Cable Street, although it's possible that he was the only one who ever used it. It reads as a war chronicle, a frontline dispatch, a description of landscape so transformed by myriad battles and upheavals so as to be almost unrecognisable to former inhabitants. He states: 'Almost all the tailors have cleared out,' by which I take to mean the Jewish population, and goes on to report: 'Their shops have become cafés, many of which cater for a particular race, forming a part of present-day Cablestrasse and helping to create the new atmosphere of the district.' Comparisons are made with Tiger Bay in Cardiff; the 'exotic new blood' injected into post-war Cable Street is celebrated: 'Cablestrasse folk are different races, outlooks, upbringing, religion, occupation and so on. Yet they mix socially as Cablestrasse citizens, with every man amiably disposed towards his neighbour.' That George finds heaven where the likes of Father Joseph Williamson and Edith Ramsay found only hell might be questioned in the light of Foulser's anecdotes:

> There is a team of men, once seamen but now all drinkers of methylated and surgical spirits, in the Cablestrasse area. Some time ago, they solved their housing problem by a pretty unorthodox squatting situation. They entered a derelict churchyard a few hundred yards from Cablestrasse and established squatters' rights in a vault. They tidied the place up by slinging a couple of worm-eaten coffins into the grassy undergrowth outside the vault. Inside five minutes they were settled in, and their house-warming party was in full blast.

With all this sort of thing going on, it seems doubtful that many of the other Cable Street inhabitants, new or otherwise, would have shared George's vision of an anarchic utopia. After all, he goes to great lengths to tell us about the 'decent ... coloured ex-seamen and their families.' He states: 'Indeed, the sight of such a family, clean and smartly dressed going out on a Sunday excursion, makes

201

the other side of life in Cablestrasse look tawdry and cheap.' Their main vice was gambling. One of the 'spielers' (a Yiddish word for a place where cards are played) that he frequented 'was quite an elaborate one, a two-roomed effort. The front room had a bar, selling tea, coffee, and booze, and it had a juke-box. The first time I entered that place I was with my mate, and I enquired naively what the rattling sound was in the next room. He answered, "That ain't church bells, man!" It was, in fact, the sound of dice being rattled in a cup.' George Foulser was in the forefront of writers who sponsored the rapidly developing mixed-race environment as something to be wholly encouraged. He finishes his article with the raised-fist declaration: 'Long live Cablestrasse!'

# 8. East of Watney Market
## Cable Street Generations

## Alexander Gander

'Five generations of my family lived and worked in Cable Street, and the London and Katherine Docks,' so began one account that was sent in response to the Cable Street Group's appeal for people's memories. Alexander Gander, living in Ruislip at the time of writing to us in late 1988, said in his covering letter: 'Enclosed are my notes on Cable Street and I hope that they will be useful to your group. You may find a mistake or two, but it is difficult to concentrate and to think when the TV or radio is on in the next room.' Mister Gander was one of the few non-Jewish people to respond to the group's initial invitation. His letter mainly concerns the shops, houses, businesses, people and pubs, beginning at the very eastern end of the street: that section barely mentioned by many of the other interviewees. Culturally and geographically, the area was closer to Wapping. He refers to, 'the Irish bands, one from St. Patrick's Church, Wapping, and the other from St. Mary and Michael, Commercial Road. There would be bagpipes and flutes, side drums and a big bass drum and they would puff and blow and practice for the East London Catholic processions and other functions. They all looked smart in their kilts and tam-o'-shanters coloured in green.'

## Childhood in Cable Street

The beginning of Alexander Gander's letter sets the tone for the level of detail that he was able to recall over more than half a century.

'For seventy years my family lived at the crossroads of Glamis Road, and Hardinge Street, and our local milkman

Mr. Warren who kept his cows under the railway arches at the back and also in a brick shed on the old Shadwell Fish Market. Next door to my house was a pub, the Hastings Arms, and on the other side a butcher's shop and another pub, the Bricklayers Arms, owned by a Mr. Pfeffer and a Mr. Siemen, both were of German origin like many descendents of the old German sugar boilers in the district.' He went on to say, 'I remember during the 1914-18 war when a lady opposite got the news that her eighteen-year-old son had been killed in action, she crossed the road with a house-brick in each hand and threw one at each window smashing the large plate glass to pieces. At that time there was great animosity shown to anyone with a German sounding name. Mr. Pfeffer was a very kind man and used to give credit to the poor people and sometimes he would cut a bill if they were ill.'

Elsewhere in his letter, Alexander Gander, wrote about a family business that still operates in East London, although no longer based in Cable Street:

*Opposite St Mary's Church was A. Tadman the undertakers, the business was founded in 1860 and young Alf was the third generation. His father, old Alf, was a very smart man who conducted his work very well indeed, but young Alf surpassed his father. With his shiny top hat, tails and white gloves, he carried a baton under his arm as the cortege passed slowly through the narrow streets of the district. Alf was known to have a good sense of humour, although he was compassionate, and when passing the sympathisers at the funeral they would give him a nod of recognition. To some he knew well, in a quiet few words from the side of his mouth, Alf would say: 'You don't look too well Tom', or: 'You're next Dick.' Alf had many nasty experiences when burying local prostitutes and he always insisted on the pimps paying before the burial. Some made excuses, but Alf made them go and borrow the money from their friends before he would take the coffin to the hearse. When he was paid, Alf would pass the cash to his coachman because on several occasions when he returned to the house for his tools and trestles, he would be 'turned over' on the stairs by the pimps trying to get the cash back.*

Alexander Gander's letter was handwritten on lined paper. His only request was that a typed version be returned to him so that he could share it with others. Jil Cove duly typed it up and Mr Gander expressed his delight at the result. In another of his letters he told us, 'I left Broad Street School in the Ratcliff Highway in 1924 at the age of fourteen having learnt very little grammar in my class of fifty-two boys, but I must say that the clerical work done by the docker-checkers was far better and legible than that of the modern lads, so we must have learnt a little to be of use to the employers'.

# George Jones

George Jones, whose father had worked at Wapping Gas Works, sent the Group a letter in 1989 from his Oxted home. Like Alexander Gander, his memories concentrated on the eastern end of the street and went back to the very early years of the twentieth century. During his childhood, all the lorries and carts travelling to and from the docks were non-motorised. The arrival of 'steam wagons' in the 1920s carried with them a sense of wonder: 'Those early giants of the road often interrupted our evening cricket and football in Cable Street. These were something novel for we youngsters to see, with their boilers up front and red hot cinder trays underneath the funnel emitting smoke above the driver and his mate. We related them to the steam trains which had possibly escaped from the railway lines.' He wrote of his family:

> *From the late 1800s, number 328 had housed my grandparents, our family joining them there about 1903, the inmates then numbering nine. By 1918 inmates numbered fourteen including the writer born on the premises in 1915. The six-roomed house had no bathroom and our only natural relief was obtained in the backyard toilet some eight yards walk in the open air from our back door.*

*All our neighbours were similarly placed and in retro-spect one wonders how the standard of respectability was maintained in such congested community, and yet it was to a high degree. Our landlords were The Mercers Company (Estates) whose offices were near Arbour Square, Stepney.*

As indicated, for those at the eastern end of Cable Street, it became apparent that their area of activity, and alle-giance, tended to be towards the Highway and Wapping. They might have been residents of the same, long, stretch of road but there was little contact with those west of Watney Market. The King Edward Memorial Park on the Highway was a shared resource however. George Jones' account highlights its importance.

*My parents, myself with a coloured waver, and younger sister in a pram stood on the pavement outside St. Paul's Church to witness and cheer King George V and Queen Mary as they drove past in a horse drawn open landau when they opened the King Edward Memorial Park. Unfettered loyalty being the atmosphere of that east end event some sixty-seven years ago, the Royal Party were accompanied by very few soldiers and a sprinkling of police. The 'New Park' was laid out on a derelict riverside open space. Pre 1921 football matches were played there, also some casual marketing took place. My elder brothers and sisters recall that small boats carrying fresh fish, sold their catches from the shore there to local people, including my family and neighbours. The 'New Park' proved to be an absolute bonus to the whole community and its planning was of the highest order, using the con-tours of levels and slopes down from The Highway to that new excellent promenade by the riverside amply provided with many bench seats and popular with senior citizens. Seen from the upper levels the huge vista of the then very busy Thames was an ever changing kaleidoscope of colour and activity, of wharves and cranes and ships from all nations.*

A final extract from George Jones' letter adds a surreal touch to Cable Street life.

*In Sage Street there was a business with warehouse buildings owned by Deppe's. Its nearness to the docks was necessary for they imported animals from abroad for zoos and other requirements. They covered the whole range and virtually all their imports passed our front door. Caged lions and tigers might sound off in passing to indicate their presence, but elephants, giraffes and llamas and the like were invariably on foot. One remembers only one escape, that of a monkey which provided the locals with great amusement. It was a fine summer's evening. The monkey had somehow crossed to the north side of Cable Street and was seen traversing the roofs opposite Twine Court and Sage Street. Policemen and others on high ladders tried to entice the monkey in to capture, all to no avail. The animal simply moved on to the next roof. We last saw it on the high roof of Kendrick's the Pawnbrokers whose shop was on the corner of Dean Street. We never knew the end of that story, it happening after dark. In 1925, a shipment of small tortoises which must have numbered thousands failed to find a market. They were sold off direct to children and parents for a penny or 'tuppence' each. Overnight the pavements were occupied by children taking their tortoises for a walk. Many neglected tortoises finished in the gutter, run over by cartwheels. They appeared under desks at school and at playtime, pretend races were arranged in the playground. Our three tortoises survived for many years living in our backyard and sleeping in a shed.*

Most of the buildings mentioned in Alexander Gander's and George Jones' letter are now gone. But there are those still living in the area who remember them. Some of those streets are now beneath the Cable Street Community Gardens, which I visited in the summer of 2010.

# A Day In The Gardens

## Jane Sill

What is it about the sight of an allotment glimpsed from the window of a speeding train that lifts the heart? Above the Cable Street Community Gardens, the Docklands Light Railway daily transports suited businessmen between the City and Canary Wharf. At least, I'm assuming they feel the same as me when they gaze down at this sizable patchwork quilt of greens and browns. Or are they just curious as to the purpose of this field of sheds and greenhouses, here and there dotted with ad-hoc seating and makeshift fencing to mark the different plots?

I had long been aware of the gardens but had not actually walked through the gate until making an appointment, which fortuitously fell on an exceptionally fine summer's day. When I first encountered Jane Sill, she had little time to talk. She was busy guiding in a load of topsoil, massive bagfuls of it that a lorry driver was dropping inside the perimeter fence from the claw of a small crane. After I had finished being roped into that job, Jane brushed the dirt from her hands and showed me some early minutes of the group that came to run the gardens. I turned on my recorder and we started to talk. Jane rarely speaks above a whisper, sometimes barely audible above the background sounds of trains and birdsong, but is effusive about her passion for the gardens and full of praise for those organisations and individuals who have supplied support and funding for it along the way.

One day in the late 1970s when Jane gazed down from the window of her top floor flat off Cable Street, without so much as a balcony, she must have had the same realisation that I did in similar circumstances: that tower block dwellers are always looking down. Horizontal living was the luxury of those who now occupied the refurbished houses of the displaced workers, or those who had served something akin to a lengthy prison sentence on the council waiting list. And, if they were *very* lucky, they might even have been rewarded with a garden. Up in the sky, it's possible to spend a whole day inside without once sniffing fresh air or placing the soles of your feet on anything like solid ground — let along breaking soil between your fingers. Unlike me however, moping about in my cell in the sky, scraping out the contents of the fridge for food, Jane made her mind up to get out there and do something about it. At a local festival, she approached a stall displaying information about the site, put her name on a waiting list for a plot and 'kept pestering' until, in 1981, she finally got one. A Liverpudlian by birth ('I lived there for the first two years of my life and then later in Birkenhead, the "One Eyed City" across the Mersey'), she came from a green-fingered family, helping her grandfather on his immaculate plot. She told me:

*Friends of the Earth had the site on a lease from the Greater London Council. The first people here in 1977 were keen environmentalists. Only a small portion of the site was used at first. They spent hours clearing away rubble and digging through the foundations of old houses. It was an informal group with people tending their own plots. There was no constitution — they didn't even have a name — and by the time I joined, many of the originals had already moved on. The gardens at that point were surrounded by a temporary corrugated iron fence. We managed, through The Environment Trust and Community Land Use to cut through lots of red tape; the GLC were handing the land over to what was then Wapping Neighbourhood and British Rail were handing over part of it to the DLR, so we had four landlords! It took about two or three years before we were finally awarded a substantial grant from Wapping Neighbourhood. We used that to fence the whole area and bring in a digger to clear the remainder of the site. We brought in good quality topsoil at considerable expense and also a tank for water. We were going to be called Cable Street Allotments but it was suggested that we adopted the name 'Community Gardens'. It was easier to get the lease because at that time allotments tended to bring in a lot of strict rules and regulations — and in some ways it reflected more what we do.*

*Some of the people who came here had never gardened before. We had our first meeting in 1982 in the old church hall. It was cold and the damp used to rise through your feet. We leafleted every flat in the area but people didn't really want to know until we had put the fence up and the top-soil arrived and they could see the produce coming out. We've had a waiting list ever since; there are about a hundred people on it. The first list had a lot of Irish people on it. And Scottish and Welsh. All Celts. I used to work with people who were long-term unemployed. People used to come into the Watney Market office for a job and also ask if they could put their name down on the garden waiting list. They thought it was all part and parcel! I became a sort of secretary and have helped facilitate the grants and do all the paperwork ever since. It's been important to have that continuity. Over the years we've got the greenhouse, the shed, concrete for the paths and water access. In 1984, after lengthy negotiations, we extended the Gardens to the north side of the arches, doubling our size. The plots were filled immediately. So from a small group of barely a dozen people we became a thriving community of well over a hundred, including family members and friends.*

*The Gardens are as important for wildlife as growing. Because we have been strictly organic for over thirty years there is an incredible diversity of birds, butterflies and insects. We have a number of small ponds with frogs, toads and newts. We also have bat and bird boxes and are about to begin beekeeping. Over the years we've made things more comfortable, mainly thanks to generous grants from St Katharine's Trust. We now have meeting sheds, concrete paths, compost bins and — at long last — an eco loo! We waited fifteen years for this. It was essential as because of all the building going up around us the girls couldn't disappear into the buddleia anymore. To help accommodate what is now a five-year plus waiting list we got funding for some raised wooden planters to put in an area where there's no depth of soil. The soil that you saw coming in this morning is to fill them.*

*If you look at the names in the minutes book here you can see the Irish names. But now we've got Japanese names, Malaysian, West Indian, Maltese, South Korean, and we've just got our first Eastern European lady from Lithuania. We've got quite a lot of Sylheti people — who are really good gardeners. Unlike many allotment groups we have many women members, also a number of elderly plot-holders, our oldest being eighty-six — still doing all his own digging and planting.*

# A Little Oasis

Over the years, the gardens have provided a little oasis amongst the concrete for a wide variety of people: a photographer who had worked in the Bollywood film industry; an accountant turned plumber, builders, nursery school workers, nuns from the local church, an archaeologist, a librarian, teachers, cleaners, artists, poets and a former boilerhouse stoker in a London hospital. In other words, the usual Tower Hamlets mix. Jane says, 'There was an elderly couple who had a grandson who was hyperactive. They lived in a tower block so they used to tire him out here. Their plot was just a little patch of grass and some flowers. There are as many different motives for being here as there are plots — a hobby, a break from the daily grind, a method of feeding the family.'

Although you will find flowers here: geraniums, roses, bluebells, poppies, lavenders, foxgloves, delphiniums, fuchsias, marigolds, 'big flashy dahlias' and even a cherry tree, most of the gardeners are rearing vegetables in their patches — some of which would have been unknown in the country only a generation ago. There are: carrots, tomatoes, sweet peas, broad beans, runner beans, kidney beans, rhubarb, leeks, chicory, wild rocket, radishes, asparagus, cauliflower, kale, artichokes, pumpkins, Brussels sprouts, plantain, courgettes, sweetcorn, peppers, spinach, parsnips, beetroot, sprouting broccoli and

climbing purple beans. People are growing lettuces, rasp-
berries, strawberries and blackcurrants and there is a
steady stream of onions, garlic and herbs. Jane observed,
'You've got the benefit of looking around and seeing what
other people are growing. What's funny is that a lot of
Sylheti people are growing more Irish things like cab-
bages and spuds and the Irish people are growing
coriander.' Jane told me about the various groups that
they have become affiliated to; they have even taken part
in the Chelsea Flower Show. And they have attracted
substantial media interest. 'Recently, a film for South
Korean television featured students on a UK visit. They
couldn't believe that Korean vegetables were being grown
in the middle of London!' At the end of the interview,
before I pressed the 'off' button, Jane pointed to my
recorder and said, 'It's a pity that you can't record the
smell of the garden on that thing as well.'

Perhaps it was the heat of the day or the butterflies
fluttering around my head, but in a moment of reverie I
began to think of Cable Street as a long snake. And if I
imagine its snarling mouth to be the Leman Street end,
with its history of prostitution and music hall, and its
twitching tail being the edgy artists studios at the
Butcher Row end, defending their territory against the
encroachment of the Canary Wharf colonialists, then I
fantasise that I have found in the Cable Street Gardens
its satisfied stomach. But I am shortly to be brought back
down to earth by an alternate tour of the site by someone
who remembers the area long before the gardens came
into being. The story of what lies beneath.

## Ray Newton

Ray Newton has a plot in the Gardens. And he was there
on the day I spoke to Jane Sill. Ray is best known locally
for digging around in a different way. He is the secretary
of the History of Wapping Trust, which over the years has

produced a steady stream of local books and postcards. They must be one of the few small independent publishers which doesn't spend the majority of their time and energy chasing grants from funding agencies. When they have the money, they publish. When they don't, they don't. They are beholden to no one except their readers. Ray tells me that they are in the final stages of the rewrite and reprint of perhaps their most successful publication, *Waeppa's People*, by Madge Darby. The group hosts a number of lectures and presentations throughout the year. Ray specialises in history walks, steering interested parties through the locale, managing to point out the most astounding things that you have never noticed before, despite walking past them every day for decades.

Ray was the only person who I was cautious about meeting while writing this book. I had put off contacting him time after time. This is because I had always associated him with the proper stuff of history, carefully sifting through ancient documents and maps and digging out those little known facts that make the History of Wapping books so engrossing, at the same time being a first-hand witness to decades of turbulent East London life — while I seem to plough quite a different field, chasing unverifiable memory and keeping an ear to the ground for rumour and gossip. I didn't know what he'd make of me. Ray immediately put me at ease however and as the day progressed he proved generous with both his time and the sharing of his vast knowledge of the locality. He is modest in talking about this lifetime accumulation. His father had chucked in his job as a docker and bought a pub and he says it was here, as a child, listening to the boozers' tales, that he ingested the history of the area.

Standing outside the Gardens on Cable Street, Ray cast an expansive hand around the immediate area. 'This,' he told me, 'was a little village.' As with others I have encountered on this journey he probably thinks — but is too polite to say so — that my Cable Street project

*Ray Newton on his plot*

is built on an artificial construct. The street was home to the many communities that lived along it but they didn't necessarily interact, or even show much awareness of each other. Ray took me on a tour:

> *I was born in a tenement on this site, Roslyn House, in March, 1938. This little area is a part of Shadwell. You knew everybody and most people worked locally. My dad was a docker and his father was a docker and my mum's family were lightermen, so I was brought up with the river. In this little area you either worked in the docks or you were a carman or you worked in a factory or something. All of the tenements were owned by the Bowes-Lyon family — the old Queen Mother's family. They owned all the land around here. There was a pub called the Red Lion next door to us and you had all the shops you wanted.*

By this time, Ray is pointing this way and that, identifying features of the lost landscape without any hesitation. 'You had a grocery shop, you had a butchers, you had a café and on this side you had a fish and chip shop. You had a bakers, a chimney sweep down the bottom and then you had a barbers here. Looking that way you had a greengrocers and a wet fish shop. And over on that side you had a sweetshop — Mrs Vernie's — and then next door to her you had another greengrocers and, of course, loads of pubs. Umpteen pubs. And then along Cable Street here was Warman's, the dairy, where I would be sent by my mother with a jug with a piece of muslin on top to get a pint of milk which they'd bring out of a churn. They had their own cows which they kept in stables in Glasshouse Fields.'

My head had begun to spin by this point. But it all underlines Ray's philosophy. He is emphatic, 'You can only understand the East End in terms of little villages. Further up was another little village with their own shops. The only thing we didn't have here was a post office. We had to walk up to one near King David Lane.' King David Lane is a stone's throw away. But such was the village's self-sufficiency that a trip to Watney Market, another few hundred yards down the road, was seen as something of an event. Interestingly, the Jewish interviewees that I had spoken also saw Watney Market — which they would have approached from the opposite end of the street — in a similar way. A no man's land. A neutral space for the opposing tribes. A border which should not be crossed because beyond here be dragons:

> When my mum wanted a speciality she would go to Watney Market. She would be there for hours talking to people. She'd meet Mrs Jones or Mrs Smith and they'd chat away. She might have gone there for some pots and pans or some material. But your everyday shopping was done here in this little area. If my mum wanted something like my dad's eels, I'd have to go to the fishmonger and get two eels. They'd get the live eels out of a dish and chop them up into pieces. They were still alive and wriggling in the paper as I carried them back home.

Ray is a man who wherever you bumped into him on the globe couldn't be mistaken for anything other than a born and bred East Ender. An insider. Several times in our wander round the streets of his childhood we were interrupted by any number of long-time residents who look just like Ray. White, stocky, grey-haired men who wanted to know the identity of the guy with the recorder — quickly sizing me up before throwing in their own tuppenceworth — then striking out on unspecified missions to the garage under the arches or the housing office. It reinforces Ray's concept of the place. There was a strong family network, supportive neighbours and a network of school friends who became work friends who became adult friends. Ray continued:

> *I didn't go to work the docks. In the 1950s my dad bought a pub in the Highway called the Cock. Most of the dockers and lightermen who used it had been in the First World War and lots of them in the Second World War. They were very interesting people. That's where I learnt all my local history. I did loads and loads of jobs but when my dad died, I became a publican at twenty-three years old. I did that for over eight years. The pub was demolished when the Highway was widened. Then my brother who had a betting shop asked me to be a manager. I did that but thought, well, I don't want to do this for the rest of my life. So I went to university and got a degree. I was about thirty-six, I suppose. I did teacher training and went to West Ham College teaching sixteen to nineteen year olds. I then went into adult education teaching computing and maths.*

## What Lies Beneath

Now, having toured the outside perimeter, my head still reeling with all the long-gone pubs, houses and shops that Ray is able to locate to within an inch of pavement, we re-entered the Gardens. And, for me, this was the most engrossing part of Ray's tour. It is as if he has a form of X-Ray vision, searing through the allotments, the piles of manure and paving, to the outline of the streets below.

'This very narrow track which goes right the way through into the allotments was Drewton Street. This was the worst street in the area — not the people — but the conditions. It was a very narrow street with no pavements. The arches were full of rags. The merchants would collect it all up and they would sell it on for people to make paper out of it. But where you got rags you got rats.' And so on. If Ray had a big enough sheet of tracing paper, I'm sure he could lay it down over the gardens and sketch out the location of the vanished streets. 'Under each of these allotments there is a home. Under my own allotment I've only got about eighteen inches of soil because of the cellars, or what we called the "aireys". When they pulled the houses down they filled them up with rubble. So I reckon in about a hundred years time when they excavate here they'll find stuff down there from the 1950s.'

One of the recurring themes in Ray's banter is his deep regret that so many of the old buildings and houses of his childhood have gone, their destruction as much down to 1960s council ideology as Hitler's bombs. The fact that those few that remain are inhabited and in good condition would seem to prove that the bulldozing of so many streets was unnecessary. Towards the end of my tour, we pondered various issues including the young people of today, and Ray has some thoughtful observations:

> When you were a young boy around here, if you behaved yourself and you weren't too cheeky, all the men liked you and they would take you around their factories. Off Cable Street in Glasshouse Fields there have been glass manufacturers for hundreds of years. In the factory there, T.W. Ide's, I'd be taken in by the night watchman and be shown all the glass being bent and all the lovely stained-glass and everything. But if you were saucy, you didn't get it. I think that the trouble with children today is that they've lost that connection with men, with adults.

It is only at the end of our wander that I discover my initial wariness had not been misplaced after all, and I realised how lucky I had been to be granted an interview. Ray usually refuses them. He is sick to the teeth of people wanting to talk about how poor it all was, how rough it all was. And although poverty and violence feature in the Cable Street story it is by no means the whole story. As a young man, Ray had his pick of jobs, all within walking distance of his home. He fondly recalled that one of his brothers had three in one day. 'He had a job that started at eight in the morning but he packed it up at the morning break because he didn't like it. He went out and found another job and packed that up at lunchtime and found another job in the afternoon. There was plenty of work.'

I left, exhausted by the weight of information. But also exhilarated by both my encounters. Earlier in the day, Jane had talked glowingly of Ray, about how he really is a walking encyclopaedia of the area. I can only agree with her. If there is anybody who should get it all down in a book, it's Ray.

# 9. Extreme Ends
# Wilton's Music Hall

## Frances Mayhew

Cable Street is book-ended by two large buildings, both labyrinthine in structure and which, from their outward appearance, give the casual passer-by no real idea of the myriad of activities which occur within. The entrance to Wilton's Music Hall is unexpectedly modest, a decorative surround on the doorframe being the only indication of a gaudy past. It is tucked away in Grace's Alley, a slim back-street by Wellclose Square at the western end of Cable Street. Wilton's is a grade II listed building and said to be the oldest surviving grand music hall in the world.

When the Cable Street Group undertook its series of interviews with the mainly Jewish people who had lived in the surrounding streets, Wilton's seemed to have little place in their consciousness. But that's not totally surprising. During the period that they lived in the area, the

Photograph James Perry

hall had long ceased to be a place of entertainment and had been taken over and used by the Methodist East End Mission. There were some recollections however. Gertrude Cass spoke about the magic lantern slide shows: 'They used to put up a sheet and turn the light off. They showed us things about drunken fathers coming home after spending all their money in the pubs and how we shouldn't go that way.' And Gerald Broer told us how he used to bunk over a fence that had been erected around it because there was 'a special tree there that was always full of caterpillars and we used to take our match-boxes and shove a leaf in and fill it up with caterpillars', only to be chased out again by the 'monks'. Interestingly, the much older Prince of Denmark pub that was the hall's beginnings, more famously known as the Mahogany Bar, has under that name become embedded in the local psyche. I have heard it referred to by people who couldn't possibly have remembered the place when it was open.

I went to talk to the current Managing Director, Frances Mayhew, amongst the magnificent decrepitude of present day Wilton's. She first stumbled across the building in 1997 as a student, working as an intern for Broomhill Opera. They had read a review of a performance of T.S. Elliot's poem, *The Waste Land,* directed by Deborah Warner and performed by Fiona Shaw; and enthused by the description of the building, arrived as a mob to stake the place out. Frances says:

> *It was completely boarded-up, covered in chipboard and scaffed together. We came in through the window and had a look around and it was amazing. Everyone fell in love with it. It was essentially derelict; most of the original features had been ripped out and looted generations ago, but it was being rented occasionally for photoshoots and the odd performance. The opera company managed to take the building over but ran into financial difficulties. I came back about six years ago under the new Wilton's Music Hall Trust, saw the electrics being put in and got its first proper license since about 1880. The original pub was called the Prince of Denmark because of the Danish*

*community that resided here then, but it became known
as the Mahogany Bar because of the wood in it, which
was a big deal at the time. When John Wilton came here
in the 1850s it already had a little music hall attached
and over a period of eight years he bought up the four
adjoining terraced houses with a vision to build a new
hall in the back yards. He knocked through the houses
sideways, leftways, upways, downways until it became
this beautiful honeycombed building. You can get quite
lost in it. The auditorium itself was begun in December
1858. It took four months to build and opened for the
public in March 1859. It ran as a music hall until 1880.
It was sold several times during its life. It was very big for
an early music hall and very glamorous.*

In its heyday, Wilton's contained a mirror-covered wall,
raked seating — with an elegant gallery above — looking
towards a high stage with a proscenium arch; all of it
overseen by a 'sun-burner' chandelier consisting of three-
hundred gas jets and 27,000 cut crystals. 'All gone —
well, most of it,' Frances sighs. But the distinctive 'barley
sugar' cast-iron pillars remain, making the hall easily
identifiable as a location in Richard Attenborough's film,
*Chaplin* and the television adaptation of Sarah Waters'
*Tipping the Velvet.* Tom Cruise also came here for his
*Interview With the Vampire.* Almost inevitably an adaptation of *The Picture of Dorian Gray* put the building to
use, as have the makers of any number of pop videos, the
most appropriate being that for the Annie Lennox song,
*No More "I Love You's",* in the 1980s. Most appropriate
because the hall where it is said that the Can-Can was
first performed in Britain — and promptly banned — was
used in the video to create a Moulin Rouge type atmosphere.

Back in its music hall days, Wilton's was the launching
pad for George Leybourne's song, *Champagne Charlie.*
Leybourne's adopted persona as a moustachioed, top-
hatted, well-dressed 'swell' saw him performing the song
on stage whilst making his way through a bottle of Moët
& Chandon. It's an image that seems to be burned into

our collective consciousness, visual shorthand for the elegant but racy style that we associate with music hall. Or, at least, the way we would have liked it to be.

## 'If you can't beat them, buy them'

The building was sold in 1880, where Frances takes up the story:

> *I suppose the landlord would have thought another landlord would buy it but actually the local Methodist Mission moved in. Even before they bought the place there are accounts of them annoying the music hall customers by coming in during the evening and banging their tambourines to warn people about the evils of drink. So they'd obviously had their eye on the place. Once they took over they called themselves The Old Mahogany Bar Mission and at one point The Prince of Denmark Methodist Mission. I know that because I found some china under the floorboard with that printed on it. During the Docker's Strike of 1889, they provided meals for literally thousands of strikers and their families. And they were here until they were forced to move out in 1956, after which it became a sorting house for rags.*

There is some evidence for Frances's assertion that the Methodists had been stalking the hall. A policy of 'If you can't beat them, buy them'. During their research, the Cable Street Group received a letter from a Mrs Shaw, then living in Arbroath, who recalled her work with the Mission. The story had come down to her about how they had also taken possession of 'Paddy's Goose' on the nearby Ratcliff Highway, 'a most notorious pub', where, it is claimed: 'One of our deaconesses knew the police officer who had to shadow the Prince of Wales (Edward VII) when he visited to watch women boxers stripped to the waist!' At Wilton's, she remembered first-hand that: 'Round the walls were some well executed murals but they were so obscene they had to be painted over. There was also a trapdoor that led into a muddy passage that went down to the river — When the sailors came ashore they, often with many months' wages, were made drunk, robbed of everything often including their clothes and then dropped through the trap door — often to lose their lives in the river. I was shown the trap door — well nailed up.' Hard now to separate myth from reality in Wilton's long history. Frances Mayhew is aware of the legends surrounding the building. But it reveals its secrets gradually — parts are still largely unexplored — and they have only recently discovered that a trapdoor in the auditorium opens on to one of the earliest forms of underground heating systems.

The poet and heritage-vigilante John Betjeman was one of those who campaigned to save Wilton's from demolition in the early 1960s. Since then it has passed through the hands of a variety of organisations, complete with celebrity endorsements, all keen to renovate and revive the building, some of them almost accidentally knocking it down in the process. After Frances' arrival, new plans and funding bids were made to keep the building going. There are concerts, theatre productions, film shows and projects conducted with local schools. Sitting in one of the rooms with its exposed brickwork and makeshift furnishings, Frances takes me by surprise when she tells me that the Trust's desire is to *not* leave their mark on the place. Any idea of a complete renovation isn't on the agenda. Or perhaps even desirable. 'The building is subsiding and it's all held up with acro-props. The bar is open but because the building is so fragile I don't think we could handle being super-popular at the moment. There's something nice about this area in that you can find little hidden gems; you stumble across a bit of history that you wouldn't see. And, in a way, we'd like to keep that. When people do come here they have quite a personal reaction. They get a feeling or an atmosphere or a vibe. And that's quite precious. We'd hate them not to feel that. They feel they've made a bit of a discovery and walked into a time warp.'

I leave Wellclose Square and Wilton's to walk the length of Cable Street for the last time: for the purpose of this book anyway. I have an appointment at the other end. As I make my way, however, I realise that although I have returned time and time again to this end of the street, I have not mentioned Sly House. It goes against my original intention of only writing about happenings within the living memory of the interviewees. But I won't deny you an account by George Simms, which he put on record exactly one hundred years before the publication of the book you are holding.

# The Old Court House

## George Sims

George Sims was born in 1847, the son of a successful cabinet manufacturer. This much-married Londoner was a gambler, a connoisseur of food and drink, a sportsman, a race-goer, a breeder of bulldogs and, for a brief period, a Jack the Ripper suspect. And it gets better. The stately, bearded Victorian was a writer of detective novels, a playwright, a translator of Balzac, a radical journalist and campaigner for social reform. He was the author of *Christmas Day in the Workhouse*, that much-mocked, much-parodied poem, thought to have been set in Poplar Workhouse. That he invented a quack cure for baldness and through bouts of charity and heavy gambling managed to dispense with most of his fortune before he died in 1922, gives us a picture of a man with boundless energy.

I have brought George Sims to your attention here due to his contribution to *Off the Track in London*, published by Jarrold & Sons in 1911, where, on foot, coming from the direction of Ratcliff Highway, he enters Cable Street, '...one end of which is Jewish and the other Irish, while the middle may be said to be English.' Along the way he makes comparisons between the communities, unfavourable to the Irish in relation to their 'barefooted, ragged, capless' children. All the Jewish children, it seems, are well-shod despite them having 'not been long in our land of liberty.' His observations extend to the women's coiffure. The Irish women are hatless with curling pins in their hair while, 'The young alien Jewess dresses her hair very much as the working-girl of Paris does. It is neatly and artistically arranged, and it frequently boasts an ornamental comb, which, though cheap, is effective and picturesque.' Sims eventually leads us to Wellclose Square and the King's Arms in Neptune Street where he visits the defunct cells of what were once The Old Court House, and supplies us with yet another tantalising tale of secret tunnels.

*Hidden away from the passing throng, unknown, I imagine, to the majority of Londoners, there are the cells and the plank beds — aye, even the fetters and the strait jackets of the days when the poor prisoner was poor indeed, the cells in which, some of the Peninsular prisoners pined, and where many a famous felon languished. The landlord of the house is amiable, and permits us to see the grim remains of a bygone day and an obsolete prison system. He takes his keys, and we pass through a side door into a hall. From the hall a fine old staircase leads to the court-house. But the cells are below. We pass down a narrow, dark stairway, through a brick kitchen, and across a paved yard, and presently we are in the cells. Here they are, as they were two hundred years ago. The door has to be unlocked with heavy keys, the massive bolts have to be unshot, and thick, black, forbidding doors have to be forced back upon their hinges before we can enter the dungeons. The old prison was known as the Sly House, because people who were seen to enter it were rarely seen coming out again. There was a subterranean passage that led from this prison to the Tower, and to the docks; and it was along this subterranean way that prisoners passed on their way to the 'Success', the famous convict ship. Standing in one of the cells with its plank bed, the heavy fetters stapled to the wall, the grating of the little window closed, and the candle lighted, we people the dismal dungeon with forms that have long passed away. Many of the prisoners handed their names down to posterity by carving them on the woodwork.*

George Sims quotes a rhyme he found inscribed there, indicative of the fact that many of those held there were debtors: 'The cupboard is empty — To our sorrow; / Let's hope it will / be full to-morrow'. On demolition, one of the cells was salvaged and is currently on display at the Museum of London. And it includes the deeply carved rhyme quoted above.

# The Cable Street Studios

## Saturday Night to Sunday Morning

The Cable Street Studios are at the far eastern tip of Cable Street just round the corner from where I currently live. A few years ago, on my regular Sunday morning visit to the newsagent, I was surprised to see so many young people up and about so early in the day.

It was only after a while that it dawned on me that they weren't up early — they were on the way home after being up all the previous night. I wondered where they could have been, the immediate area not (in my mind) being associated with the club scene. Then one morning I found out. I spotted a stream of people emerging through the gates of the large open yard in front of the studios, among them, several hive-topped drag queens in spiky stilettos blinking into the harsh light of the morning. Later on in the week, I dropped into Jamboree, a small bar housed in one of the units on the courtyard. There I watched a series of acoustic neo-punk bands playing to a small audience of their girlfriends and mates who sat around on a variety of battered chairs and sofas. The staff were welcoming and the atmosphere friendly. I found an echo of Wilton's here in the bare walls of the partially-decorated room; abstract artworks stared down at the clusters of tables, illuminated by a collection of incongruous Tiffany Lamps. But this was just one unit of many. What was happening in all the others? I needed to find out. My book wouldn't be complete without it.

# 'An East End Elysium'

In a previous life the studio building was a sweet factory called Batger & Co Ltd. The firm was established in 1748 in Bishopsgate but was obviously already well-established in Cable Street by 1887, because that was the year when, in *Every Girl's Annual*, Florence L. Henderson wrote an account of her visit there entitled: *An East End Elysium*. Florence would appear to have been a volunteer at the nearby 'Young Women's Help Society' who became curious about the working conditions of the cold and hungry girls who came there in the evenings to sup pea soup and practice their needlework. With an unnamed lady companion, she trudges through the pelting autumn rain, arriving at the gates of 'Batger's Metropolitan Confectionary Works', passing through the yard full of wagons, to be received by a fawning management. They are steered around the huge revolving cauldrons 'containing every sort of coloured almond' and bubbling rows of coppers and, in a variety of rooms off the courtyard, the preparations of a wide range of products. The account is highly detailed and slightly breathless, with the whole wide-eyed Willy Wonka experience slightly offset in a single paragraph towards the end. At certain times of the year there were as many as six hundred 'hands', male and female, toiling in the 'blinding atmosphere of odorous steam' of the works. One of them, who Florence recognises as one of her 'Help Society' girls, scampers up to ask the ladies, 'Do you like it. Ain't it nice?' Adding, 'For you at least, not for us.' Batger's is a name still recalled by older Cable Street residents (sometimes referred to as 'Badgers'). But over the years, like Wilton's, ownership of the building has passed through a number of hands via amalgamations and acquisitions; although locals still remember confectionery being manufactured there, certainly into the 1950s.

# Inside the Studios

Since I've lived in the immediate area, the huge, 88,000 square foot building has had the title and number 566 THAMES HOUSE emblazoned about half way up its tall central tower. Lower down, above the arch which opens onto the courtyard, there is a later addition: CABLE ST STUDIOS + GALLERY. On the inside wall of the arch are a number of battered tin letterboxes with the names of some of the inhabitants scrawled on them. Below them, on the cobble-stoned ground: the familiar urban phenomenon of piles of dumped telephone directories, obscenely bloated by rain seeping in through their corrupted plastic wrapping. The ground floor windows are protected by wire mesh and there are several smashed panes in the tall windows embedded in the redbrick above them. With loose wires dangling out of holes all the way up the walls, one gets the feeling that whatever's going on inside the building is far too interesting for anybody to care much how it looks from the outside. It is four storeys high, its sprawling shape hard to ascertain due to the structures that have been built up around it. At the very top is a green dome with a flagpole sticking out of it and around that, four red-painted, non-working, wrought-iron clock faces in various states of disrepair.

Unlike Wilton's, where Frances Mayhew provides a pleasant and media-friendly focus for the theatre and all its component parts, the Cable Street Studios does not have a representative at the beck and call of nuisances such as me. Various names and numbers were filtered to me along the line as possible contacts but mostly my calls went unanswered, and even those I got to talk to had moved out of the studio orbit by the time of my second call. Sometimes they would provide me with another name, which I would dutifully pursue only for the process to repeat itself all over again. Eventually, the fates must have taken pity on this human pass-the-parcel because I received a call from somebody called Brook Cronin.

# Brook Cronin

Although only in his late twenties, Brook Cronin is seen as something of a veteran at the Cable Street Studios. That's because of the high turnover of artists who've been through the place. Brook, originally from Devon, talked to me about that generation who were here in the 1980s as if they were people from a dark and distant age. My interview with him was conducted in the courtyard where he led me around the various, constantly evolving spaces. He said:

*I first came to this building in around 2003, to a big electronic music underground party. And apart from some of the artists and musicians still here from the 1980s there were just two clubs, a fetish club on the top floor and one for transvestites called Stunners, on the ground floor here. We were sitting down outside and we saw these men in women's clothing, and leather-clad businessmen on leads and we thought —* Wow, this is a crazy place! *Me and some friends who were working in design and art projects took over this large space here. At that point we weren't actually paying anything to the landlord. People were living here as well as working so every now and then we'd have to lock everything up and turn the lights off and hide when the owners came to look around. Eventually we started to rent studios properly and my friends started a nightclub here called Unit 7. We'd throw really amazing cutting-edge techno-music parties, not quite illegal but not quite fully legal either, using temporary events notices. We had capacity for a thousand people more or less — well, legally, six hundred and fifty. I started working with them about a year into the project and we started to make it a much more serious venture. We were interested in using profits to fund arts, design, interactive experimental technology, within the space. The studios really started filling up as well, a whole new batch of people renting and decorating and renovating. But the place was full of rubbish: there was a lot of heavy machinery left over from an old print studio and squatters had been chucking bags of rubbish out of the windows for ten years. Thirty-seven skips worth had to be taken out before we could get started. There had been a lot of pirate radio stations based here as well but they cracked down on that. When we were building computer networks, we'd be on the roof laying some new cables for the Internet and we'd meet Ofcom people up there looking at the old ones. We'd tell them what we were doing and they'd say, 'That's all right, we're tracing the pirate station'. It was a time of fascinating transition — we got a full venue license and we were running big events every week with big sponsorship deals. We had international DJs and people flying in from all over the world. Other clubs were using spaces but unfortunately one of them — their entrance was out on the street — had been getting more and more trouble until in the end somebody was shot and killed outside it.*

The incident that Brook referred to was the gunning down of a thirty-six year old man outside Club Red, in the summer of 2008. He was hit with up to six shots to the head and neck at around 3.45 in the morning. The event continues to be marked by that other modern urban phenomenon; a roadside memorial of wilted plastic-wrapped flowers taped to a lamppost. A twenty-nine year old man was later charged with the murder. Back to Brook:

*We'd run for three years and had 35,000 people through the doors. The police had only come to the venue once — and that was when we'd called them to get rid of a drug dealer that we'd kicked out of the place. But after the incident outside Club Red, the council came in and hit us with a stop notice and shut everything down. There were going to be no more big raves in Cable Street. We were always a private initiative because it's so hard to get funding without restraints. So this was a way to fund the artists who wanted to work in the building. As you can see, what was our nightclub is now divided up into a mosque and a children's jungle gym. I would say that there are about a hundred and fifty studios here across four floors including the ground floors. These are all of varying sizes and shapes: some shoeboxes and some really beautiful studios with original parquet flooring and metalwork. The building is a real labyrinth inside. It's easy to get lost up there — you're never really sure what you're going to find. When people moved in here there were very few amenities, so everybody's made their own showers, toilets and bathrooms. When I was here we brought in the digital and multi-media artists. At the moment there is a mix of performing and recording artists, writers, sculptors, painters, dancers — a really broad creative class. You've got people who started here as struggling artists who've done really well for a while and then come back here to be struggling artists again.*

As I wandered around the courtyard with Brook, I saw that it hadn't been given over entirely to the arts community; there are mini-cab firms and manufacturing businesses. The owners, as Brook indicated, remain fairly anonymous and communication, such as there is, is filtered though a property agency. Every now and then plans for redevelopment of the site crop up, only to disappear and replaced with yet another sketch for yet another unrealised giant skyscraper. Brook says, 'At some point they are going to redevelop this area. Even when I was living and working here there was always the feeling that this might be the last year and they are going to say — *All of you. Out!* I came here for the first time when I was about twenty-two. It's been a major part of my life ever since really. It's full of friends and memories.'

# Epilogue
## Cable Street Insurrection

In the days after recording my final interviews for this book, I started to think about how I could bring all the stories together: I had been certain from the start that a unifying theme would emerge. Looking for inspiration in the street itself, I found myself returning to the Battle of Cable Street Mural on the side of St George's Town Hall. As mentioned, it has provided the backdrop to any number of gnarled veterans, thrusting local councillors and people like me with a book to flog, who have come to have their picture taken in front of it. It appears in a wonderful eight-minute film, *The Battle of Cable Street*. Made by Yoav Segal in 2006, this award-winning short is based on the director's relationship with his own grandfather. The story is told through the eyes of a child, doodling onto a pad in the back of a car as his granddad regales him with Battle tales. The boy imagines himself in the heart of the conflict, the main events deftly sketched in as the pictures come to life. The film ends as they arrive at the foot of the mural. The boy is told, 'Look up, see the world around you. Find a voice, express yourself.' And maybe it's as simple as that: self-expression as the theme of this book. Cable Street Politics. And if I describe that as a form of insurrection, I'm not talking the Russian revolution, suffragettes manacled to the gates of Number Ten or Robin Hood and his Merry Men. My Cable Street insurrection is, I suppose, a revolt against expectation. Don't expect us to bring down the shutters while the Bully Boys march past. If you think we're just a bunch of troublesome black boys then we'll make a film and show you our side of it. As truants, drop-outs and no-hopers we've become poets, playwrights and publishers. We make music in cellars, we paint pictures on gash hardboard, we take photographs of old men in the markets and, oh, any number of things. The people of East London make their own art and their own history: they don't like others imposing it on them. They don't like people telling them what they should say or think. They don't toe party lines. They are frequently off-message, out of line and in trouble. They are a myriad of things: angry and affectionate, awkward and accommodating. In a place of constant flux they claim that nothing ever changes. Life swirls around them; and everything that has ever happened to them has, at some time or other, happened in Cable Street.

# Appendix

## A Historical Perspective — The Origins of Cable Street
*by Derek Gadd*

*I have included here the work of Cable Street Group member Derek Gadd. In it, he underlines the fact that the street, or sections of it, have appeared under various guises in its long life.*

The thoroughfare, more than a mile long, running from the Royal Mint to Ratcliffe, first had the name Cable Street applied to it at the end of the seventeenth century. Accurate small scale maps of the area were beginning to appear at about that time and Mason and Paynes Survey of London of 1745 shows that the name Cable Street was given only to a very short section immediately north of the newly laid out Wellclose Square. Of the remainder, different sections had clearly come into being at different times — Rosemary Lane, Knockfergus, Bluegate Fields, Sun Tavern Fields and Brook Street, these last two appearing on the survey to be little more than farm tracks.

It was not until 1937 that the name Cable Street was extended over the entire length from Rosemary Lane — which was renamed Royal Mint Street — right down as far as Butchers Row.[1] Brook Street is mentioned in Parish registers in the middle of the seventeenth century[2] but the precise date of origin of any of the sections that make up the modern Cable Street is impossible to determine with any accuracy. Likely dates must be based on our knowledge of the development of settlement in the area.

London was founded by the Emperor Claudius' invading Roman army in 43AD at the lowest bridging point of the River Thames. Further east the alluvial plain of the river was marshy as far north as the gravel terrace and on the junction between the two. One of the many roads that radiated from the City ran from a gate in the City wall just north of the (later) Tower along the line of the modern Highway to meet the river at Ratcliffe and possibly beyond. Most of the land south of the road was prone to flooding while to the north of it was well drained gravel.

The Roman practice of prohibiting burial within city walls resulted in the development of extramural cemeteries, especially immediately outside gates. Three main cemeteries existed around London, one to the north between Bishopsgate and Moorgate, one to the west towards the River Fleet and a third in the east around the Minories. The first recorded discoveries in the burial grounds were made at the beginning of the seventeenth century –

> *Within the parish of Stepney in Middlesex, in Radcliffe Field, where they take ballast for ships; about some fourteen or fifteen years ago there was found two monuments, the one of stone wherein was the bones of a man, the other a chest of lead, the upper part being garnished with scallop-shells and a crotister border. At the head of the coffin and the foot, there were two jars of a three foot length, standing and on the sides a number of bottles of glistening red earth some painted and many great vials of glass, some six some eight square having a whitish liquor within them. Within the chest was the body of a woman, as the chirugians[3] judged by the skull. On either side of her there were two sceptres of ivory 18ins long and on her breast a little figure of Cupid, neatly cut in white stone. It seemed (said Sir Robert Cotton from whom I had this relation) there were bodies burned (sic) about the year of our Lord 239, being there were found diverse coins of Pupienus, Gordian and the emperors of that time.[4]*

The location 'in Radcliffe Field, where they take ballast for ships' was narrowed down by the compilers of the Royal Commission volume on Roman London to 'the angle of Love Lane and Cable Street.[5] Love Lane became Brodlove Lane in 1937[6] at the extreme east end of Cable Street and the existence of burials at the Shadwell end of Cable Street was thought to represent a distant extension of the main cemetery at Goodmans Fields just to the east of the Minories. More reports of finds crop up in other eighteenth century works. John Strype reported in his 1755 edition of Stow's Survey –

> *In Goodmans Fields without Aldgate was a Roman burying place, for since the building there about 1678, have been found there (in digging for foundations) vast quantities of urns and other Roman utensils ... Some of the urns had ashes of bones in them, and brass and silver money: and an unusual urn of copper, curiously enamelled in colours red, blue and yellow.*[7]

Gough in his edition of Camden's *Britannia* noted that –

> *In the foundations of the new church in Goodman's Fields among many parcels of bones were found urns.*[8]

These cemeteries were in use for the whole of the Roman occupation of Britain from the first century to the beginning of the fifth. The discovery of burials immediately outside a Roman city could have been expected but the location in 1974 of the foundations of a signal tower south of the Highway opposite St George's swimming baths was extremely unusual. The eight metre square masonry tower was built in the late third century and was probably part of a series of installations controlling river traffic and relaying warnings of raiders possibly from the forts of the Saxon shore around the south coast. Timber buildings sprang up around the tower and in the backfill of a small wood-lined pit associated with these a Roman leather bikini was found.[9]

From the end of the Roman occupation in 410AD into the medieval period there is no real evidence for any settlement on the gravel terrace around Cable Street.

However one analysis of the place name evidence has suggested that it was the site of a Saxon settlement. The name Wapping first appears in the documentary record in the thirteenth century but is Saxon in its origins and means the settlement of Waeppa's people.[10] The first maps, of the eighteenth century, show Wapping where it would be expected in the area occupied by the London Dock at the beginning of the nineteenth century. However such sites on the alluvial plain with a high risk of inundation were nowhere attractive to Saxon settlers. For that reason it has been put forward that the settlement of Waeppa's people lay north of the Highway on the gravel terrace.[11] The shift in the name is accounted for by the introduction of the term Wapping atte the Wose or Wapping in the marsh in the fifteenth century to differentiate the old settlement on the gravel terrace from the newly growing riverside hamlet. In the first half of the sixteenth century, a Dutchman, Cornelius Vanderdelft, drained the marsh and the consequent riverside expansion so outstripped the original settlement on the gravel terrace that it appropriated the name entirely.

The creation and growth of the satellite villages around London in the sixteenth century is normally accounted for by the ready market for agricultural produce that the city supplied.[12] To this was added the increasing volume of goods coming into the Port of London from international trade and the stimulus to the growth of mercantile crafts in the riverside settlements such as Wapping. John Stow writing at the end of Elizabeth's reign points to a more macabre reason for Wapping's expansion.

*Wapping in the Woze, the usual place of execution for hanging of pirates and sea rovers, at the low water mark there to remain, till three tides had overflowed them was never a house of standing within these forty years: but since the gallows being after removed farther off, a continual street, or filthy straight passage with alleys of small tenements or cottages builded, inhabited by sailors, victualers, along by the river of Thames, almost to Radcliffe, a good mile from the Tower.*[13]

The 'continual street' is clearly a reference to the Highway, and Stow goes on to indicate that most of the new building was taking place to the south by the river. In his one reference to the area to the north he returns to the macabre –

> *...now one note on the north side (of the Highway) also concerning pirates. I read that in the year 1440 ... certain persons with six ships brought ... fish to victual the city of London ... and ... a number of sea thieves ... cut their throats, cast them overboard; took their money and drowned their ships ... Two of these thieves were after taken, and hanged in chains upon a gallows set upon a raised hill, for that purpose made, in the field beyond East Smithfield, so that they might be seen far into the River Thames.*[14]

During the Civil War, Parliament empowered the City Corporation to encircle London with a ring of defences fortified with bastions at intervals after bands of marauding royalist cavalry had harried parts of the City after the battle of Edgehill in 1642.[15] An engraving made by Vertue in 1738 depicts the fortifications of East London. Whitechapel High Road remained open but all the roads between it and the river were cut by the defensive bank and ditch. What was to become known as Cable Street was pierced just east of Cannon Street Road and a bastion was constructed at Gravel Lane roughly where the News International Plant is today.

With the Restoration, these defences were abandoned and levelled, and the suburban sprawl of London continued unhindered through the second half of the seventeenth century. One of the earliest small scale surveys, Bowles and Carvers, dateable to the 1690s shows the newly laid out Wellclose Square with the Danes church in its centre designed by the sculptor Caius Julius

239

Cibber. The leases entered into for the creation of Wellclose Square by Nicholas Barbon of the Fire Office[16] refer in 1695 to 'a certain new street called Cable Street heretofore called Knockfergus.'[17]

Although there has been a suggestion that the existence in a parish register of 1629 of a resident called Mary Cable could mean that the name derives from a personal name, most authorities are agreed that it reflects rope manufacture in the area.[18] On Gascoigne's map of 1703 a 'rope walk' is marked parallel to its north side and the growth of mercantile craft suppliers in the riverside parishes from Stow's time has been commented on elsewhere.

The squalid reputation that Cable Street was to gain in later years appears to originate at the same time as the name first appears. Daniel Defoe, writing thirty years later, commented that the area was –

*So remote from houses, that it used to be a very dangerous place to go after it was dark, and many people have been robbed and abused passing it.[19]*

# Notes

1. London County Council *Names of streets and places in the administrative county of London* (1955).
2. Registers of St Dunstans and All Saints Church, Stepney High Street (P93 / DUN) Baptisms 1568-1954, Marriages 1568-1962 and burials 1568-1929.
3. A surgeon.
4. Weever's *Funeral Monuments* (1631) 30.
5. Royal Commission on Historical Monuments (England) *An inventory of the historical monuments in London III Roman London* (1928) 163. The identification of 'Radcliffe field where they take ballast for ships' to the extreme east end of Cable Street is useful if confusing. Weever was reporting discoveries made eighty years before the name Cable Street was first used.
6. Op. cit in n. 1.
7. John Stow *Survey of London II Appendix 23* (1755) published by John Strype.

8. William Camden *Britannia* (1755) 11, 17 published by Richard Gough.
9. Tony Johnson 'A Roman signal tower at Shadwell E1 — An interim note' *Transactions of the London and Middlesex archaeological society 26* (1975) 278-280.
10. The English Place Name Society *The Place-Names of Middlesex* (1942).
11. K.G.T. McDonnell *Medieval London Suburbs* (1978) 10.
12. Christopher Hibbert *London the biography of a city* (1969) 35-53.
13. John Stow *A Survey of London* reprinted from the text of 1603 by Charles Kingsford (1908) 70-71.
14. ibid.
15. H.L. Smith *The History of East London* (1939) 283-4.
16. John M Sims 'The Trust Lands of the Fire Office' *Guildhall Miscellany* 4 Oct 1971-April 1973.
17. W.J. Hardy (ed.) *Calendar of the Sessions Books 1689-1709* (1905) 145.
18. S. Fairfield *The Streets of London* 1983 et al.
19. Daniel Defoe *A Tour through England and Wales 1724-6* Everyman edition (1928) I 328.

# Selected Bibliography & Notes

**Caroline Adams**, *Across Seven Seas and Thirteen Rivers: life stories of pioneer Sylhetti settlers in Britain* (London: THAP Books, 1987)

**Michael Banton**, *The Coloured Quarter: Negro Immigrants in an English City* (London: Jonathan Cape, 1955)

**The Basement Writers**
*The Boxer Speaks* by Stephen Hicks (1973), *Never Had It So Good* by Tony Harcup (1974), *Follow Me* by John Schroder (1974), *Bedwritten* by Debbie Carnigie (1974), *Breaking Through* by Gladys McGee (1975), *Living in the City,* a songbook by Dave Swift (1975), *Up the Docks,* 'a cartoon melodrama' by Alan Gilbey (1974), *The Basement Writers' Poetry Show,* an anthology (1975), *Mendoza For Ever!* A play by Chris Searle (1975), *Ink Slinging* by Alan Gilbey (1976), *Sometimes You Can Hear the Birds Sing* by Leslie Mildiner (1976), *Tall Thoughts* by Deepak Kalha (1976), *Paper Talk* and *Window on Brick Lane,* both by Sally Flood (1979), *Tuesday Night,* an anthology (1979), *He Don't Know 'A' From A Bull's Foot: Cockney Slang of the Thirties* by Jim Wolveridge (1979), *No Green Leaves* by Robert Hamberger and David Amery (1979), *Running In* by Bruce Norris (1980), *Moonlight and Roses,* an anthology (with The Tower Hamlets Arts Project, 1985), *Just a Cotchell: Tales From a Docklands Childhood and Beyond* by Liz Thompson (1987), *In My World and Other Poems* by Sally Flood (1989), *Joined Up Writing: New Poetry and Prose from the Basement Writers* (1990), *Wiggerly Words: Poems for Children* by Joan Vicente (1992), *Take It From Me* by Sean Taylor (1992), *XX Years in the Basement,* an anthology (1993)

The frenzy in which Basement Writers publications were produced, the smallness of print-runs and their instant distribution (no one thought to keep any copies back for posterity) means that few copies of any of them exist outside private hands. Even I don't have copies of some of the titles I helped to produce. The above list is almost certainly incomplete.

**Andy Beckett**, 'Return of a Class Hero' *Guardian*, November 19th, 1997.

**Simon Blumenfeld**, *Jew Boy* (London: Jonathan Cape, 1935, reprinted by Lawrence and Wishart in 1986 and London Books in 2011)
*Phineas Kahn* (London: Jonathan Cape, 1937, reprinted by Lawrence and Wishart in 1988)
Simon Blumenfeld occasionally dropped into the THAP Bookshop when I worked there. With a large, florid moustache and a smart hat, tilted at a rakish angle, he carried with him a theatrical élan. For many years, under the name of Sidney Vauncez (the Yiddish name for moustache) he wrote regularly for *The Stage* newspaper, becoming the oldest working columnist in the country. He died in 2005 at the age of ninety-seven.

**E.R. Braithwaite**, *To Sir, With Love* (London: Bodley Head, 1959)

**The Cable Street Group**, *The Battle of Cable Street* (London: The Cable Street Group, 1995, new edition published by Five Leaves Publications in 2011)

**Peter Catterall** (ed.) Witness Seminar: The Battle of Cable Street, *Contemporary Record* 8.1 (Summer 1994) (London: Frank Cass, 1994)

**Joseph Cohen**, *Journey To The Trenches: The Life of Isaac Rosenberg* (London: Robson Books, 1975)

**Elvis Costello**, 'Less Than Zero' on *My Aim is True* (Stiff Records, 1977)

**Andy Croft**, *They Shall Not Pass* (Edinburgh: Barrington Stoke Ltd, 2009)
A book for children. Illustrated by Alan Marks.

**Madge Darby**, *Waeppa's People: A History of Wapping* (London: Connor & Butler on behalf of The History of Wapping Trust, 1988)

**Geoff Dench, Kate Gavron, Michael Young**, *The New East End: Kinship, Race and Conflict* (London: Profile Books Ltd, 2006)

**The Desperate Bicycles**, *The Medium Was Tedium* (Refill Records, 1977)

**William J. Fishman**, *The Streets of East London* (London: Duckworth, 1979, reprinted by Five Leaves Publications in 1998)
'A People's Journée: The Battle of Cable Street (October 4th 1936)' in Frederick Krantz (ed.), *History from Below: Studies in Popular Protest and Popular Ideology in Honour of George Rudé* (Montreal: Concordia University, 1985)

> *The Battle of Cable Street*, a forty minute documentary in the BBC *Yesterday's Witness* series was broadcast on the 4th of January 1970. There is a transcript in the Tower Hamlets Local History Library. Produced by Stephen Peet and directed by Michael Rabiger, it features Professor Bill Fishman and Oswald Mosley, for whom a ban on television appearances was lifted for the occasion. Having come to it some years after its initial broadcast, it was something of a shock to see people who I had only read about in books or pictured in photocopied newspaper articles — people such as Phil Piratin and Edith Ramsay — talking on the screen. It somehow felt as if I had stumbled across hitherto undiscovered footage of William Shakespeare or Queen Boadicea.

**Patrik Fitzgerald**, *Poems* (London: THAP Publishing, 1979)

**George Foulser**, 'Cablestrasse' *The Observer*, 28th August, 1960.

**Alfred Gardner**, *An East End Story: 'A Tale of Friendship'* (London: self-published, 2002)
*'Watch Your Fingers': An East End Cutter's Chronicle, 1956-1973, Part One* (London: self-published, 2006)

**Greenwich Mural Workshop**, *Murals in London: A Guide to London Murals Since 1976* (London: Greenwich Mural Workshop, 1987)

**Caroline Grist and Katy Ferguson**, *No Way In Wapping: the effect of the policing of the News International dispute on Wapping residents* (London: National Council for Civil Liberties, 1986)

**Florence L. Henderson**, 'An East End Elysium' in A.A. Leith (ed.) *Every Girl's Annual,* (London: Routledge, 1887)

**Nigel Henderson**, *Photographs of Bethnal Green 1949-1952* (Nottingham: East Midlands Arts and the Craft Advisory Council, 1978)

**Stephen 'Johnny' Hicks**, *Sparring For Luck* (London: THAP Publishing, 1982)

**Stan Hugill**, *Sailortown* (London: Routledge & Kegan Paul, 1967)

**Richard Humm, Dan Jones**, *A for 'orses: a comic alphabet* (London: THAP Books, 1981)

**Joe Jacobs**, *Out of the Ghetto: My Youth in the East End: Communism and Fascism 1913-1939* (London: Janet Simon, 1978, reprinted by Phoenix Press in 1991)

> The account given by Sam Berkovitz in the 'Witnesses' section of my book, on the events leading up to the Battle, closely follows that of Joe Jacobs in his book. But it is hardly undisputed. In May 1991, a seminar was arranged by the Institute of Contemporary British History at the Institute of Historical Research, bringing together veterans and historians to share their views. There, Phil Piratin claimed that Jacobs' book 'exaggerates' the author's role and that Communist Party plans to take on the BUF marchers were already being laid out, rather than coming about through a last-minute turnaround. Piratin recalled that Jacobs was, 'OK in his way.'

**Dan Jones**, *Blood on the Streets* (London: Bethnal Green and Stepney Trades Council, 1978)

**Chris Kelly**, *The Cable Street Gardeners* (Maidstone: CK editions, 2005)

**Anne J. Kershen** (ed.) *1840-1990 150 Years of Progressive Judaism in Britain* (London: The London Museum of Jewish Life, 1990)

**Bernard Kops**, *The World is a Wedding* (London: MacGibbon and Kee, 1963, reprinted by Five Leaves in 2000)

**Tony Kushner and Nadia Valman** (ed.), *Remembering Cable Street: Fascism and Anti-Fascism in British Society* (London: Vallentine Mitchell, 2000)

> In Tony's Kushner's essay in the above: *Long May Its Memory Live!: Writing and Rewriting 'the Battle of Cable Street'*, he points out that while the phrase: 'The Battle of Cable Street' was minted on the very day itself, in a celebratory speech by Communist Party activist Pat Devine, it didn't immediately become common currency, not appearing in print until 1961,

in Colin Cross's book *The Fascists in Britain*. He goes on to state that the memory of the Battle itself lay dormant as 'useable' history for years and that it was only in the 1970s that it took on the status of something approaching myth. He also hints at political opportunism: 'The attempt to utilise the memory of the "Battle" for multi-cultural, as well as explicitly anti-racist and anti-fascist purpose, began in earnest with the fiftieth anniversary celebrations in October 1986'. This invaluable volume also contains the full script of Simon Blumenfeld's play, *The Battle of Cable Street*.

**Anthony Lam**, *Notes from the Street* (London: Camerawork, 1995)
Photographs and interviews relating to Bangladeshi youths in the Shadwell area of Cable Street.

**Langdon Park School**, *The People Marching On* (London: Langdon Park School, 1976)

**Kenneth Leech**, *Through Our Long Exile: Contextual Theology and the Urban Experience* (London: Darton, Longman and Todd Ltd, 2001)
*The Anglo-Catholic Social Conscience: two critical essays* (London: The Jubilee Group, 1991)

**Shaun Levin**, *Isaac Rosenberg's Journey to Arras: a Meditation* (London: Cecil Woolf Publishers, 2008)

**Nick Lowles** (ed.) *From Cable Street to Oldham: 70 Years of Community Resistance* (London: Searchlight, 2007)

**Gladys McGee**, *Old Age Ain't No Place For Sissies* (London: THAP Publishing, 1986)

**Gavin McGrath**, *Cinemas and Theatres in Tower Hamlets* (London: self-published, 2010)
In the essay by Jim Wolveridge, 'The Acme of Imperfection' included in my book, he states that the Cable Picture Palace was destroyed during the blitz. In the above book it states it was demolished after 1941.

**Roger Mills**, 'The Art of Cable Street', *Rising East: The Journal of East London Studies* 1:1 (London: Lawrence and Wishart, 1997)
Parts of this article have been incorporated into my book, mostly in the sections about the mural and artists' interpretations of the Battle.

**Dave Morley and Ken Worpole** (ed.) *The Republic of Letters: working class writing and local publishing* (London: Comedia Publishing Group, 1982)

**Roi Ottley**, *No Green Pastures* (London: John Murray, 1952)

**Phil Piratin**, *Our Flag Stays Red* (London: Lawrence & Wishart, 1948, reprinted by the same publisher in 1978)

**Martin Pugh**, *'Hurrah For the Blackshirts': Fascists and Fascism in Britain Between the Wars* (London: Pimlico, 2006)

**Millicent Rose**, *The East End of London* (London: The Cresset Press Ltd, 1951)

**Harold Rosen**, *Are You Still Circumcised?: East End Memories* (Nottingham: Five Leaves Publications, 1999)

**Michael Rosen and Susanna Steele**, *Inky Pinky Ponky*, illustrated by Dan Jones (London: Granada Publishing Limited, 1982)

**Chris Searle** (ed.), *Stepney Words 1 & 2* (London: Reality Press, 1971)
A single edition of both the above books, with photographs by Ron McCormick, was published by Centerprise in 1973.
*This New Season* (London: Calder and Boyars, 1973)
*Classrooms of Resistance* (London: Writers and Readers Publishing Cooperative, 1975)
(ed.), *They Shall Not Pass: A Poetry Anthology to Celebrate The East Enders Victory over Fascism — Oct 1936* (London: Reality Press, 1975)
*The World in a Classroom* (London: Writers and Readers Publishing Cooperative, 1977)
(ed.), *Bricklight: Poems from the Labour Movement in East London* (London: Pluto Press, 1980)
'Spanning two languages: The legacy of Isaac and Joseph' in *Race & Class, Volume 28, Number 1* (London: Institute of Race Relations, 1986)
(ed.), *One For Blair: An Anthology of Poems for Young People* (London: Young World Books, 1989)
*None But Our Words: Critical Literacy in Classroom and Community* (Buckingham: Open University Press, 1998)
*Lightning of Your Eyes: New and Selected Poems* (Middlesbrough: Smokestack Books, 2006)
*Race & Class, Volume 51, Number 2, Chris Searle: the great includer. A Festschrift on his sixty-fifth birthday* (London: Institute of Race Relations, 2009)

**Barnett Sheridan**, *King Sol* (London: Chatto & Windus, 1939)

**Lazarus Sheridan**, *Twelve a Penny* (London: AZAL Press, 1997)
Of all the discoveries I made during my research, the most jaw-dropping for me personally was that I had actually met Barnett Sheridan (a.k.a. Lazarus Sheridan and Laza Shrensky) without realising it. He was the headmaster of William Patten Primary School in Stoke Newington when I was a pupil there in the mid 1960s. I recall a firm but encouraging presence, keen to guide us to the library, particularly extolling the virtues of Mary Norton's *The Borrowers*.

**Paul Simmonds**, Lyrics to 'Ghosts of Cable Street', on *How Green is the Valley*, The Men They Couldn't Hang (MCA Records, 1986)

**George R. Sims**, *Off the Track in London* (London: Jarrold & Sons, 1911)

**Ashley Smith**, *A City Stirs* (London: Chapman & Hall, 1939, updated the above in a 1951 edition, published by Cleaver-Hume Press Ltd)

*The East-Enders* (London: Secker & Warburg, 1961)

**Stepney Books**

*'Ain't It Grand' (or 'This Was Stepney')*, Jim Wolveridge, 1976

*Victoria Park* (published with Centerprise), Charles Poulson, 1976

*Memories of Old Poplar*, John Blake, 1977

*Under Oars* (published with The Journeyman Press), Harry Harris, 1978

*Looking Back — A Docker's Life*, Joe Bloomberg, 1979

*Tough Annie*, Annie Barnes, 1980

*Children of the Green*, Doris M. Bailey, 1981

*Rego & Poloakoff — Strike Songs* (published with Centerprise), 1983

*Edith and Stepney*, Bertha Sokoloff, 1987

*My Poplar Eastenders*, Carrie Lumsden, 1991

*In Letters of Gold*, Rosemary Taylor, 1993

*Brick Lane 1978: The Events and their Significance*, Ken Leech, 1994 (originally published by AFFOR, 1980)

*Outside the Gate*, Malcolm Johnson, 1994

**Rosemary Stones and Andrew Mann**, *Mother Goose Comes to Cable Street*, illustrated by Dan Jones (London, Kestrel Books, 1977)

**Rosemary Taylor**, *Hannah Billig: The Angel of Cable Street* (self-published, 1996)

**Peter Townsend** (ed.) *Art Within Reach* (London: Thames and Hudson, 1984)

**Various,** *Auschwitz and East London* (London: The Tower Hamlets Arts Project, 1983)

**Various**, *Writing* (London: The Federation of Worker Writers and Community Publishers, 1978)

**Ray Walker Memorial Committee,** *Ray Walker* (London: Coracle Press, 1985). Published for an exhibition of the artist's work at the Royal Festival Hall.

**Arnold Wesker**, 'Chicken Soup with Barley' in *The Wesker Trilogy* (London: Jonathan Cape, 1960, available from various publishers down the years, more recently in an edition by Methuen in 2001)
*As Much As I Dare: An Autobiography* (London: Century, 1994)

**David Widgery**, *Beating Time* (London: Chatto & Windus, 1986)

**Aaron Williamson**, *Splitting the Atom on Dalston Lane*, (London: Eel Publications, 2009)

**Joseph Williamson**, *Father Joe: The Autobiography of Joseph Williamson of Poplar and Stepney* (London: Hodder and Stoughton, 1963)

**www.reelstreets.com**

# Five Leaves' books on the Battle of Cable Street

**Battle for the East End: Jewish responses to fascism in the 1930s**
by *David Rosenberg*
978 1 907869 18 1

**October Day**
a novel by *Frank Griffin*
978 1 907869 15 0

**Everything Happens in Cable Street**
oral history from *Roger Mills*
978 1 907869 19 8

**The Battle of Cable Street**
by *The Cable Street Group*
978 1 907869 17 4

**Street of Tall People**
a children's book by *Alan Gibbons*
978 1 907869 23 5

Available from bookshops or, post free, from Five Leaves, PO Box 8786, Nottingham NG1 9AW, www.fiveleaves.co.uk